THE BLOODY
BATTLE FOR
TILLY

NORMANDY 1944

THE BLOODY BATTLE FOR

TILLY

NORMANDY 1944

KEN TOUT

SUTTON PUBLISHING

First published in 2000 by
Sutton Publishing Limited · Phoenix Mill
Thrupp · Stroud · Gloucestershire · GL5 2BU

British Library Cataloguing in Publication Data
A catalogue record for this book is available from the British Library

ISBN 0-7509-2475-6

Typeset in 12.5/16 pt Garamond 3.
Typesetting and origination by
Sutton Publishing Limited.
Printed and bound in England by
J.H. Haynes & Co. Ltd, Sparkford.

Contents

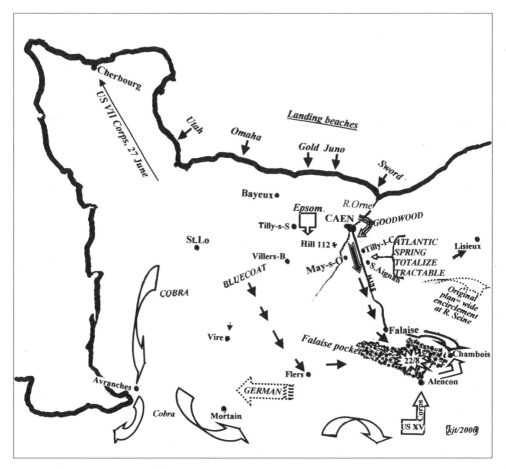

Normandy, June–August 1944.

Acknowledgements

When the idea of this book was taking shape with Jonathan Falconer, ever helpful at Sutton Publishing, the Canadian research looked to be a mammoth and complicated task. In the event I was overwhelmed by the response. Two people especially 'saved my bacon'. Maj Peter Williams, RCA, on a posting to RSA on Salisbury Plain, had shared with me a Normandy tour and then promised, and delivered, a list of Canadian contacts and sources. He in turn recommended to me Professor Terry Copp who not only heads the Wilfrid Laurier centre but also edits *Canadian Military History*. At short notice, Terry set up a tour of Ontario for me, opened vast treasures of information and, with Linda, offered me hospitality of home and office.

Others who helped me practically in Canada, in addition to those quoted in the text and Notes, included (in civilian style alphabetical order): T. Roy Adams; Maj W.R. Bennett, CD; Capt G. Blackburn, MC; Lt H.N. Brosseau; Cliff Brown; Drs J.L. Granatstein, R. Sarty and War Museum staff; Dr G. Hayes; Maj D. Learment, DSO; Col J. Martin, DSO; Dr W. McAndrew; M.J. Morin; Lt-Col J.W. Ostiguy, DSO; Lt-Col D. Patterson, CD; Brig S.V. Radley-Walters, CMM, DSO, MC, CD, OLd'H; Lt-Col F.H. Wheeler; Brig D. Whitaker, DSO, CM, ED, OLd'H. Begging their several pardons for any errors of rank or honours.

Willing assistance from France was forthcoming from the Mayors of May, St Andre, St Martin, and Tilly-la-Campagne, and adjoints, Messieurs Grard, Poulain and Samson. Also from Jenny Bourrienne and

Guy Merle. A 'thank you' too, for German responses from Gevert Haslob, Manfred and Hazel Toon-Thorn and Gerhard Stiller. Advice and help in Britain was offered by Mrs M-L. Bush (Keele University Air Photo Library); Col Hugh Cuming, MBE, JP; Lt-Col A.M. Cumming, OBE; Lt-Col A.A. Fairrie; Lt-Col S.J. Lindsay; Bob Moore, MM; Maj James Nairne; Sir Patrick Nairne, GCB, MC; Dr Tom Renouf, MM; Pat Shurmur. From my own regiment, among many, I am indebted to Lt-Col Rt Hon. Lord Boardman, MC, TD, DL; Joe Ekins; Rex Jackson, MM; Sid Jones, Les 'Spud' Taylor and Reg Spittles.

Photographs and other illustrations in the book are credited in the captions and include copyright photos used by permission from the Imperial War Museum (IWM), Public Archives of Canada (PA) through the good offices of the *Canadian Military History* editorial, the RAF (Ministry of Defence – Keele University), and Queen's Own Highlanders Museum. My wife Jai gave me valuable help in navigating the Normandy battlefields once again, and taking photos, not only for publication but also to refresh the writer's mind as memory tended to fade or become confused with too much detail. My son Roger found a treasure trove of yellowing newspapers from July 1944 (!) when renovating an old workshop for his surfboard business in Bude, and sent me this most useful hoard.

Thank you again also to all those quoted in the text! The turn of the millenium is a critical time for Second World War memoirs. Memories and veterans fade. Frank Cox of the Royals died before he could send me his recollections. That angry Tilly survivor, Charles Kipp, completed his contribution although very ill, but has since gone to his Last Parade.

Introduction

1944 – for four years most of Europe had been occupied by the Nazis. Now the Russians were advancing from the east and allied forces were probing up the spine of Italy. Then on 6 June, D-Day, Allied armies stormed ashore in Normandy.

A few miles inland from the beaches, that is to the south, lay the important city of Caen. In addition to its own intrinsic value, it stood at the strategic crossroads of the region. An advance south-east would take the Allies to Paris, and on through the Low Countries to Germany. It was therefore essential for the Germans to defend the Caen sector to the utmost of their ability.

Field commander Montgomery had hoped to capture Caen on D-Day itself. The task eventually took a month. But, having liberated the city, the Allies looked optimistically at the terrain ahead. If they could cross the River Orne, which circled south of Caen, beyond it lay the enticing gentle slopes of the Bourguebus-Verrieres Ridge, so much like Salisbury Plain where much British tank practice had taken place. Montgomery's strategy was therefore to attack hard south of Caen with his British and Canadian armies on that left flank. This would draw the elite German panzers to the area and allow the Americans on the right to break through weaker German defences. It looked as though the Americans would be advancing into the Cherbourg peninsula cul de sac, but a quick advance and a left swing would bring them behind the main German army pinned down around Caen.

In the Caen area the allies had only one bridgehead over the Orne through which tanks could advance and this was actually north-east of the city. So it would be necessary to cross that bridge, circle the city outskirts and then face up the ridges ready for an all-out armoured charge. This task would be undertaken with the code name Goodwood by the three British armoured divisions.

Meanwhile, the Canadian army would walk south through Caen's ruins, fight their way across the unbridged Orne, and enable engineers to push Bailey Bridges over the river. So in the Caen sector, looking south, the British were on the left and the Canadians on the right (with the Americans even farther to the right). Also coming ashore soon, in mid-July, would be the leading elements of the Polish armoured division. Against these around Caen would be lined up the best of Germany's panzer divisions, including the 1st SS Panzers LAH (the initials signifying Hitler's own bodyguard) and the 12th SS Panzers Hitler Youth.

What was worrying to more percipient observers was that in almost every element of ground equipment the defenders had the advantage – more powerful tank and anti-tank guns, demoralizing multiple mortars, the fastest firing machine-guns, ammunition causing less flash and smoke, and long battle experience. Against this the allies had command of the sea and air, plus an almost inexhaustible supply of materiel, especially tanks, however outgunned these might be.

As the two sides prepared for the anticipated Allied break-out from Caen in mid-July many of the best formations had been involved in bitter fighting in the close country just in from the beaches. The Germans, dug in along the ridges, had evacuated civilians from villages and turned the stone cottages and farms into formidable small fortresses dominating all the open land in between. There was little room for the attackers to spring surprises as the British, led by their three armoured divisions, the Guards, 7th and 11th, together with the Canadian 2nd and 3rd infantry divisions, prepared their weapons on the north bank of the Orne.

Note: The armoured divisions normally consisted of an armoured brigade of three tank battalions and a motorized battalion, plus a brigade of infantry to support the tanks. An infantry division consisted of three infantry brigades, each of three battalions, without tanks. In practice the infantry divisions were generally supported by other tanks from independent armoured brigades.

CHAPTER ONE

In the Foot-slogger's Boots

They struggled with the ferocity that was to be expected of brave men fighting a forlorn hope against an enemy who had the advantage of position . . . knowing that courage was the one thing which could save them.

(*Julius Caesar, 57 BC*)

'They told us this was to be our gradual initiation into battle', said the sergeant, 'and one Hell of an initiation it turned out to be.'[1]

'Hell?' responded a rifleman. 'After Tilly, Hell would be a holiday camp.'[2] A German trooper felt the same way. 'Up to this point I had only fought on the Eastern Front. Nothing from my previous experience could have prepared me for what happened at Tilly. The tactic of unbroken artillery barrages lasting for hours was gruesome mental and physical torture.'[3] The war-hardened, war-worn Desert Rats, sent to Normandy, concurred.

> Under Canadian command, within enemy artillery range, in a very small area . . . the next eight days were as unpleasant a time as the troops were to have throughout the whole North-West Europe campaign. Shelling was incessant, all movement could be observed by the Germans, there was a steadily mounting roll of casualties . . . the infantry could only sit in their trenches, watching the first salvoes throwing up their mushrooms on the ridge, the range increasing every few salvoes and searching out every nook and cranny of the ground.[4]

The tough men from the wild coasts of northern Nova Scotia described it graphically:

Soon the night was a bedlam of noise. Enemy guns began shooting from all angles. The dug-in tanks began shooting at fixed targets. Machine-gun fire came from emplacements concealed in haystacks, from the tin-roofed building, from the orchards, from everywhere. The Germans shouted and yelled as if they were drunk or drugged and the North Novas pitched into them with bomb and butt and bayonet in one of the wildest melees ever staged. . . . Soon voices were calling in many directions and most of them were groans or pleas for mercy.[5]

Men from the prairies of the Canadian mid-west knew the same horrors:

The South Saskatchewan Regiment are driven back over the ridge on their bellies through the wet grain and mud, seeking only to escape the savage machine-gunning and the crushing tracks of rampaging Panther and [54 ton] Tiger tanks. And even as they crawl through the three-feet-high wheat, the insensate steel monsters, with engines roaring horribly, follow them, trying to squash them or flush them out where their machine-guns can get at them.[6]

Yet another writer records that 'all that dusty day of July 25th the men kept crawling back, with raw knees and arms and minor wounds. The whole affair had been more or less a nightmare. . . . Those who escaped were they who crawled like snakes on the ground. It was one of the worst death traps soldiers had tried to cross, with practically every foot of ground ranged for machine-gun fire.'[7]

No more unlikely place could be found for such grisly happenings than those gentle, fertile slopes south of Caen. A ridge whose dual name would be carried as an honour on more than forty regimental standards: Verrieres-Bourguebus. A ridge but not a mountainside. A pleasant incline up which to take a summer afternoon stroll across fields high with golden corn in 1944. A panorama speckled with innocent-looking villages of sandstone cottages, busy farms and long vistas. Places with attractive sounding names: Tilly-la-Campagne, Fontenay-le-Marmion, Beauvoir Farm, May-sur-Orne. Places with religious sounding names: St Andre, St Aignan, St Martin, St Sylvain. Perhaps also places with ominous sounding names: Hubert Folie, Ifs, Grimbosq.

Then, in that July and August of ripening wheat, those slopes were blasted by raging fire and jagged, screeching steel splinters. The sky was darkened with smoke and dust, and then illuminated by lurid flashes, briefer but more frequently lethal than lightning. Flashes of guns firing and shells bursting and tanks exploding. Now flashes only of unwelcome memory in the minds of survivors. Flashes that persist into a new Millennium. Flashes of recollections they are reticent to share. Unless the records pay tribute to the quickly forgotten dead, and warn of the barbarity and inanity of war.

A Highlander recalled the insane ferocity of battle:

Everyone was shouting, screaming, swearing . . . someone said look at the ground for spider mines, someone said look at the sky for the flashes, shells were coming all ways, the man next to me got hit through the shoulder, he fell down. I looked at him and said 'Christ' and then ran on. I didn't know whether to be sick or dirty my trousers.[8]

Cpl Charles Kipp, of the Lincoln and Welland regiment, had no illusions about the reality of battle. For him it was:

dog eat dog, no quarter asked and no quarter given. It was a fight to the death. And I did lose many comrades killed, wounded and missing. And was very lucky to have lived through it. The German firepower was superb. Well directed and in the right place. They knew what to do, and how to do it. It was devastating . . . too terrible![9]

It was indeed hand to hand in the most literal sense. One Canadian company, seeking their own dead, found an enemy infantryman in the middle of their own. The German had no wound of bullet, shrapnel, burns or blast. He had been throttled by hand in the midst of the battle. It could even be eye to eye:

We had a hole dug atop the bank for our Bren gun . . . one night I was on the Bren gun at this post when Jerry opened fire at me. Their machine-guns do fire at a very rapid rate and this time about every fifth bullet was a tracer and it appeared with the path they were coming at me that I was going to be hit right between the eyes and what a cracking sound as the bullets went by my ear.[10]

There was no respite. The savagery went on and on and on. When the Royals thought that they had experienced the worst, and that there was nothing conceivably worse, it became worse:

Every night the Germans would lay down heavy smoke on our flanks and penetrate the Canadian line to encircle our rear. Each morning we'd find the Regiment surrounded till we were able to force the Tiger tanks to withdraw. And, every night, the enemy also sent Fighting Infantry Patrols deeply into our positions, and then would leave snipers behind everywhere. Each morning Royals had to spray all the trees with machine-gun fire to rout them out.[11] [There were no 1914–18 continuous trench lines or clear No-Man's-Land but only networks of two man slit trenches.]

Even sleep guaranteed no escape as gunner George Blackburn records:

You're surrendering to the sweetest of sleeps when Jerry starts lobbing over something of very large calibre. You only can guess it's one of their larger-calibre Nebelwerfers firing their rocket-propelled mortar bombs, one bomb at a time. You can hear one coming from a long way off, growing louder and louder – sounding remarkably like a bus humming towards you at high speed on a highway while you stand at the side of the road. But just as the sound suggests it's going by, it lands with a wicked flash and a horrendous roar that make the ground shudder and sifts sand from the bunker ceiling . . . once more there's a plaintive cry of 'Stretcher!'[12]

The tiny slit trench, accommodating two men, was the most convenient refuge at the point of battle, but even that was not foolproof, as a bomb or shell descending vertically could drop right into the trench, the explosion's flesh-rending power increased by being confined within the narrow walls of the six-foot-deep slit. John Martin of the Lincs and Wellands, then a Lieutenant, is not ashamed to admit that:

My most vivid recollection of the night [at Tilly] was the intense shelling . . . how terrified you all were in a slit trench and just anxious to dig yourself further into the ground. Every time there was a break in the shelling you could peek out of the trench and someone would be screaming and someone yelling for a stretcher bearer. I'm not sure how we survived.[13]

Stan Whitehouse, an English Oxs and Bucks reinforcement for the Scottish Black Watch temporarily under command of the Canadian II Corps, also recorded a similar sentiment:

Relaxing uneasily in my 'slitter' up front, it was impossible to unwind completely . . . a chill moved through my body. I began sweating heavily and the sweat turned icy cold . . . During the day I was too busy protecting life and limb to dwell on morbid thoughts, but now, crouched below ground, I reflected on our two lads lying dead back there . . . an occasional spasm of trembling ran through my limbs and I wondered when my number would be up too.[14]

Even back, but not so far back, at headquarters there is no respite, no relief. The officer responsible for entering up the war diary of the Stormont, Dundas and Glengarry Highlanders of Canada at their HQ had his pen poised to write down his regiment's experiences when he was given an unwanted opportunity to get 'bang up to date':

All Hell breaks loose! The RSM's ammo dump is hit and catches fire: small arms and grenades go up in fire and smoke. Our BHQ office truck is perforated with shrapnel. Several are wounded and suffering from shock. Shelling continues at intervals, *id est*, at 11.15, 11.40, 13.25, 13.30, 13.45, 13.50, 14.00, 14.25, etc.

At this period of July, a month after D-Day, Allied troops were still coming ashore and being given the 'Quick march!' almost straight into battle. The Royal Regiment of Canada had disembarked on 6 July and by 10 July were in front line positions. There was no time for gentle introductions. For many there was a ghastly (and sometimes mortally brief) initiation by dirt, desperation and death:

This vicious baptism of fire upon green troops fed with uncooked compo-box rations, little drinking water (none for washing or shaving), with sleep impossible and ravaged by ground-lice was a shocking initiation to war. Our Tanks were no match for the Tiger, our rifles were inferior to their Mauser, his 88 mm was legendary and his Nebelwerfer six-barrelled mortar sequentially fired six 150 mm 70 lb bombs nearly four miles. During these [first] five days, with little [attacking] activity from our prepared positions, the Royals had 1 Off & 29 ORs killed and 3 Off & 71 ORs wounded, mostly from direct hits. . . In one of these 'Moaning Minnie' attacks on our HQ, our Doctor, Capt I.P. Weingarten, MD, was killed.[15]

For those who, like the author, sat in the vulnerable Sherman tanks, at least with armour proof against bullets and with a big gun to fire at 800 yards range and having the ability to retreat at 25 mph, the thought of fighting German tanks was frightening. What must it have been like to confront the same monsters at 20 yards range, having only a puny rifle and a tiny tin hat, and needing to crawl away through the crops in order the escape the gargantuan fury? Maj L.L. Dickin, 'D' Company, South Saskatchewans, wrote it all down in a dispassionate report next day:

Enemy tanks appeared over our left flank, shooting all hell out of everything in their path. They moved up and down on our left flank. This area is completely flat and there is no cover provided except by grain. In the wheat fields the tanks had the advantage of height, which gave them vision, while our weapons could not see because of the standing grain. Three [of our static] 17 pounders began shooting blind after beating down the grain in front of them. They were knocked out in a few minutes. I next called for the PIATS [infantry anti-tank bomb tubes] . . . two of them tried to fire standing up. They were soon dealt with by the tanks.

A Canadian Highlander who wanted to remain anonymous wrote down what his impressions were at such a moment:

Ah, yes, ha ha! This is some joke. They said this was perfect tank country, wide open spaces to charge across with the PBI [poor bloody infantry] safely behind our tanks. And there are those tanks all blasted away and the poor buggers burning inside them and without our tanks we're just sitting ducks for their tanks. And those bloody great Tigers! It was plain murder. And if you got up and tried to run away through the wheat that was plain suicide. . . . You daren't even poke your little hose over the top of the slit to pee. Jerry snipers loved that.[16]

The Tigers had 88 mm guns, originally designed to shoot down aircraft flying at 15,000 feet. Now they were used point blank. There were also 88 mm guns in self-propelled hulls and more 88 mm anti-tank guns which were towed into battle. The Lincs and Welland history states that 'so impressive were the enemy's 88 mm guns that one man in the Mortar Platoon informed Battalion HQ that the shells were burrowing into the twelve-inch [thick] stone walls and stopping with their noses poking through'.

Tank men looked in awe and fright on the infantryman's sufferings and sometimes themselves became involved in the vicious encounters of man versus machine. This has been graphically described by Cpl Reg Spittles, a tank commander with 2nd Northamptonshire Yeomanry:

The Germans, Panzer Grenadiers, were jumping on the tank and all sorts, fierce buggers, but some only looked about 16, boys, you know. They had sticky bombs and that was their delight to stick a bomb on your tank. It had a little projectile inside, like a bullet. The charge drove the projectile, which was like a bolt, straight through the armour: it didn't explode and it didn't necessarily damage the tank, it depended what it hit inside the tank! It was like being in a small room with a hornet, because when they came inside, they flew round and round until they hit something. If it hit a human being it could go on and hit another one, so you could have two or three wounded crew in an undamaged tank, or a tank totally out of action but nobody wounded.

Meanwhile we are tossing hand grenades and phosphorus bombs out. They were like little paint tins; you took the cap off and there were two tapes with lead weights on. You threw it up in the air and the tapes flew undone; when it hit the floor it . . . went off like a firework and the phosphorus would spray out and cover an area of 10 or 12 feet, and if a spot got on you, you started to burn and could not stop it. We were chucking them out like rain. . .[17]

One occurrence involving man and machine was recorded by the Royals who saw a Sherman tank burst into flames. 'The hatch flew open, emitting clouds of black smoke, and those of the crew who could do so threw themselves out. One man came out backwards, catching his knee on the edge of the hatch, and hung there for a moment, blazing like a torch, before he fell to the ground on his head. The burning trooper actually set the wheatfield afire, and the stretcher bearers who rushed forward had to put out these flames as well as those covering the body of the man.'

Waiting to go into action the atmosphere in Bourguebus was most sinister. 'The village was virtually destroyed, and every wall, every hole, every skeleton of a tree sheltered one of the men of the North Nova Scotia Highlanders, whose helmet was covered with net bristling with branches so as to assure perfect camouflage.[18]

Many infantrymen actually found some security advancing out in the open if they could 'lean into' their own artillery barrage which moved forward at a constant pace. This was in spite of the risks from faulty shells or shrapnel spinning back. It had dangers as one battalion commander pointed out. 'A disadvantage of the highly concentrated artillery fire is the dense smoke and dust raised. In one instance the assaulting infantry were unable to see the exploding shells and walked right into them: in another they waited too long and lost their support because they couldn't see through the smoke. Defenders began firing back almost immediately.'[19]

Then there were the perilous minor individual tasks, as when Stan Whitehouse was issued with a prodder with which to dig into the earth as one crawled along searching for mines:

Schu mines were triggered by the slightest tread and could easily remove a man's foot. As he fell sideways he often exploded another mine which blew off a hand or an arm. Flail tanks deal with the mines easily enough but were not always available. It was asking a lot of a squaddie, to go into action poking about with his prodder like a blind man, while at the same time keeping an eye on the enemy ahead and somehow having his personal weapon handy. I still marvel at the accoutrements we had to carry into battle. Even without the prodder they must have weighed well in excess of 60 lb.[20]

There was nothing certain, nothing definite about battle. 'Uncertainty is in the very air which a battle breathes . . . the uncertainty of the enemy's whereabouts, the uncertainty of falsehood, the uncertainty of surprise, the uncertainty of your own troops' actions, the uncertainty of a strange land, the uncertainty of rescue and the uncertainty of confusion itself.'[21] There was an all-pervading fear of 'the bullet in the back':

> A wounded lad was put on a door and two cooks carried him out, only to walk into five Germans armed to the teeth. [The cooks] had no Red Cross bands but the Germans waved them on their way. They walked forward stealthily, placing each foot carefully on the ground and expecting a bullet between the shoulder blades at any moment.[22]

Even when the enemy surrendered, extreme caution was the order of the day. It was generally accepted that the Wehrmacht would obey the agreed laws of war, but with the SS that could not necessarily be assumed. Les 'Spud' Taylor, a tank man with 1st Northamptonshire Yeomanry was not so sure about taking prisoners:

> I heard someone crashing through the brushwood, cocked my gun, and came face to face with a German. That Kraut would never again come closer to getting himself punched full of bullets . . . we had got a prisoner. He was a tall thin man and in spite of the hot summer weather he was wearing an overcoat that reached down to his ankles. Mike had his revolver out and began to interrogate him. I am sure the poor sod was convinced he was about to be shot. He wore a Red Cross armband but that did not impress us: we had heard of it many times before. After putting the fear of God into him, we sent him to the rear . . . I believe he was glad to give himself up.[23]

For Spud and his crew there was a moment of almost elation in having captured one of the feared enemy. There could even be moments of humour which helped some men remain sane a little longer. The Regina Rifles were waiting behind a railway embankment to advance on La Hogue. Even in that partial refuge bombs and shells were dropping vertically. L/Cpl Pretty was buried up to his neck in one violent explosion. He had to be dug out but was otherwise unharmed. Banter began immediately. 'Pretty was not looking pretty!' and 'It was not a very Pretty sight!' and rather less printable comments.

Such moments in the front line could provoke almost hysterical yet therapeutic laughter. After long hours of ultimate warring the adjutant of the Black Watch was sleeping, sprawled at the side of the road, pallid, almost motionless, one unseeing eye half open. Two stretcher bearers approached and thinking him mortally wounded, lifted him on to their stretcher. Thus shaken and wakened and finding himself about to be carried off for burial, the adjutant addressed himself to the stretcher bearers in a variety of epithets that only a Canadian Highlander adjutant could summon up. The surrounding troops found it hugely amusing . . . for a moment or two.

Even in ostensibly front line positions, when the main focus of battle was elsewhere, there could be moments of almost idyllic peacefulness. 'The slit trench is usually a humble abode but in a day or two there are compartments in one for kits; bunkers for cooking; a sliding roof; straw lined beds. One boy adopted a cow, milked her twice a day, gave her salt, water, changed her pasture regularly.'[24] But not on Verrieres Ridge where some men had to dig new slit trenches three or four times a day and the cows were all dead, swelling balloons of stinking gas or bleached skeletons with four legs pointing to the sky like anti-aircraft guns.

Sometimes amid the torment errant sleep would come tardily:

Men have learned to carry on by grabbing sleep whenever the opportunity arises . . . even during the worst bombardment Able Troop has yet endured. Infantrymen have described falling asleep while continuing to walk robot-fashion up a road. And you know from experience that a man can fall asleep standing up, have done so yourself on more than one occasion recently while leaning over the artillery board.[25]

Spud Taylor remarked on the relationship of sleep with death:

> Crossing the field we came upon a British Tommy lying there, to be factual, the top half of the soldier, the remainder having disappeared. My mind by that time was numb . . . In the rear wood we saw our infantry . . . it was very difficult to tell the living from the dead. Some lay asleep, other ominous bundles lay in a row, wrapped and tied in army blankets. The rest sat around, subdued and quiet, not talking, not a sound.[26]

For Lt John Williamson of 15 Platoon, the Royal Hamilton Light Infantry, sleep could have been fatal one night. After many hours of waking battle he had to crawl across a road, accompanied by a sergeant, to cut some wire in the far ditch. As they were lying on the road about to cut the wire they were stopped by German voices coming from the same ditch a few feet away. The two 'Rileys' froze. They lay *rigor mortis* still, deathly silent in the dark. Suddenly Williamson was wakened by the sergeant feverishly pulling his sleeve and whispering, 'You were bloody well snoring!' It was not very funny at the time.[27]

But when sleep came, came also the nightmares evoked by the sights seen, sounds heard and foul odours smelled everywhere. A CANLOAN officer, Lt S.A. Kemsley (on loan to the British Army) with the 1st The Royal Norfolk Regiment remembered that 'suddenly m-gs cut loose so we hit the ground and the only shelter in the field were dead bloated cattle – I well remember the bullets thudding into the dead cow and the stench that came out'.[28] For Charles Kipp the bodies were not only animal. 'Our front in Bourguebus was littered with dead Germans and horses and all stank to high heaven. The bodies bloated up and rolled around and one exploded about 20 feet out in front of me. What a smell!'[29]

Again Spud Taylor was able to record a similar impression most graphically:

We came upon yet another burnt out Mk IV Panzer. Three of the crew had managed to bale out, one lay on the engine covers, another by the side of the vehicle's track and the other a few yards nearer to the road. All of these pathetic remains were stark naked, black as coal and burned to a cinder, each and every part of the corpses reduced in size until they looked for all the world like small puppets or little black apes.[30]

Of course none of this was worse than what the medics saw, and had to deal with, in desperate attempts to save the lives of those who looked to be damaged beyond human endurance, as Canadian surgeon John Hillsman described:

We saw the tragic sights from which we were never to be free for ten long months. Men with heads shattered and grey, dirty brains oozing out from the jagged margins of skull bones. Youngsters with holes in their chests fighting for air and breathing with a ghastly sucking noise. Soldiers with intestines draining f[a]eces into their belly walls and with their guts churned to a bloody mess by high explosives. Legs that were dead and stinking – but still wore a muddy shoe . . . Boys who lived long enough for you to learn their name and then were carried away in trucks piled high with dead.[31]

Most front line infantrymen had helped to tend one such tragic remnant of a human life or had gathered portions of a mate's body to bury him in a decent temporary hole. And there were always the two kindred thoughts in their minds: 'it's always the other chap who gets it' but also, 'is my name going to be on the next bullet?' It was this constant stress which developed an awful vision in the mind of one FOO (Forward Observation Officer), the forward artillery officer whose duties took him into the 'Forward Defence Localities' (FDLs) of the infantry and sometimes beyond:

I was haunted by a vision of my own psychological collapse, lying gibbering at the bottom of the slit trench while the infantry were desperately calling for artillery support and then being wiped out because I had gone insane and failed them. So I carried a small bottle of rum inside my battledress blouse in case at the final moment of crisis a small nip might restore my balance of sanity. Fortunately I never needed the nip, although I was the only FOO of my regiment to survive the whole campaign.[32]

The North Novas' adjutant outside Tilly, Don Ripley, writes: 'You ask if any of us were truly sane? I think not. We were all caught up in a withdrawal from reality and subject to aberrated behaviour. Our lives were redirected. However, I think that those of us who dodged the bullet and returned were better men.'[33]

Dr Bill McAndrew is one of the leading experts on battle exhaustion and has written much on the subject, more pertinently about the days of the Verrieres/Bourguebus engagements.

Many, wounded or not, were driven into the state known to the troops as 'bomb happy', but in reality a very sad and horrific assault on their very sanity. The War Diary of the Canadian Exhaustion Unit set up to deal with these cases immediately behind the lines recorded:

21 July 1944: Yesterday 59 patients were admitted. Today has been as heavy. We have admitted over 80 patients and they are still coming in. Our routine sedative Sodium Amytal is exhausted and most of a bottle of Medinal which we borrowed is gone. However the day has been saved by the arrival of 2000 capsules of Sod. Amytal.
22 July 1944: One hundred and one cases of exhaustion were admitted . . . our convalescent ward and the 'morgues' are filled [with exhaustion cases] . Those in the morgues have to sleep on blankets spread on the ground. The rain has been pouring down and the majority of the men are wet and muddy.[34]

And all those incidents contributed to a casualty roll such as, 'on the morning of July 26, 1944 Fifth Brigade began the first day of its second week at the front. More than one thousand men, roughly one fifth of the total strength of the brigade and more than half of its infantry rifle strength, were killed, wounded, prisoners of war or exhaustion casualties'.[35]

What this rate of casualties meant in one particular company and one particular platoon is well illustrated by the then Lieutenant Charlie Forbes. For three days Le Regiment Maisonneuve (the 'Maisies') at St Andre had been in 'constant battle, constantly submitted to firing by artillery from both sides, constantly submitted to patrolling by infantry and minor probing attacks by tanks, constantly under observation, continuous violence day and night'. Charlie was called forward from 'A' echelon to reorganize one company which had been reduced to 42 men, about a third of its normal size. There were no officers left, no sergeant-major, no senior NCOs. L/Cpl Mario Bijet had promoted himself to sergeant, sewn on two extra stripes and taken charge. When a new company commander arrived, Charlie was the only officer platoon commander (18 Platoon), Sgt Gay commanded 17 Platoon and 16 Platoon was non-existent.[36]

What this rate of casualties meant to a battalion and to a regiment, is nowhere better illustrated than in the tragedy of the Black Watch, (the Royal Highland Regiment of Canada) on 25 July 1944. According to Charlie Forbes of the Maisies, on arrival in Normandy the Black Watch were 'a bloody good regiment, extremely efficient, everything done by the book, the crack unit'. They had already undertaken two quite successful actions in the preceding days. They had a highly esteemed commander, Lt-Col S.S.T. Cantlie. They were to attack Fontenay-le-Marmion.

At 0400 hours Lt-Col Cantlie held an Orders Group (O group) in an orchard on the outskirts of St Martin-de-Fontenay to plan the attack. Present also were two company commanders and the intelligence officer, Capt J.P.G. Kemp. Suddenly there was a burst of enemy machine-gun fire which penetrated the orchard, killing Cantlie and badly wounding Maj Motzfeldt. The next senior officer, 24-year-old Maj Philip Griffin took charge. Griffin was reputed to be a brilliant officer and very positive in his actions. The brigade commander, Brig Megill (pronounced M'gill, not Meg-ll) came up to discuss the situation with the young but confident Griffin. The two officers stood on a verandah looking out over the ground the Black Watch must cross. From St Martin there was a fairly level road to May-sur-Orne along which the battalion could march, then making a left incline towards Fontenay. The high shoulder of the ridge ran to the left of the road to May but Fontenay was hidden beyond the ridge shoulder and at a lower level.

However, there were various delays and Griffin needed to agree with the artillery on a new schedule of barrage. The way through May, which was being cleared by the Calgaries, was not yet known to be open. The tanks of the 1st Hussars which were to support the Black Watch were assembling in the orchards but would become susceptible to 88 mm fire from enemy tanks on the ridge once the Hussars broke cover. In the circumstances Griffin was proposing to avoid the dog-leg through May and march straight up over the shoulder of the ridge and down into Fontenay. At the same time he ordered his own patrol into May to take out an enemy machine-gun reported there.

The situation was fraught with all the imponderables of battle against the odds. In later years Megill was inclined to think that he might perhaps have cancelled the advance.[37] The deciding factor was the confidence of Griffin and the efficiency of the battalion. Megill allowed Griffin the choice of 'go or stay'. So Griffin set about his preparations which meant a march across open fields to reach the transverse road which was the theoretical start line, before climbing, again across open ground, the ridge which at that point is perhaps at its steepest. The land beyond the hill brow was out of sight.

Griffin formed his battalion, two companies up, about 320 men, the total front line rifle strength after some initial casualties from clearing snipers in St Martin. At 0930 hours the Black Watch stepped forward in drilled open order towards the start line beyond which the artillery barrage would lead them. Enemy fire began to come from in front, from the ridge to the left, and from industrial buildings near on the right. Other enemy gunners on the far side of the River Orne to the west were on elevated ground and could fire across the river. One by one Highlanders began to fall as the advance continued with measured pace, just over 800 yards to the start line and then another 800 yards to the brow of the hill. Beyond the hill across the unseen land perhaps another 1,000 yards into Fontenay.

At the so-called start line, great gaps had appeared in the ranks. Artillery, tank guns, mortars, machine-guns, snipers all fired from south, east, and west. Men fell one by one – past the start line now, but enough rifles still to continue forward with Griffin calling 'Forward men! We've got to keep going'. Like an aircraft in trouble over an ocean the advance had reached a point of final 'No Return'. To halt in that exposed place would be suicidal. To retreat would be as costly as to advance. Advancing, there was always the possibility in war that the forlorn hope would flourish. Later one of the survivors was asked why they kept on going. He replied 'I suppose because that was what was expected of the Black Watch.'

The thinning ranks moved remorselessly on up the steepening slope to the hill brow and then, like mountaineers disappearing into the mists of the ultimate peak, some sixty Highlanders walked on and on over the ridge and disappeared from view. The noise of battle continued beyond that horizon. Wireless communication had been cut off but a wounded officer returned with a message from Griffin. 'Don't send reinforcements: we have too many men trapped here now.' The remnants of the battalion had advanced into a further encirclement of dug-in guns at the edge of the town. Capt E.R. Bennett in St Martin gathered cooks and drivers to form a firm base and receive survivors. Cpl W.J. Steele and Piper J. Mitchell exceeded the call of duty in moving along the slopes to find the wounded.

German sources suggest that some of the enemy had at first watched in wonder and sympathy at the bravery of the advancing men, before ordering their guns to fire. Now unseen, Germans came forward on the level field at the top of the ridge to take in prisoners.

Griffin lay amid the rest of his dead, beyond the brow but short of Fontenay. Of the more than 300 men, some were gathered in wounded from the lower slopes. Only about 16 survivors found their way back from the upper ridge. Of this darkest of days the Black Watch war diary, with typically tight upper lip, stated bleakly:

July 25: The Bn under the command of Maj. Griffin, acting O.C., formed up and went in on the attack, but the COYs were able to get no farther than the ridge overlooking the town when they ran into a heavy concentration of fire, and of the fwd. Companies, practically all are missing.

July 26: [The tight lip begins to tremble] A few, a very few of those missing have managed to make their way back to the Bn and of these, the large majority have been wounded.

July 27: [The human emotion breaks through] No more news of the missing boys.

July 28: We have had no more news of the missing.[38]

Because of the confusion, survivors writing home sometimes erred in references to the fate of comrades. On 10 August a battalion order was necessary to prevent erroneous and worrying information being passed to next of kin, as 'it is kinder to send no information than to send incorrect information. There must be no writing home with details until the CO has been able to send his letter to the next of kin.'

The repulse of the Black Watch, and of other battalions similarly agonizing, would be only temporary. Within two weeks, Canadian and British tanks would roll up and over and beyond those ridges and stand behind the defiant German defenders. Scottish and Canadian Highlanders would at last walk into the charnel villages of Tilly, Verrieres, May and Fontenay. Elite German troops, held along the ridges to counter the incredible bravery of the advancing infantry, would be rushed too late to halt the equally incredible advance of the American armour swinging wide around the circumference of the Falaise battle zones.

So much happened on those slopes about Verrieres and Bourguebus, those pleasant, fertile, blasted, infernal slopes. Four persons, among many, studied the ridge and expressed their own grim sense of trepidation:

Cpl Doug Shaughnessy of the Rileys, at the start line, thought, 'My God, we'll never make it up those slopes.'

Sgt W.R. Bennett of the Royals, between Bourguebus and Tilly, feared 'those of us who are on these slopes will never leave them'.

Maj Jacques Ostiguy, of the Maisies, admitted, 'Looking back up those slopes, I've no idea how on earth we managed to get up them. But get up them we did.'

And another private added, 'A miracle it must have been, walking all the way up those slopes with the 88s and the Moaning Minnies and the machine-guns and dozens of snipers waiting and their artillery registered on every square foot of ground we had to tread on.'[39]

Surprisingly, among all the horrors and technical details of battle, the war history of the Royal Regiment of Canada sounded a kind of requiem for those who never left those slopes where a war cemetery now crowns one of the highest areas around Cintheaux:

High on a hill above Ifs a wayside shrine, miraculously intact in the midst of so much fire, was a ghostly landmark silhouetted against the sky. The figure of Christ seemed to look down with dejected compassion on the battle scene below.

Another war diary noted philosophically 'whoever said "there are no atheists in foxholes" knew whereof he spoke'. Appropriately it was the diarist of the Black Watch of Canada who wrote that note.

CHAPTER TWO

Departure Point 'Despair'

The battlefront was not formed according to rules of military theory but as necessitated by the emergency and the sloping ground of the hillside.

(*Julius Caesar, 57 BC*)

Take 'the finest fighting army of the war, one of the greatest the world has ever seen', place it among defences that 'were as formidable as any encountered in the entire war',[1] and give it total observation from on high of what their opponents were doing. What expectations then might those opponents entertain? The opponents in this case being the British and Canadian armies looking out from Caen and viewing the wheatfields of the Verrieres-Bourguebus ridge.

The History of the 10th Canadian Infantry Brigade gives an interesting description of the view in 1944:

The Caen-Falaise road was a first class broad stretch of pavement. It led up and down gently sloping hills, was sunken between ridges in spots, and long stretches were lined with the traditional high poplars. Small towns lay to right and left, and their crossroads formed barriers of defence all along the way. All these villages however had been under intense bombardment by our artillery and air forces and were just jagged mounds of dust-caked rubble. The only bits standing were the not quite indestructible church spires . . . many a harrassed forward observation officer probably praised these houses of God for an accurate bearing.

For a month after D-Day the Allied armies had fought yard by yard through the restricted bridgehead within the approximate line Caen-Caumont-St Lo, except for the American dash into the cul de sac of Cherbourg. Then the pivotal city of Caen fell and the British and Canadians viewed the promised land of open plains, thought to be 'typical tank country'. The ruler-straight road in front led to Falaise. From Caen other routes led to Rouen, Paris and Berlin. The massing Allied divisions around Caen presented a dangerous challenge to the Nazi regime.

Furthermore, a breakthrough via Falaise or Lisieux could begin to encircle the German forces. So if the German generals responded to the Caen challenge and placed their elite Panzer forces there, the Americans on the Allied right might break through a weaker defence screen and charge around the enemy, completing the encirclement somewhere near Falaise. Montgomery's strategy was calculated to retain the mass of Panzers in front of Caen, but could only do so by mounting attacks strong enough to threaten a breakthrough to the Seine and Paris. Feint attacks would not serve.

From the German point of view it was equally important to halt the Allies by fortifying the dominant ridges south of Caen. The British generals seem to have believed that they could prevail by rolling masses of tanks along the plain, so like Salisbury Plain where many tank regiments had trained. But, as pointed out by Brig 'Rad' Radley-Walters, who commanded a tank squadron there in 1944, 'good tank country is where there are few anti-tank guns'. Or, in other words, 'good tank country' is better anti-tank country if the defenders have the best guns. And the Germans had.

The commander of Canadian II Corps south of Caen, Lt-Gen Guy G. Simonds, made his own appreciation of the situation:

The ground is ideally suited to full exploitation by the enemy of the characteristics of his weapons. It is open, giving little cover to either infantry or tanks, and the long range of his anti-tank guns and mortars, firing from carefully concealed positions, provides a very strong defence in depth . . . In essence the problem is how to get armour through the enemy gun screen to sufficient depth to disrupt the German anti-tank gun and mortar defence, in country highly suited to the tactics of the latter combination.

The dominance of the more powerful German guns was further enhanced by their siting at the start of a long incline which, with a few dips and sharper rises, continued for some 15 miles before the next considerable descent. The River Orne, soon to run into the sea, lay between Caen and Bourguebus. Just south of the Orne, Cormelles stood at an elevation of only ninety-eight feet above sea level. Where the D80 minor road crossed the main road some five miles south of Cormelles the ridge had risen to 413 feet. In between, three miles from the 1944 Cormelles, on the first brow of the slopes, sat the tiny village of Tilly-la-Campagne, just off the main road. The view was extensive and the Germans had the best field glasses in the world. Also their backs were to the sun, whereas the British with their more ponderous binoculars ran the risk of the sun glinting on their lenses when they dared stare up the hill.

Nature and industry had added other hazards for the attacker. Towards St Andre-sur-Orne, the slopes of the ridge as they merged into the river banks were serrated with caves and quarries. More quarries had been opened on high ground. Apparently unknown to the planners, an extensive system of iron mines ran under the ridge from the Orne to the main road. These mines were worked along high galleries with trains carrying both ore and personnel. There were access and egress of those mines in what were to be strategical locations. On the maps issued to Canadian staff the large mine complex at St Martin-de-Fontenay was described as a 'Factory'.

The quarries of May-sur-Orne were nationally famous and had produced the paving stones for the Palace of Versailles. A very hard type of sandstone was quarried and used for all the domestic and farm buildings in the area. Even when ruined by shell fire the sandstone walls and rubble provided excellent fortress bulwarks. Other hindrances to progress included a number of sunken roads and a railway which ran diagonally past Tilly with embankments and cuttings. And everywhere the wheat grew tall, an instant hiding place for machine-guns and snipers. With a minimum of digging, even a Tiger tank could disappear turret down in the corn. The ingenious defenders also noted the abundance of haystacks and realized that snipers could lodge in them and tanks could be disguised as them.

The brain behind the general defence system was that of Rommel. His typical defence structure has been described as:

a line of infantry to absorb the shock,
a supporting line of tanks immediately behind them,
a line of strong points with anti-tank guns,
strong artillery concentrations in concealed positions,
and a second line of strong points with mobile reserves (including panzers) some miles behind.[2]

It was the Royal Regiment of Canada's history which declared that 'the enemy defences were as formidable as any encountered in the entire war'. It was the eminent historian, Max Hastings, who wrote that:

the Allies in Normandy faced the finest fighting army of the war, one of the greatest the world has ever seen. This is a simple truth that some soldiers have been reluctant to acknowledge, partly for reasons of nationalistic pride, partly because it is a painful concession when the Wehrmacht and SS were fighting for one of the most obnoxious regimes of all time. The quality of the Germans' weapons – above all tanks – was of immense importance. Their tactics were masterly: stubborn defence; concentrated local fire-power from mortars and machine-guns; quick counter-attacks to recover lost ground. Units often fought on even when cut off, which was . . . sound tactical discipline.[3]

The Canadian official historian also pointed out that 'the Germans held particularly strong ground, and old mine shafts and tunnels gave special advantages to the defence. Enemy guns and mortars, powerfully seconded by tanks dug in on commanding positions from which they had perfect observation, cut the attacking battalions to pieces. 88 mm [guns] had the roads taped, dropped concentrations on orchards and fields, and then searched systematically.'[4]

Another historian, D'Este, details more specifically the situation south of Caen at the middle of July 1944:

Panzer Group West had disposed the forces of I SS Panzer Corps and LXXXVI Corps in four defensive belts nearly ten miles deep, with a fifth as the reserve. Within the axis of the [Operation] Goodwood advance there were two infantry divisions in the first belt and two panzer grenadier regiments [German regiment = equivalent to a British brigade] of 21st Panzer Division in the second. The third belt was a series of villages heavily fortified with anti-tank guns and infantry and some 270 Nebelwerfers. . . The fifth belt, well out of range of the British guns . . . held some sixty to eighty tanks as his mobile reserve.[5]

Polish Maj-Gen Maczek calculated that on 8 August there were 4 kilometres of first defences, but at Soignolles and Quesnay Woods there were tank traps and pill boxes at 8 to 10 kilometres beyond the first line.[6] A tank troop leader during Operation Goodwood was amazed to learn that the German defences then were 'two and a half times as thick as what they were opposing at that time to the Red Army'.[7]

Among the main forces awaiting the advance south of Caen were the 1st and 12th SS Panzer Divisions and the numerically strong 272nd Infantry Division. The two SS panzer divisions were the only units in the German armies to include the name of Hitler in their titles and to wear his name on their sleeves. They were regarded as the elite and were two of the three most decorated divisions in the

German armies (2nd SS Panzer Das Reich was the third). The 12th SS Panzer Division carried the title 'Hitlerjugend' (Hitler Youth). This was recruited from picked youths of fifteen, who were thoroughly trained and most of whom were eighteen when they first joined battle near the Normandy beaches. The Canadians had already clashed with Hitlerjugend and knew their fanaticism and military skills.

The 1st SS Panzer Division was the proudest of all, having originated from Hitler's personal bodyguard of the 1920s, which was given formal status as the Chancellery Guard in 1933. It carried the designation 'Leibstandarte Adolf Hitler' (LAH). The highest standards of fitness were required and the division had priority in all matters of reinforcement and equipment replacement. It had served with distinction throughout the war and its surviving hardened veterans, leavened by younger recruits, were ready to engage with the somewhat less warlike troops about to attack them.

It is necessary to note that 'the old cinema pictures of vast battalions of Nazi storm-troopers goose-stepping past Hitler . . . gives a false impression of the preparation of Hitlerjugend. The youths . . . were indeed subject to a high degree of Nazi indoctrination but the traditional type of "square-bashing" was prohibited. The Hitlerjugend regime developed . . . a very high level of weaponry and fieldcraft . . . was almost prudishly puritan. Boozing, smoking, visiting brothels and even serious "girlfriending" were officially denied, while a major emphasis was put on sport and fitness. The entire mode of training . . . emphasized technical skills, strict self-discipline and a cool ability to employ tactics like allowing the enemy to pass by and then attacking from the rear.'[8]

Many Allied soldiers recognized, if somewhat grudgingly, the military skills of the best German soldiers, although not agreeing that all German soldiers were better than all Allied soldiers, nor all German units better than all Allied units as some critics seem to have implied. Capt Maurice Berry of the Royal Regiment of Canada writes, 'German infantry fighting in a defensive role were very good, difficult to locate, lots of ammunition and m-gs. They could also call for very heavy and accurate mortar fire on any group of men. The German tanks were very frightening and for us to see many British and Canadian tanks knocked out did not help our morale.'[9]

The then lieutenant Don Learment (North Novas) saw an amazing example of the toughness and endurance of German soldiers. When his company was surrounded by the enemy earlier in the campaign he was taken prisoner and was interrogated by the notorious 'Panzermeyer' of whom more later. The SS leader surprised him as being very proper in his attitude to the prisoners (remembering later that Meyer was accused of shooting prisoners). Don Learment was able to escape but not before spending one night with his guards after trudging miles. They all sat down and took their boots off. Not one of the guards had a full set of toes. Two had no toes at all. They were all frost bite cases from the Russian front but were soldiering on as though toes were unnecessary appendages.[10]

Maurice Berry was correct in saying that the German tanks were frightening, even to Allied tank crews opposed to them. A simple comparison of the two largest German tanks commonly seen with the Allied workhorse tank, the Sherman, illustrates this in terms of total weight of the tank and its thickest armour, usually frontal:

Panther	armour: 4.72 in	weight: 99,868 lb
Tiger	armour: 4.33 in	weight: 125,441 lb
Sherman	armour: 3.00 in	weight: 71,175 lb

Turning to the gun, at 1,000 yards the Sherman 75 mm could penetrate 60 mm of armour, but the Tiger 88 mm could penetrate 102 mm. Again, at that range the Sherman could penetrate 60 mm but the Tiger had front armour of 100 mm. The Tiger could penetrate 102 mm but the Sherman frontal armour was only 76 mm.

Making a different comparison, a Tiger was seen to knock out a Polish Sherman tank at 2 kilometre distance with the shot going right through the turret and out the other side. There are instances of Sherman 75 mm shells bouncing off Tigers like tennis balls at short range. The Panther had a 75 mm gun but it was an upgraded high velocity weapon with a performance not much less impressive than the Tiger's. The smaller German Mark IV tank, about equivalent in size to the Sherman, also packed the higher velocity gun.[11]

The situation was only balanced to some extent when the larger high velocity 17-pounder gun was mounted on the Sherman (which hybrid was then called the 'Firefly'.) The Firefly could respond to the Tiger, gun for gun, but still suffered the handicap of 'corned beef tin' armour and the propensity for exploding into a mass of flames if hit in the engine. As a rule in battle the Firefly was kept hidden behind the other three Shermans of a troop until needed. Being a new gun the 17-pounder also had teething problems, both just before and after D-Day, but when it did fire it began to restore the confidence of Allied tank crews.

Another infantryman, George Cooper of the Regina Rifles, sums up the 88 mm gun, whether mounted on a tank, or as a self-propelled gun, or towed into battle as an infantry anti-tank gun. 'German guns were fearful weapons when we first encountered them. Their 88 we could only respect for its velocity, its smokeless propellant, and its versatility. The sound was terrifying – the muzzle blast and the exploding shell at some distance crashing almost simultaneously.[12]

As terrible in its psychological effect, but even more terrible than the 88 mm in terms of casualties caused, was the *Nebelwerfer*. This was a mortar tube which fired a rocket propelled bomb which would drop vertically on to or into a target. It could be fitted with a siren giving it the name 'Moaning Minnie' or, for the French-speaking Canadians, 'La Vache'. It was commonly fired from multi-barrelled tubes, six to ten together. The bomb loads of the three sizes of *Nebelwerfer* were huge. The three sizes, with weight and range were:

150 mm	weight 75 lb	range 7,300 yd
210 mm	weight 248 lb	range 8,600 yd
300 mm	weight 277 lb	range 5,000 yd[13]

The 272nd German infantry division had three regiments of *Nebelwerfer* at the ready, in total about 200 mortars of the various sizes.

When it came down to small arms, the Germans were equally well supplied. While the merits of respective rifles could be argued, the 'sub-machine-gun' type saw many Allied soldiers carrying the Sten, a simple weapon which could be, and was manufactured in small, poorly equipped workshops. Some troops were happy with the Sten but it had a bad habit of choosing when it would fire, sometimes jamming and sometimes firing without trigger pressure, resulting in numbers of casualties. The German equivalent Schmeisser was a stronger, technically excellent job. All German ammunition used powder which had less flash and smoke than that used in Allied guns, making them far less easy to spot.

The light machine-guns with which the normal infantry units were supplied varied in style and purpose. The Allied Bren was a magnificent weapon of Czech origin which could be fired with the accuracy of a rifle, but at a low rate of fire (500 a minute). The German Spandaus (MG42) were used in a spraying fashion and with a rate of 1,200 a minute could cover a wide area with a mass of bullets in a kind of woven pattern. When it is remembered that a German infantry company carried sixteen of these ferocious bullet-sprayers, some idea will be gained of their ability to develop what might look like a solid blanket of fire across a field. While the Bren and other machine-guns had a regular thudding sound, the noise of the MG42 was likened to ripping calico, or a greatly magnified, hastily pulled up zip!

Several infantrymen facing the Germans on the ridge noted how astute were the tactics used by the enemy in employing their superior weapons. Maj L.L. Dickin commanding 'D' Company of the South Saskatchewans observed the enemy's machine-gun tactics:

The enemy dig shallow pits, 4 feet square by 1½ feet deep, where two men can lie safe from artillery fire. One man pops up, observes, ducks down, and then orders fire, while the other shoots the LMG [light machine-gun] through the wheat. This means that at the moment of firing neither man is looking up, so the fire is hard to pinpoint.[14]

Capt Chapin of the Queen's Own Cameron Highlanders of Canada noticed similar tactics on the part of the enemy tanks:

German technique was to bring three tanks facing west to cover their exposed flank, then five looking north fired into the quarry (where were located our tanks, MMGs [medium machine-guns] and mortars). They would drive up to the crest, take aim and fire, then return to the low ground [behind the crest]. Even under the fire of 17 pdrs and our tanks, Jerry was very audacious. He salvaged tanks from in front of our eyes, getting out and hooking a tow chain on and driving off in the face of our fire. He was in the habit of dismounting and walking around his tanks frequently. His normal procedure was to dismount, walk up to the ridge making a recce and then come back to the tanks and engage his target.[15]

Lt-Col MacLaughlan commanding the Calgary Highlanders detailed how continuous German firing at previously observed target areas made the attackers feel as though they were visible and exposed when they were not:

. . . technique of having his gunners sight on a target and then duck down, firing their guns without observing their targets. This meant we were engaged by weapons which were extremely difficult to locate. He sent fire raining down on any likely attacking position, whether he could observe it or not. The effect was to make one feel under the most skilled and complete observation at all times with 'observed fire' coming from extremely well hidden positions.[16]

Was this then a totally perfect army without failings or indecision? One might ask, 'Was it not disheartening, now that the Allies were securely ashore in Normandy, to know that your own army was likely to be overwhelmed by the vast Allied resources of materiel and personnel, however indifferent their quality? Surely defeat was inevitable?'

The Nazi hierarchy was quite aware of the problems of morale likely to arise. In late 1943 and early 1944, on the initiative of Col Gen Jodl, Chief of Operations at OKW [Supreme HQ], they were already working to match up propaganda and reality in the armed forces: the propagandists proclaiming 'we are winning' and the soldiers complaining 'no we're not'. A task force of instructors termed Nationalsozialistischer Fuhrungsoffizier (NSFO) was sent out to boost the morale of the troops by any means. By December there were 1,074 full time and 46,000 part-time NSFOs.[17]

One of the most loyal Nazis and effective commanders, the newly promoted young general Kurt Meyer, known as 'Panzermeyer', remembered the qualms of the period:

We have often talked of the futility of conflict during the last few weeks and cursed this horrible inhuman war. Why do we not put an end to it? . . . Officers and grenadiers clearly foresee defeat. . . . The political aims of the Allies are felt to be even more awful than the cruellest death. Death has lost its horror a long time ago.[18]

True or not, the German soldiers heard stories about Allied attrocities which angered them. A young SS corporal commanding a mortar crew, Karl-Heinz Decker, was told by supposed eye witnesses about Canadians shooting prisoners. He had no opportunity to check on the truth of the reports but they certainly made him fight more fanatically and consider surrender more dangerous than fighting to the last. His resolve was finally confirmed when he heard that Stalin, Roosevelt and Churchill had agreed that Decker's home region of East Prussia should become a part of the Soviet Union. He now had no home to which he could return. (Eventually he settled in Wales!)[19]

One weakness in the German army, including SS units, was the need to supplement German nationals by recruiting 'foreigners', volunteers or pressed men from occupied countries in Europe, including those vast regions of Russia which had been occupied by the advancing German troops. One of the SS divisions recruited from the Balkans had to be disbanded before it ever received its cap badge because of indiscipline. While some of the foreigners were volunteers with fascist sympathies, many had no desire to fight. They did so only under extreme compulsion and were quick to surrender if the opportunity arose. A message pad, dated 31 July 1944, from the commander of 2 Company 20 SS Panzer Grenadiers was captured, and read: 'Company sector difficult to hold since Ukrainian volunteers can only be kept in line by force.'[20] The next day the deserters from the same regiment (of the 9th SS Panzer Division Hohenstaufen) reported that they had been 'told by their own officers they would be shot and if they succeeded in getting to our lines we would shoot them'. Other foreigners on surrendering were only too anxious to give information to their captors.

The manner in which Hitler himself interfered with decisions in the field is well known and needs little elaboration. Even the highest of German officers found themselves frustrated by commands which were misguided or outdated. Few German soldiers were more highly esteemed than von Runstedt but even he was hog-tied by the insistence of Hitler on deciding even the smallest issues. A friend of von Runstedt wrote about 'the suffering caused him, how it robbed him of rest and sleep to have to stand by in impotent rage while blunder piled on blunder, while our last powers of aggressive action were wasted'.[21]

The chaos caused along German communication lines by Allied bombing was exacerbated by sabotage. Some of that sabotage hindered the ability of the Luftwaffe to strike back at the Allied air forces. Underground cables were cut by French saboteurs and the telephone land-line laid by French technicians had numerous faults built into it. Farther back in occupied Europe saboteurs were also at work. Some

Allied soldiers had cause to thank those unsung heroes directly. On 21 July 1944 five 105 mm shells landed among the lines of battalion HQ of the Royal Regiment of Canada. None exploded. Had they done so tremendous damage would have been caused. Battalion armourers examined the shells and found them to be of Czech origin. The Royals muttered heartfelt prayers for the safety of the Czech saboteurs responsible.

So much for the German defenders. The major part of the forces attacking the ridge was Canadian supported by British elements and, for Operation Totalize, Polish troops. They enjoyed the blessing of air cover by the superior Allied air forces, although the Luftwaffe was not totally absent from the skies as some commentators may have implied. The effectiveness of the air support for ground forces was marred at times by an unwieldy system for requesting air support. In one incident which will be explained a tank officer spent most of a day trying to direct air support on to a promising target. One historian summed up the problem of normal routine at the time, remembering also that the RAF and Royal Canadian Air Force were under separate command to the USAAF:

A unit being hit had to inform Brigade Headquarters; they would tell Divisional Headquarters; Divisional Headquarters would pass the message on to Corps Headquarters; and Corps Headquarters would pass it on to Army headquarters. The message would be given to the Senior Air Staff Officer who would relay it to the appropriate authorities in Bomber Command. Meanwhile the bombers were flying at about 250 miles an hour, Squadron after Squadron, dumping their bombs on friendly troops.[22]

A present-day general has pointed out the distinctive nature of the Canadian Army in Normandy in 1944:

Every man had volunteered for overseas service. . . . The policy had two effects: first, motivation was high; second, there was a serious shortage of reinforcements available to replace battle or other casualties. The shortage of reinforcements had in turn two serious consequences – a man who had been highly trained in a specialist role could hardly be spared to replace a basic infantryman, and as the campaign progressed, this produced serious undermanning in front-line units; and the army on the battlefield felt increasingly that their sacrifices were being made in isolation from the rest of the nation.[23]

From a manpower point of view the Allied armies were also most affected by what one critic has called 'the ineluctable growth of the armies' "tail"'. More soldiers were needed to get a combat man into battle than were actually operating as combat men. An infantry division needed 17,000 men but only 4,000 of those 'actually carried rifle and bayonet'. And, even so, while the British and Canadian armies in North-West Europe at the close of 1944 numbered 514,000, the Supreme Headquarters structure of 21st Army Group required 302,000 personnel on Lines of Communication duties.[24]

The question as to whether the Allies or the Germans were more highly motivated is a subject for endless debate. The various elements of motivation for the Germans were powerful in combat: sheer fanaticism in some cases; absolute draconian discipline in most cases; fatalism related to the inevitable outcome of the war; and, in the better units, superb training and absolute confidence in, and loyalty to, their field commanders.

The motivation for Allied soldiers, although usually based on an abhorrence of what they understood the Nazi regime to be, tended to be more muted and also confused by the desire to achieve demobilization in a victorious country looking to a better world. For most, there was a strict drilling in obedience to orders and a sense of performing an important duty. This is well summed up in the words of one platoon commander, who stated that 'a burning desire to kill Germans was lacking among the soldiers of the North Shore [Regiment]. I am not suggesting that in battle they were hesitant to carry out their tasks.'[25]

It must be noted that many Allied soldiers in 1944, like the author himself, young and poorly informed, did not have full access to gruesome reports about such matters as the inhuman conditions in Nazi concentration camps. These now familiar reports, magnified by war crimes trials and amplified by radio, cinema and television, were not yet divulged in their full horror to the world in general. Many Allied soldiers saw Hitler as more of a figure of fun, and 'Jerry', 'Fritz' or 'Heinie' as an old antagonist come back for a replay of the mortal combat of 1914–18, 'like in our Dad's time'. It tended to be more senior commanders who referred to 'The Hun'. Warnings about the SS 'not playing the game' did not at first inspire any great blaze of berserk hatred in battle, unless and until the individual soldier had experienced some act of unacceptable military behaviour.

Having said this, there was in most soldiers a sub-stratum of patriotism which they found difficulty in expressing. In the final accounting of battle it was the old climactic truth: destroy or be destroyed. Who shoots first and straightest survives. Many fought with apparent ferocity not so much against the German *personlich* but against his power to kill very efficiently.

Maj Jacques Ostiguy won the high distinction of a DSO for his actions on the ridge and is entitled to speak about bravery under fire. He says:

> You weren't naturally aggressive. You had to make yourself aggressive or at least make yourself look aggressive. It was always the quiet men who achieved the toughest tasks, not like in the film 'The Dirty Dozen'. The boasters soon disappeared in one way or another. Look at me, a little, relatively frail man, I would never qualify for the Dirty Dozen.[26]

At the highest level of command there was pressure on Montgomery, commanding all the Allied troops in Normandy, to hurry on his left flank of British and Canadians around Caen. The American press trumpeted that their troops had raced to Cherbourg in less than a week and were fighting in the most dense Bocage areas. Montgomery's Chief of Staff recorded that the Supreme Commander, Eisenhower was therefore under pressure from his own compatriots, some of which pressure he had to pass on to 'Monty':

> Eisenhower was being subjected to a pretty violent press campaign in America about the slowness in Normandy and the results achieved by the American troops compared with those by our men. 'Why don't the British do some fighting?' . . . Eisenhower, of course, knew Monty's plan, but he couldn't announce to the world what was going on.[27]

It may be that such pressure tilted the balance in leading Montgomery and others to make over-optimistic statements, announcing substantial victories before they were consolidated, and extending expectations of planned operations to targets which were clearly unattainable. Had Montgomery, Simonds and others been less optimistic in their plans it is possible that subsequent criticism might have been less harsh. If one says one is 'going for Falaise' then one fails if one does not arrive there within the time frame appropriate to the plan.

These were the human and strategic parameters out of which the Verrieres-Bourguebus mathematics would develop, in lives mourned and lives destroyed, ground gained and ground conceded, tanks brewing and tanks brewed up, and, later still, historians praising and historians condemning. All in what many considered, and the Royals' scribe expressed as 'some of the fiercest fighting of the whole war'.

With that enemy awaiting them on that terrain with those guns all loaded, the Allies' departure point on 18 July 1944 might well have been code-named Despair.

CHAPTER THREE

Operation Atlantic – in Deep Water

He sent out a force of infantry and cavalry in three columns to pursue the fleeing enemy. . . . They had advanced some way . . . when dispatch riders brought news from Atrius of a great storm

(Julius Caesar, 54 BC)

The British had their minds on horse racing while the Canadians were thinking about the boat journey home. At least that is the impression which might be given by the choice of code words for the dual operation south of Caen, commencing 18 July 1944. The British called their attack Operation Goodwood, having already used Epsom. The Canadians called their share Operation Atlantic. The two words described a simultaneous two-pronged attack. The Germans knew perfectly well that it was coming, whatever the code words.

Canadian troops had taken part in the D-Day landings but now, five weeks later, more formations were landing. On 13 July the main part of the Canadian II Corps headquarters came ashore, including the signals element, with nearly 800 personnel and 350 vehicles. That same day Second Army commander, Lt-Gen Dempsey met with three corps commanders, Lt-Gens Crocker, O'Connor and the Canadian Guy G. Simonds. There they discussed the forthcoming operations.

On 17 July Dempsey issued the formal orders which would send three British armoured divisions, with some 800 tanks, rolling across the River Orne, over bridges already occupied, to the east of Caen, then wheeling right before dashing across the level Caen plain between Giberville and Bras and on up the slopes of the Bourguebus

Ridge. Destination Falaise! Or at least that was what many people thought at the time. The Canadian 8th Infantry Brigade would wheel inside the British right, turn and clear the outskirts of Caen on the south side of the river. Meanwhile the Canadian 7th Infantry Brigade would cross the broken bridges in the southern outskirts of Caen itself and move forward on the right flank of the entire massive operation.

The Goodwood attack would be made by tanks, culpably deprived of sufficient infantry support. The Atlantic attack would be infantry-intensive but with tank support. The vast assembly of troops and vehicles gave everyone encouragement although some foresaw traffic jams. Typically the South Saskatchewan Regiment, which had landed only on 8 July, thought 'that with tanks in front of us there would not be heavy opposition', according to their war diary.

In the general area of Caen racecourse (not ironically in the Goodwood sector!) and the railway station it would be the Reginas and the Black Watch of Canada who would dare the river crossing over or under the smashed bridges. The Regina Rifles, who would become the Royal Regina Rifles in 1982, were more familiarly known as the 'Farmer Johns' or just the 'Johns' from out on the great prairies. They derived their ancestry from the 95th Saskatchewan Rifles, which sent the 28th Battalion to France in 1914–18, there to win no less than thirteen DSOs, while one of their lieutenants had moved to another battalion and won the VC. The Reginas had landed on D-Day and taken part in difficult battles north of Caen.

Parts of Caen had been turned into mountains of rubble by the huge RAF raid prior to liberation. The author experienced something of this when the tank in which he was the gunner, 3 Baker of C squadron in 1st Northamptonshire Yeomanry, was sent in after the raid as lead tank to try to enter Caen. Attempting to cross the rubble the Sherman tank eventually drove down into a multiple crater so deep that the crew, standing on top of the turret, could not see up to ground level. This destruction meant that there was no possibility of 800 tanks from the three armoured divisions driving through Caen. Therefore they had to loop to the east. Equally it meant that the Canadians by the railway station at the southern edge of Caen could not expect major tank support as they attempted to rebuild the bridges.

Just before midnight on 14 July, the Reginas' scout officer, Lt Bergeron had taken a patrol across what was left of the Epron railway bridge near Caen station. He was therefore the ideal man to lead the Atlantic attack when it commenced on the 18th. French guides were attached to the battalion and given uniform. Two of the French guides were men of heroic stature: Pierre Chatelain and Guy Merle.

Chatelain was attached to 'Bergeron's Boys', a group who had volunteered for the hazardous job of patrolling, who were described as 'unkempt and slap happy' but who would 'make many a platoon officer and sergeant breathe easier, knowing that the scouts would be assigned to do the patrols'.[1] Bergeron with Chatelain and fifteen men crossed the bridge which was useable only by crawling men. They reached the south bank with the loss of one man but then five enemy machine-guns opened up at close range and laced the crossing with bullets at a combined rate of 100 per second. The support group carrying the 46 wireless set was unable to cross. Chatelain, clinging close to the girders, crawled back and forward several times to pass information to headquarters.

At 1500 hours Able and Dog companies arrived at their start line after their own cockroach scrabble over rubbish heaps and uprooted railway lines. Bergeron and Chatelain decided to try to construct a link across the gaps in the bridge. As Chatelain crossed one more time he was killed by the incessant machine-gun fire. By 1700 the carriers had found a way through the ruins and their own machine-guns and mortars were able to subdue the German fire. Able and Baker then crossed fairly easily but Dog was delayed because they were to have used assault boats which the German gunners had riddled with bullets and sunk.

Meanwhile Guy Merle was attached to Lt 'Buzz' Keating's 18 Platoon which was in the lead. Buzz describes Guy as 'a very fearless young boy'. He himself had been in action only three or four days and still could not distinguish between 'our' shells and 'theirs'. He found everything 'very scary and very noisy'.[2] Guy Merle continues the story:

Passing through the buildings of an old exhibition fair we soon arrive close to the water . . . twenty metres wide and up to eight deep. Not an easy place to cross. The few kapok boats which we have are found to be pierced. It is necessary to make a decision and make it quick because the barrage of artillery has ceased and the 'Boche' who still occupy the Caen station will soon counter-attack us. The lieutenant gives the orders and the soldiers quickly lay some planks on the rails that remain of the railway bridge. I follow the lieutenant closely and after a little trapeze exercise, not without wetting my feet, I arrive again on firm land.

Next we make an excursion into the goods section of the railway station . . . a German m-g opens fire . . . our m-gs fire, sweeping under the abandoned goods waggons . . . slowly we progress! . . . an order – four men detach to the right, go throwing smoke bombs into the immense warehouse. This moment, like from an anthill, 'fritzes' flood out. We profit and take a leap towards the waiting room. After a serious cleansing of the cellars we round up 69 prisoners. The station is totally occupied.[3]

As the Reginas push forward on all sides, Rifleman F. Court also has sudden bursts of excitement:

clearing out snipers . . . we were pinned down and unable to move ahead. We knew where the problem was. We couldn't get at them with small arms fire. They were too far away for hand grenades. By this time I had been carrying the PIAT [Projectile Infantry Anti-Tank] for what seemed like a lifetime. I looked at it and said to our sergeant 'You give me some covering fire and I'll get those SOB's out of there.' The sergeant asked 'How are you going to do that?' I said, 'You see that shutter on that window? I'll try to hit that.' He said, 'It sounds crazy but try it.' I prepared the PIAT, received the covering fire . . . fired the PIAT. . . . Bull's eye! Out came three Germans, ass over applecart, shouting 'Me Polack'.[4]

Amid the heroics of those whose lot it was to walk directly at the enemy guns, as the casualties mounted the extraordinary heroes were the stretcher bearers (often regimental bandsmen). Although they wore a Red Cross on their arms, screaming bombs and spinning shrapnel and searing blasts were no respecters of such symbols. One of the 'Johns', Sgt George Cooper, paid tribute to their courageous deeds as among the noblest of acts seen on the battlefield:

Noted a stretcher bearer calmly going into the open field while shrapnel was still scattering all around to attend to a bleeding soldier; staying in the open to apply a tourniquet and then remaining crouched over the wounded soldier until the shelling moved on. Only then did he come back to get a volunteer to help carry the wounded one back to where we crouched in our slit trenches. No time to write a citation.[5]

In fact, not far away from George, a Service Corps driver won the Military Medal, first of all amid devastating shellfire moving wounded soldiers from a canvas shelter into a safer house and then, still under intense fire in the street, changing the shattered tyres of the ambulance in order to evacuate the wounded more quickly.

Another of the Reginas recalled how disheartening it was to survive a ground battle and then be fired on from the air by accident, as described by that most fraudulent term 'friendly fire':

A short while later on this same road a lone Spitfire flew by and then to our sudden amazement came round from our rear and with its guns blazing strafed our column. It passed so low overhead I think I could have reached up and touched the plane . . . then with our yellow smoke and us waving yellow scarves he flew by dipping his wings up and down as to say, I'm sorry for the mistake and then he took off. A few minutes later this lone US Thunderbolt plane at our rear released its bomb, we could see it dropping and it landed among Cdn army ammunition trucks so as to cause deaths and wounded.[6]

At the same time as the Reginas were assembling at their start line the men of the Black Watch of Canada were waiting to move from the racecourse at Caen. It has already been seen how, one week later, the soldiers of this regiment had the *esprit de corps* to walk steadily through a death trap. It is therefore pertinent to explain the background of some of these very proud Canadian regiments. The Canadian Army at first consisted entirely of part-time volunteer militia, but those volunteers claimed roots which dug back to the beginning of Canadian history.

In 1756 the Scottish Black Watch had been sent to Canada, and entered Montreal in 1760 at the end of the war between Britain and France. The regiment stayed in Canada until 1767 and then returned during the War of American Independence. Numbers of British soldiers took their 'demob' on that side of the Atlantic and settled in Canada. On 12 June 1775 authority was given for raising in North America a corps of 'Royal Highland Emigrants' from these ex-servicemen, to defend the border of Canada.

Under the First Volunteer Act of 1855 the Canadian Army was modernized with a structure of twenty-two companies. In 1862 the embryo 'Black Watch' was designated as the Royal Light Infantry, and later as the Royal Highlanders of Canada (RHC). In some war diaries of 1944, the battalion is still noted as the RHC, although it formally took the name 'Black Watch' in 1907. It served in the First World War, and was awarded six VCs.[7] Such links are the elements which fuse to produce regimental pride.

Now, on 18 July 1944 the Black Watch waited for last light near Franqueville with their revered commander, Lt-Col S.S.T. Cantlie. They were to cross the River Orne on assault boats and a kapok bridge, but without artillery support – which often served to warn the defenders. But the enemy was alert and opened fire with machine-guns and mortars. There were heavy casualties, boats were wrecked and the fragile bridge was attacked by the Luftwaffe as it was being assembled. The two parts of the bridge failed to meet. Lt T.K. Dorrance was commanding the lead platoon which was unable to cross the big river. Dorrance immediately dived in, swam out to hold the two pieces of the bridge together. His men hurried across the bridge while the soaking wet officer exerted all his force to stay afloat while holding the bridge in place. The platoon cleared the way for the battalion to advance and occupy its objective, the southern suburb of Vaucelles.

On the extreme right of the Allied advance the intention was to take the village of Louvigny, south-west of Caen but still on the Caen side of the River Orne. From Louvigny another crossing might be made if others failed. The task was given to the Royal Regiment of Canada, another proud regiment, under the command at the time of Maj J.G.H. Anderson. The regiment was originally an initiative of skilled artisans who, at a meeting in December 1861 formed 'The Toronto Engineers and Mechanics Rifle Corps', to enlist men from those professions. After three months the corps was formalized into the 10th Battalion Volunteer Rifles and the next year the designation Royal Regiment was incorporated into the title. The regiment had landed in France with the first Canadian contingent in 1915 and had won two VCs by 1918.

Now their route to Louvigny lay through an orchard of the local chateau, past the chateau and into the village. The orchard was protected by a seven foot high wall of large boulders, so tanks of 10th Canadian Armoured Regiment (10 CAR, Fort Garry Horse) would blast holes in the wall from a distance. Dog company under Maj J.D. Fairhead led the way at 1800 hours and found the German machine-guns and mortars apparently slow to respond. All went well until they passed through three breaches made by the tank fire, when enemy fire blasted forth in full spate. Maj Fairhead was killed just inside the wall, as was the only other officer in the lead, Lt E.J. Chellew. Sgt O.C. Tryon of the mortar platoon reorganized Dog company and advanced through the orchard into the chateau, for which he was awarded the Military Medal.

However, the defenders were well sheltered throughout the orchard in aerial bomb craters. All the Royals' wireless sets had gone dead so there was no way of calling for artillery fire. The brigade commander, Brig Lett, with liaison officer Lt L. Patterson came forward to make contact. Another burst of mortar fire killed Patterson and badly wounded the brigadier. The forward companies had continued to push forward through the trees and hedges, men falling as they went. With the companies so dispersed Maj Anderson sent Sgt Corbett in a carrier to make contact but the carrier was blown up on a mine and the driver killed. Corbett walked back bringing two prisoners with him.

Lt L.H. Gage and 8 Platoon had forced their way into the north of the village itself through continual crossfire and encountering enemy infantry every few yards. Then some French refugees met the soldiers with the news that a large enemy force was moving through from the south of the village. It was therefore decided to reform in the orchard as a firm base. It was during this fighting that a German infantryman was throttled in hand-to-hand fighting of the most desperate kind. Yet, at first light, Baker company moved forward cautiously, as Charlie company cleared the chateau grounds, and found that the enemy had withdrawn from the area. Fifty-five prisoners had been taken but the Royals had suffered 111 casualties.

On the Canadian left flank the French-speaking Regiment de la Chaudiere faced a task that was immense in every sense: they were to clear the immense Colombelles steel works. The author remembers firing a Sherman 75 mm gun, together with some sixty other tanks of 1NY (the 1st Northamptonshire Yeomanry), each gun firing some thirty shells and, at the end of the bombardment, there was no significant visible damage to the vast complex. This included smelting furnaces, rolling mills and, towering above all, high and apparently indestructible chimneys with a view for miles around. Truly a ready-made fortress if ever there was one.

Once named the Provisional Battalion of Dorchester, then the Beauce Regiment, the regiment assumed the title 'de la Chaudiere' in 1936. It is unlikely that anyone on the staff noticed the pun, for a meaning of *chaudiere* is boiler, and here was one of the largest complexes of furnaces in France. And once the regiment had dealt with the steel works there was still a large chateau nearby manned by the enemy. In bitter fighting the French Canadians lost half of their 'B' Company, then a quarter of both 'A' and 'D' Companies in subduing the extensive defences.

Alongside the Chaudiere men, the Queen's Own Rifles of Canada, with support of two squadrons of the 1st Hussars (6th CAR) found a sensitive place in the enemy line and swept into their Giberville objective, suffering 78 casualties but counting up 600 prisoners taken and 200 of the enemy left dead in and around the village. But this kind of battle accounting was irrelevant to the man in the slit trench. The elimination of 800 enemy could not compensate for the tragedy of one lost comrade, as a caring CSM, Charlie Martin recorded:

Heavy fire was coming from the village. 'A' Coy achieved its objective but lost all three newly-arrived platoon commanders who had been promoted from the regiment's ranks via an Officers' Training Unit. The company mourned the loss of Rifleman Buck Hawkins, 39 years of age and a tower of strength, six foot two and 190 pounds. Corporals had taken over 8 and 9 platoons and some of the men had moved forward from the objective to what looked to be a better position at a hedgerow and railway line. Just then two enemy companies, about 400 men, burst out of the wood and counter-attacked. CSM Charlie Martin went forward to order the isolated men back and also called for smoke cover. Most of the men pulled back safely but only because Buck, with one or two others, had stayed until last to give covering fire. When all ammo was used up the tiny rearguard began to pull back but Buck was hit and killed by a fierce burst of machine-gun fire. Later colleagues went out through the continuing fire to bring back Buck's body.[8]

The Stormont, Dundas and Glengarry Highlanders had been brought forward to share with the Chaudiere men the attack on the Colombelles chateau, beyond the steel works. As at Louvigny there was a walled orchard with enemy defence posts dug deep in craters and pits between the trees, which were thick with lush leaves and ripening fruit. The CO, Lt-Col G.H. Christiansen, always concerned for his men, called for tank support. He was told that none were available (indeed there were only about 950 tanks located within two or three square miles of the orchard!). So he stepped outside the orchard, stopped two Cromwell tanks of 2nd Northamptonshire Yeomanry (2NY), and persuaded them to 'brass up' the orchard, while the infantry fought yard by yard through the trees.

Due to traffic jams away down the supply lines, the Stormonts had only one hard biscuit and one slice of spam each all that day. Having fought throughout the day, and watched through the night, they were alert by 0400 hours next morning clearing the last snipers from the chateau. The new dawn brought them no encouragement for, as they completed their own task and looked out across the opening plain, they were disillusioned to see some hundred or more wrecked British tanks and only fifteen derelict enemy panzers. Something must have gone sadly wrong.

Something had! One commentator wrote, 'The Canadians had made good progress' in the Atlantic element of the twin plan.[9] The Canadians had achieved the plan to 'capture and hold Vaucelles and Giberville . . . and build bridges over the River Orne at Caen'. The British element coded Goodwood was to 'establish armoured divisions in Vimont, Garcelles-Sequeville, Hubert Folie, Verrieres and patrol south in direction of Falaise'.[10] But the date of 18 July 1944, together with the morrow, would go down in the annals of British armour as 'the Death Ride of the Armoured Divisions'.

Much has been written about the disaster of Goodwood. A force of three British armoured divisions, with about 800 tanks available, was launched across the plain near Cagny and Cormelles on 18 July, with the intention of advancing rapidly up the Bourguebus Ridge. Over three days about half the tank strength was lost but the advance failed to achieve the totality of Montgomery's own injunction of 15 July 'to dominate Bourguebus – Vimont – Bretteville and armoured cars to push far to the south'. Rain and mud completed the disappointment.

There were two main factors in the Goodwood shambles. The first was the failure to recognize the perils of sending weaker tanks en masse across open ground towards more powerful armour, and without adequate infantry support. The second was a text book movement schedule for enabling the divisions to arrive on time, which ignored the obvious factors of narrow bridges, restricted roads, destroyed villages, cratered land, and the propensity of machines to break down and of the enemy to cause disruption. Support troops were delayed while the forward tanks were being decimated.

Sgt fitter Sid Jones (2NY) in his carrier was ordered to follow his squadron through the railway arch near Soliers. The embankment was high and 2NY had advanced unmolested behind it. Now the nineteen tanks and the fitters' armoured recovery vehicle (ARV) passed through the arch. The Germans waited until the entire squadron was in the open: then unleashed their guns at long range. Ten Shermans were brewed up in minutes and only nine returned from the killing ground. Sid Jones found himself more urgently called on to stem bleeding wounds that to repair machines. The worst 'bleeder' had a lip ripped off by shrapnel and Jones's crew did not have the skills to staunch the flow of blood.[11]

On the narrow roads across the plain advancing troops were involved in traffic problems with ambulances evacuating burn cases from brewing tanks. A Canadian officer, Gordon Brown, was appalled by what he saw:

I went to a British field hospital near Reviers . . . they couldn't remove the tiny piece of shrapnel that had struck a vertebra behind my throat. So I left hospital and returned to the regiment [Reginas]. While I was in the hospital there were 300 British tank soldiers arrived. All wounded and in many cases burned very badly. I went with one of the Medical Officers to see the wounded men. It was one of the most sad experiences that I have ever had . . . I had great admiration for our tank crews who lived very much on the edge, and who suffered terribly when their tanks burst into flame.[12]

The Canadian infantry on the Allied right could face the dawn of 19 July with some confidence in their achievements of the previous day but with many worries about the British armour lagging behind on their left. On 18 July the Canadians had advanced on a wide front stretching from Louvigny to Giberville, a good five and a half miles. The British armour had now swung across much of that front and turned to face up the Bourguebus part of the ridge. Three Canadian infantry battalions would therefore advance towards the Verrieres part of the ridge, to the right of the main Caen to Falaise road, on a front of less than two miles around Fleury and Ifs.

Cormelles village, now linked into urban Caen, was then a separate locality but, with its large car factory, was a complicated area to clear of enemy snipers. On 19 July, the Highland Light Infantry of Canada had to complete this operation, which it did successfully, in order to allow three other battalions to advance. The British armour was now scheduled to sweep across the front of the HLI.

At 1300 hours the Regiment Maisonneuve was due to set off down the Caen to Fleury road and almost ran into disaster immediately. The 'Maisies', as they were known, took their title from Paul de Chomedey de Maisonneuve (1612–76), also known as the Sieur de Maison-neufve, the first governor of the island of Montreal. He had recruited settler-soldiers from France in 1653 to defend Montreal against the raids of Iroquois Indians. Now the French-speaking 'Maisies' assembled with Able and Dog companies up, at what was perceived to be the start line. It proved to be some 200 to 300 yards too far forward and . . . down came their own artillery barrage on top of them.

Maj L. Brosseau, commanding Dog company, attempting to sort out the situation, was killed, as was Capt A.L. Orieux. The CO, Lt-Col H.L. Bisaillon, came forward and ordered the other two companies to take over the roles of Able and Dog, which they did. Meanwhile Capt G. Vallieres reorganized Dog and got them moving again. Supported by a squadron of Sherman tanks of the Sherbrooke Fusiliers (27 CAR), medium machine-guns of the Toronto Scots and guns of 20 Canadian Anti-tank Battery, the force reached La Haute with relatively few casualties, and by 1630 had consolidated on the objective.

The infantry were still moving forward with considerable panache at this stage and, at 1715, it was to the ancient skirl of bagpipes that the Calgary Highlanders stepped out. Entering Fleury they were then directed on to a strategic stretch of high ground, la Poudriere, between Fleury and St Andre. On the hill they dug-in quickly but the enemy had now opened up with heavy mortar and machine-gun fire and by 1830 a panzer counter-attack was on the way. Maj F. Baker, soon to be wounded, had pushed forward a patrol led by Lt Vern Kilpatrick, carrying one of the awkward and not too reliable PIATs. The German battle group hit Kilpatrick's small patrol but the PIAT fire knocked out three panzers. This sounded a clear alarm to the main Calgary body who resisted a fierce attack until dark. Kilpatrick was killed.

Moving at 1900, and also supported by Sherbrooke tanks, the Black Watch completed the day's operation by capturing the important village of Ifs, now 2½ miles beyond the point where they had crossed the Orne. The battle appeared to be progressing favourably although Maj 'Rad' Radley-Walters of the Sherbrookes saw panzers milling around on high ground too far away to begin shooting.[13] There was plenty of incentive for everyone to dig in deeply.

It might be thought that in fertile agricultural country like Normandy digging in would be easy. George Cooper did not remember it as so:

Digging in Normandy soil reminded us that this wasn't Canadian prairies. The Normandy clay was slow tough digging in most places. A good thing some planner was alert enough to provide man-sized spades and picks and remove what would have been useless from our kit – the folding shovel. Nothing like a hole in the ground to soothe the infantryman's fears of enemy fire.[14]

This impression was confirmed by Evert Nordstrom who recalled 'the hard time of trying to dig a hole in the hard based ground on the attack towards Falaise'.[15] Gunner George Blackburn observed that the infantry soon worked out the best scientific ways of acquiring shelter. For instance, if enemy fire was coming from the south it made sense to dig the slit trench running from east to west across the line of fire, rather than north to south along the line of falling shells.

While the Canadian infantry sat along the line of objectives on the Verrieres feature, the three British armoured divisions were still deep into their 'death ride'. Maj Gordon Brown observed this with both comradely sadness and keen disappointment:

> I was taking D company towards Bourguebus when I noticed dozens of British tanks just ahead of us and off to the right in a field. 'Great!' I thought to myself. 'We finally have a lot of tank support.' But when we had reached our position I learned that all those British tanks had been knocked out in the massive British advance.[16]

At that point in the proceedings it seemed that the heavens had tired of the puny human tumult of pseudo thunder, sham lightning or mock gales of hissing bullets, and had decided to give a full-blooded demonstration of real celestial anger, noise, flame and floods which would stun the humans into inactivity. The hot weather had given birth to the inevitable semi-tropical storm which arrived to interfere with the best assessments of generals and colonels. Just to complicate things a little more, during the night the Reginas were hit by a 'buzz bomb', one of the V1 flying bombs intended no doubt for London. It was sufficiently astray to cause debate as to whether Hitler might be planning to use that weapon in the battle lines.

In fact it was not to buzz bombs that the German commander Gen Eberbach was looking. During the evening of 19 July he had ordered into the Canadian area a Mk IV tank battalion and a panzer grenadier battalion. About midnight he also decided to order forward a Panther battalion, a recce battalion and another artillery battalion. God and Mammon appeared to be conspiring on Verrieres Ridge for the dawn of the 20th.

While the British 5th Royal Tank Regiment was slogging up to Bourguebus in the dying urges of Goodwood, 6th Canadian Infantry Brigade (6CIB) had made its plans to defy the enemy and the elements. It would fight with all three battalions up, Queen's Own Cameron Highlanders on the right, South Saskatchewans centre and Les Fusiliers de Mont-Royal left. Essex Scots, on loan, would be in reserve and two squadrons of the Sherbrookes would give support. Up the hill the enemy's numerically strong enemy 272nd Infantry Division waited. Many of its men were conscripted Russians and so there was a shadow of doubt about its reliability. But giving the 272 support and a measure of compulsory resolution was 'Hitler's Own', 1st SS Panzer LAH with 70 tanks available. The Canadian plan was to start shelling at 1007 hours and attack at noon.

Sometimes the impression is given that the Western Front of 1914–18 or the Eastern Front of 1941–45 were more bloody than the Normandy campaign. No doubt in aggregate they were, but in instances of maximum intensity the slopes of Verrieres-Bourguebus were of that ilk. This can be detailed specifically in terms of artillery bombardment, as a 1944 witness and 1990s historian George Blackburn relates:

At Passchendaele in 1917 guns fired 78.8 rounds per gun per day over 18 days. At Valenciennes in 1918 firing, according to Maj-Gen McNaughton, a weight of gunfire approximating that used in the whole South African war and exceeding that fired at Jutland, they averaged for two days *146* rounds per guns per day. The Canadians from 20 to 27 July 1944 [at Verrieres] averaged *385* rounds per gun per day. (The entire 21st Army Group averaged 78 rounds per gun per day, which was considered worryingly excessive).[17]

While the three British armoured divisions were well behind schedule for their Goodwood objectives, one forward troop achieved success which caused some disruption in Canadian plans. It looked as though some tanks of 4th County of London Yeomanry (4CLY) had forestalled Les Fusiliers and captured Verrieres Ridge ahead of time. The British tank officer, John Cloudsley-Thompson remembers:

We continued our advance, mopping up more enemy infantry as we went. One sergeant tank commander captured a small ridge firing a Sten gun from the turret of his tank when both the Besa machine-gun and 75 mm had jammed. We crossed the [main Caen] road and captured a small wood on the slope beyond. German infantry were hiding in the corn all round us: we fired at them with machine-guns and high explosives, and took many prisoners. We were shelled and mortared heavily the whole time. Then we entered the wood, our Cromwells facing outwards in all directions and waited.[18]

What John did not know at the time was that the Canadian guns were lined up to pound the ridge on which he was sitting. Indeed he might have held the ridge himself if the Goodwood planners had not risked a tank attack with insufficient infantry support. What happened within his small command was, 'the sun shone warmly and I could barely stay awake. At length we were ordered to withdraw. A big Canadian attack was scheduled and our presence upset their fire plan.' He then moved back and proceeded to fight German tanks from a distance. The big attack was retimed from noon to 1500.

As the guns roared out the Queen's Own Cameron Highlanders under Lt-Col Norman Ross, set off, passing through the Calgary lines and down the slope of the hump towards St Andre-sur-Orne which was, at that moment, just one more village on the way to Berlin. Immediately the White (carrier) rear link was hit by anti-tank fire, killing the intelligence officer and the OC of HQ company. The colonel led his men on through fierce fighting down into the village. The other two battalions were also going well. The South Sasks (Lt-Col F.A. Clift) were on their objectives by 1700. Although they had not eaten a meal for twenty-three hours, Les Fusiliers Mont-Royal (Lt-Col J.G. Gauvreau) with five Sherbrooke tanks had collected twenty-five prisoners by 1605 in the course of capturing the vital Beauvoir Farm on a transverse road.

It might be expected that the Germans would counter-attack. What was not so easily foretold, on the evidence of the previous two days, was the power and ferocity of the attack. The 'South Sasks' were temporarily commanded by Maj G.R. Matthews as Lt-Col Clift was commanding the brigade after the wounding of the brigadier. They moved fast for 1,000 yards until encountering opposition based on what the war diary describes as a 'wireless station' but which local historians consider must have been a halt shed on a light tramway. Still they pushed on, discovering, as many soldiers would, that from the top of every fold of ground a higher ridge would come into view. They reached the D89 road at la Moulin de Voide.

At 1750 enemy tanks and the gods of thunder attacked almost in tandem. German mortar bombs and heavier shells rained down with the more celestial floods. Maj Matthews and his intelligence officer, Lt D.C. Pedlow died from the same direct hit. Maj J.S. Edmonson of Baker company reported later:

At the high point, with 10 and 12 platoons mopping up and the enemy running back in the wheat 4 tanks appeared over the ridge and another materialised from a haystack, closing to 25 yards. Altho' 1 tank KO'd and another hit by PIATs of 11 pl. (Lt Pulley) Edmondson withdrew B 150 yards but could only watch btn's a-t guns being KO'd as they were set up.[19]

Another participant, platoon commander Lt Matthews also reported:

'A' forward in 3 leaps. 1st OK. 2nd ran into many enemy positions in manure piles, haystacks and in the tall wheat. On 3 leap op. m-g posts every few yards. Enemy rocket planes flew over firing heavily & probably delayed [our own] tanks. Brens affected by weather, first heat wave dust settling on guns, then heavy rain which turned dust to clogging mud, then no chance to stop and clean guns.[20]

'Enemy tanks appeared over my left flank, shooting all hell out of everything', stated Maj L.L. Dickin of 'D' Company. Capt Lane, the mortar officer, was horrified by the way 'electrical storms played havoc with radio transmission'. In their moment of direct need the South Sasks were being isolated by those gods of thunder. Maj Edmonson in desperation appealed to the artillery carrier, on which the radio was operating intermittently, and passed a message to brigade asking for support against the panzers. Time passed with the free ranging panzers driving over hastily dug slit trenches and crushing bodies lying exposed in a pea field or hidden in wheat. His CO missing, his wireless defunct, his front swamped by innumerable enemy infantry, and his shallow slits flooded with storm water, Edmondson ordered all whom he could contact to withdraw. Dickin saw that 'the period of withdrawal was chaos. The CO, the IO, the comds of A & C coys were all killed and in addition many platoon Os were lost.'[21]

The Essex Scots in reserve had arrived behind the South Sasks and dug-in. As the prairie men now withdrew through the Essex Scots the full fury of the enemy counter-attack fell on the latter. Bomb and shell craters helped in forming a defence line and the Essex diary records one crater 30 feet in diameter by 15 feet deep. Now the particular enemy attack expended itself in heavy casualties on both sides. From 2100 to midnight stragglers and wounded were crawling back through the downpour, both natural and manufactured, and as late as 2200 small groups of South Sasks were still fighting a retreat in front of the Essex firm base. There was to be no respite from the dual lightning during the night. Able company of the Essex lost all its officers and most of its NCOs. Charlie company reported eight enemy tanks behind its lines and four on the right. Dog company reported another seven panzers to its rear, but the German infantry had lost casualties too and could not reinforce the encircling tanks. It was stalemate.

The hungry Fusiliers Mont-Royal had also suffered the disillusionment of high achievement and deep despair. With their five supporting tanks they had overrun Beauvoir Farm and dashed on down the slope. Behind the forward troops, German infantry appeared out of the vast cellars of the farm and hit the Fusiliers from the rear. Some Shermans were knocked out by well hidden panzers at close range. At 2000 hours other men of the Fusiliers were 'having a hard time' at another farm close by, Troteval.

Typical of the Fusiliers' resolve and tenacity were the actions of Lt Gilles Gamache. He commanded the leading platoon into Beauvoir Farm. Many of his men were killed or wounded in the advance and he himself was very badly wounded. Within striking distance of the farm he reorganized his remaining men, took a Bren gun himself and entered the farm shooting. He set up an all-round defence of the farm and then beat off the counter-attacks from front and rear. Eventually he collapsed unconscious from loss of blood and was evacuated. Most unusually for a lieutenant he was awarded the DSO.

Meanwhile the scout platoon had moved well ahead of the farm down a slight declivity and were followed by Dog company. Panzers were waiting in camouflaged dens on the surrounding slopes, together with panzer grenadiers in the wheat. Dog company was cut off and the artillery FOO was killed, thus delaying access to support from the guns. German infiltration continued between troops standing fast.

In this situation the weather favoured the defenders, who were well set in prepared defences, against the attackers who were splashing through attrocious conditions, digging into holes which filled with running water, and finding their wireless links almost entirely out of contact. At 1500 the Camerons had reported 'raining very heavily', the Black Watch noted 'very heavy rain', and Cloudsley-Thompson who had experienced difficulty in staying awake inside a roasting, closed-down tank in the heat wave, saw that 'quite suddenly the sun went in, and it started to pour with rain'.

At such close quarters, with opposed troops overlapping, the fighting was as described by Charlie Kipp, of the 'dog eat dog' nature. The Canadian 1st Hussars reported enemy raising white flags and then jumping back into their holes and firing machine-guns. A corporal of the Essex Scots was detailed to escort three SS prisoners back to headquarters. At an opportune moment the three men jumped the corporal, grabbed his bayonet and started stabbing him. The corporal drew his only remaining weapon, a knife and killed all three of the prisoners before dying himself later.

Perhaps most ominously, Maj Radley-Walters with his squadron of Shermans could see evidence of worse to come. Gunner Op Ray White says, 'To us Major "Rad" was the chief tank buster of Normandie. He was respected, and yes, even loved by his men. "Rad" had the marvellous ability to "see" the battle develop', as at this point.[22] Looking ahead from St Martin to yet another upward fold in the terrain, they could see 'numbers of Panthers milling around at 800 yards, but they had no infantry with them and came no nearer'. Later one group of eight and another of ten Panthers tried to encircle Rad's 'A' Squadron which was down to about half a dozen Shermans but reinforced by two troops from 'B' Company. Over three days they KO'd twenty-two Panthers with the help of a troop of RCA 17-pounders. But at 2,000 yards even more panzers were manoeuvring out of range.

The morning of 21 July dawned even more dismal in every way. The impetus of Goodwood had petered out with a loss of up to 400 tanks on the British sector.[23] The Atlantic troops, now thoroughly swamped, were still ordered to move forward from village to village. The North Novas, although not due to attack, cursed the weather. 'Weather VERY WET and muddy underfoot. The dust on the roads has been turned into pure mud and many choice expletives are being issued about its tenacity. We are really getting to hate this mud.' With the tanks, Cloudsley-Thompson found that 'in a short time the tracks became so bad that no wheeled vehicles could move and armoured fighting became impossible. We sat in holes under our tanks, shivering.'

Up front the Essex Scots were still ordered ready for action, but they found that 'slit trenches accumulated water, the fields became muddy and the task of keeping weapons in working order was almost impossible. The men worked continuously on the LMGs, even tearing off their shirts for rags in a futile attempt to keep them in order.'

The new day was going to be another experience of utter devotion to duty and horrific suffering for those engaged in such conditions. A glimpse at the war diary of 6 CIB 'the Iron Brigade' reveals the drama of the day:

01.10   message from 7 Bde = going into Tilly to see if occupied.

10.29   Cam[erons]. Enemy coming in on all sides of us.

11.10   Es[sex] Sc. Cannot hear but will keep sending.

11.14   Es.Sc. wireless truck cannot be moved for MUD and mortars.
(still stuck at 22.43)

14.10   Identified [German] 93 Gren. Regt from newly dug graves with crosses.

14.31   Es.Sc. 1 operator left – no means of communication.

19.22   Fs/MR – left forward company overrun – 8 Tigers and inf. Regt.

21.25   To F/MR 'have CO here as soon as possible' – reply 'Wilco. When last seen was leading coy into attack.'

22.00   Maj J.L. Carnegie B[rigade] M[ajor] (fatally) and Maj J.M. Sutherland GSO III, mortar casualties.

22.45   F/MR strafed by 1 German plane.

Fortunes varied and the state of battle was not consistent across the front. Success and defeat came intermingled. The Black Watch, having marched up, together with tanks of the Hussars, to reinforce the Essex Scots in their despairing fight against encirclement the previous night, now put in what was described as a 'text book attack' with 'B' Squadron of the Sherbrookes to retake point 67, at le Moulin de Voide. Sgt W.E. Kitching of the Fort Garry Horse, remembers the annoyance of being sniped at all day long from three directions as he watched from his tank turret. Fortunately, he thought, the snipers were poor shots and there were no enemy tanks in sight of his squadron.[24]

The high command was, in fact, in the process of closing the Goodwood operation, and with it Atlantic. However, the Canadians along the road from St Andre to Hubert-Folie were still having to contend with strong German attacks as the brigade diary indicates. The enemy had obviously not heard the bell for the end of the round.

In the outskirts of St Andre, Radley-Walters commanding 'A', Sherbrookes, saw that the distant panzers of the previous day were still perched out of range on high ground. As light improved under grey clouds at 0700 he counted no less than forty-four Panthers, a formidable force. Rad called for an air strike. Here was an extraordinary target for the vaunted rocket-firing Typhoons. But an air strike could only be organized at divisional level. Brig Young came up to have a look and decided to fetch the air liaison officer from divisional HQ to come, see and coordinate. However, in his jeep the brigadier became entangled in one of the frequent traffic jams, exacerbated by stranded vehicles on the flooded countryside. Not until 1700 hours, ten hours after the first sighting of the day, did Rad see the brigadier's jeep approaching with the air officer in it. But by then the prey had vanished.[25]

The Camerons were still holding on grimly in St Andre overlooking the Orne. At the opposite end of the Canadian line, the 'Glens' (Stormont, Dundas and Glengarry Highlanders) had taken over from a small motorized group in the village of Hubert Folie, just a mile from the dominant hill brow on which sat the tiny hamlet of Tilly. The Essex Scots south-west of Ifs had lost 'C' Company cut off by enemy tanks and infantry in force. Les Fusiliers, at the two farms, had been temporarily overrun in the mud. When their 'C' Company was surrounded, Maj Mousseau continued firing a Bren after all his men had been killed or wounded before he too was lost, as reported by the FOO who managed to escape the trap. Patrols were sent out in the night to find survivors of two Mont-Royal companies but high grain and appalling weather conditions made this impossible.

For one Maisie officer the worst of all was the continual affliction of lice and dirt which, on top of the physical battering, made one feel that the end of psychological control was near at hand. All was indignity and physical disgust: 'in the slit, if you wanted to excrete, you had to do it ducked down in the trench and then throw it out over the lip of the slit as you would probably be sleeping on the floor of the trench'.[26] The flooding had the effect of returning the surrounding sewage, faeces from live humans and worse from dead bodies, back into the tiny slit trench.

North of St Andre the Orne bulged eastwards to narrow the Canadian front at Verrieres. On the other bank of the Orne the enemy still held hill summits from which they could enfilade the Canadian bank. Nearly two miles behind the FDLs of the Camerons, German infantry held on to the lower riverside village of Etavaux opposite a particularly strong nest of enemy resistance in Maltot. The British 43rd and 59th divisions had been advancing in some of the worst infantry action of the campaign to clear the area west of the Orne including the infamous Hill 112. Etavaux was virtually untenable for the Canadians while the enemy held the heights around Maltot. But while the British divisions made one more attempt to clear Maltot, it would be helpful to distract the German troops in Etavaux. The Maisies were therefore ordered to threaten Etavaux on 22 July by making a strong patrol of two companies towards it. On 21 July a small patrol of Maisies had reported the village empty although the Calgaries had found it strongly held a few hours earlier. Had the Germans allowed the patrol to enter and depart unscathed in order to bluff the attackers, which they were quite capable of doing?

Maj Vallieres commanded Dog company while Charlie was led by Maj Jacques Ostiguy, who had until recently been directing the 2nd Division sniper school. Now newly promoted he did not look much like an officer. A general order pointed out that German snipers and machine-gunners would aim first for any visible officers. So officers were encouraged to make themselves as anonymous as possible in ranker's uniform. Ostiguy carried an ordinary soldier's rifle and had also worked out that officers could be distinguished when making obvious hand signals. He therefore commanded by means of whistle signals. He moved forward accompanied by his wireless operator and batman. Nearby was Sgt (later RSM) Benoit Lacourse.

There was a considerable amount of enemy machine-gun fire so that the infantry advanced by short sprints: diving to the ground, head down crawling from shelter to shelter and making more short rushes. A typical massive Normandy hedge loomed ahead, dominating a field of peas. To his amazement Ostiguy saw the patrol ahead swing to the right and go away in the wrong direction down the side of an orchard. He and Lacourse were left facing the hedge. At that moment an enemy artillery stonk came down (a stonk being a series of shells landing in a planned line rather than in a circular group). The batman dived into an empty slit trench and, as he did so, his Sten gun went off without trigger pressure and shot him three times in the legs.

Ostiguy now says modestly that he needed to find safe shelter for his servant and the only place available was the series of pits from which the German machine-guns were firing their 1,200 rounds per minute. Be that as it may, both Lacourse and Ostiguy made a wild dash straight at the hedge.

In 1944 the typical hedge was planted on a bank two to three feet high. The hedge itself could be ten to twelve feet in height and of a thickness and density commensurate. A hand grenade thrown straight at the hedge might not penetrate it. The machine-gunners had dug pits into the hedge roots on the far side and only the muzzles of their guns appeared through the leaves. There were eight guns spaced about ten to fifteen yards apart. Sprinting the last twenty yards or so the two Maisies then had, as it were, to 'hand deliver' their grenades through the hedge and into the pits. Lacourse took out three of the guns and won the DCM. Ostiguy accounted for the rest although in the madness of the moment he realized that he had started off with only two grenades. He also used his rifle. It could be that the final machine-gun nest was speedily evacuated by its owners preferring discretion to valour. Ostiguy also was honoured, with the DSO.[27]

Sadly Maj Vallieres leading Dog company did not survive. The raid had been launched at about 1500 to synchronize with the Maltot action. At 2300 the Maisies' other companies, Able

(Maj Dugas) and Baker (Maj Massue), were able to attack in force, occupy Etavaux and take eighty-six prisoners, with more filtering in next morning.

Back in the area of St Andre a Sherbrooke tank commander was also distinguishing himself with the same kind of selfless determination against ostensibly more powerful German panzers. Sgt L.W. Cuddie was in one of seven Shermans which took on eight Panthers. At first the panzers prevailed, setting three Shermans ablaze, damaging another two, and leaving one able to move in bottom gear only. Cuddie's tank was the only fit Sherman remaining. He knocked out the leading Panther, drew the enemy fire and then retired slowly. This led the eager and unexpecting Panthers under the guns of the partially disabled Shermans, so that the remaining seven Panthers were also brewed up. A DCM went to Cuddie. It seems that the Sherbrookes were crack shots, for Maj Radley-Walters' tank alone is said to have accounted for some twenty-two panzers over the period. The Queen's Own Camerons had also knocked out two panzers around St Andre.

The night had seen the agonies of Les Fusiliers continue. At 0045 the enemy was in possession of Troteval farm and three panzers had penetrated into Beauvoir Farm. Another twenty-five tanks were reported in the area. A message from the Fusiliers timed at 0200 did not reach brigade until 0945 due to a failure of wireless sets. It reported that 'A' Company had dug in short of Beauvoir but 'B' and 'C' Companies were believed lost. After Etavaux the Maisies had now lost more than 200 riflemen in total (with a normal front-line strength of somewhere over 300) and were having problems because of a lack of French-speaking reinforcements in the 'pipeline'.

The effect that such casualties had on units is well illustrated by the experience of Rfmn F. Court. After wounding he had been posted to the Reginas but had requested return to his own regiment, the Canadian Scottish. When the Reginas had their first shower bath on D + 46 he was advised that he could return to 'his own mob'. Delight was followed by disillusionment as he tells it:

When I arrived at the Canadian Scottish, I looked for my buddies; I could only find one man who I knew. He said 'Go back to where you were! There is no one here except me, all the rest you knew are dead or wounded.' So I reported back to the Johns, who said, 'Welcome back'.[28]

The echoes of the now aborted Operations Goodwood and Atlantic continued dully across the muddy slopes, and at 2249 on 22 July further mortaring resulted in the Camerons' CO (Lt-Col N.H. Ross) being hit. Maj J. Runcie took over a colonel's job which would soon appear to be jinxed at Fontenay-le-Marmion.

Even at this climax of human violence, men still preserved a strain of ordinary humanity. John Cloudsley-Thompson remembers amid the shells, and bullets, 'Mosquitoes gave us no peace again that night. The Canadians were putting down a barrage and a dog decided to come and sleep with us. The wretched animal was shaking with fear and at every explosion tried to climb into our sleeping bags. We had not the heart to turn it away.'[29]

The gods of war are fickle. During the brutal battle of the Essex Scots many officers and men were lost, some literally 'lost', dead in the waist-high grain. Lt Morgan survived but was taken prisoner. But the train taking him to a prison camp in Germany was strafed by the RAF and Morgan was killed.[30]

CHAPTER FOUR

Tilly – the Epicentre

They had fought from midday till near sunset and the issue was still in doubt. Their losses were everywhere heavy and when dawn came they had failed to penetrate the defences at any point.

(Julius Caesar, 52 BC)

'In Tilly one wrote, chance allowing, a "Farewell from this World" letter every day. And every day you were surprised that you had outlived the yesterday.' So said a panzer driver who was within the ramparts.[1]

'The memories are now fifty-six years old but the colours of this little French village are not faded', continued the same man, Manfred Thorn. 'The time I spent there was sheer Hell, and far worse in comparison with the War I knew in Russia, my war experience until then.'

'Tilly must be much larger than when I knew it in 1944, if it now has a mayor', said a Seaforth veteran.[2] In fact, every separate French community, however small, has a mayor. Tilly-la-Campagne AD 2000, population less than 100, has a mayor, as had Tilly-la-Campagne 1944, population of less than 100. And on 14 July 1944 it was the mayor who came knocking on the doors of all the locals, at the behest of the German commander, to order them to pack up ready for evacuation the next day. Madame Odette Colin had just been noting the prices of her weekly meat and groceries in her diary when the mayor called. She wrote 'evacuation' under the price list. She was not to know that a few weeks later her evacuated son would be killed by an RAF fighter machine-gunning him and other cyclists, thinking they were German soldiers.

In St Martin-de-Fontenay the Germans toured the streets in a truck, using a loudspeaker to tell the inhabitants about the evacuation. Little Andre Grard was sent on the iron mine train through the mining galleries on the first stage of his 200 kilometre journey to safety. In May-sur-Orne German soldiers were billeted in most of the houses and they were told to order their hosts to pack up. Some of the miners and families hid in caves from Etavaux to May. The chief mining engineer gathered eighty like-minded civilians, descended to the lowest level of the mine and barricaded themselves in to wait for liberation.[3] As the civilians moved out soldiers began to blow up some of the rugged stone buildings at strategic sites to form instant and formidable ramparts.

As Caen had fallen the Germans knew full well that the next wave of attacks would sweep down either side of the main Caen to Falaise road. On the east of that road the dominating village at the top of the first slopes was little Tilly. On the west of the road Verrieres stood in a similarly vital location. Farther west, along the River Orne, the lower-lying villages of St-Andre-sur-Orne, St-Martin-de-Fontenay and May-sur-Orne would be a triple bastion to secure the flank.

Rarely can such a tiny huddle of houses have been the centre of such intense military action as Tilly-la-Campagne in late July and early August 1944. Stand at the corner of the T junction around which Tilly clusters and it is all there for even a short-sighted person to see. In 1944 there was the large church of St Denis, a modest Mairie (town hall), a bar/estaminet, a small food shop, seven farms and about a dozen independent houses which constituted the village, except for the farm of M. Marie a little way away.

From the T junction to the furthermost farm to the west-north-west (the D230 Rocquancourt road) was a mere 90 metres. From the T to the south-west (the D230a Garcelles road) there were houses for some 170 metres. The 'long' stroke of the T was the Bourguebus road (also D230) along which houses extended for 90 metres with a gap of

140 metres to the Marie Farm and another 80 metres to a huge barn. To the left of the road, le Clos Neuf, wheatfields extended from the last vast hedge of Tilly some 800 metres to the first hedge of Bourguebus. To the right of the road, les Terres Noires, open land looked towards three equidistant woods at La Hogue, Secqueville and Garcelles, which offered good cover for enemy tanks.

On the Rocquancourt road, about 100 metres beyond the last farm, ran the iron ore railway track, with a small halt for Tilly. At that point the line lay between two low banks which would shelter machine-gun pits. The line then bent away from Tilly, northwards between Bourguebus and La Hogue, going along an embankment and then through a deep cutting. The D230 itself turned south-west beside the railway, but another country track ran west to the farm of le Noyer on the main Caen to Falaise road. On the railway side of Tilly there was an area of orchards. Behind the church six farms formed an unusually tight maze of cottages, barns, walls, hedges and fruit trees. With several outlying buildings blown up the perimeter was solid. Under the farms, often down two sets of stairs lay deep cellars where from time immemorial Calvados had fermented and Camembert had matured.

Standing on sentry-go or even dug down into an machine-gun pit the German soldier looked down on all the visible world. Tilly was set between the 75 metre contour and 69 metres. Bourguebus church, about 1,200 metres from Tilly church, lay at 50 metres. Bras was down the slope at 43 metres and Soliers at 30. (Metric measurements used to conform to sources.) Beyond them, the southern Faubourg of Caen was in plain view. German gunners behind Tilly could also enfilade the Royals to the west as they tried to swing around Verrieres. The area was not virgin of war for on the nearby slopes Duke William of Normandy had fought the English before 1066, and Caesar's legions had marched against the Lexovii before 55 BC.

The C-in-C, Montgomery, Dempsey (1st Army) and Crerar (Canadian Army) had resolved that the next surge forward should not be 'tank intensive' as in Goodwood but that the infantry should clear the vital villages, with armour available should a breakthrough be deemed feasible. The Canadian corps commander, Guy Simonds, was served the hot potato. Having seen the havoc wrought on Goodwood armour by the more powerful German guns on the ridges, Simonds determined that the attacks should take place by night. This might cause confusion to the attackers themselves but it would reduce the range advantage enjoyed by the enemy. They would not be afforded a clear view and easy target of tanks appearing 2,000 yards away.

The North Nova Scotia Highlanders were selected for the first attack on Tilly. This would launch Operation Spring, at the same time as other thrusts were being made in the Verrieres and May-sur-Orne areas. The war diary of the 6th Canadian Infantry Brigade recorded that a reconnaissance had been made towards Tilly on 21 July. The 'Novies' would be sending out their own patrol to check the situation.

Divisional orders were issued to Lt-Col Petch, the Novies' highly respected CO at 1500, 23 July for the attack on 25 July. At 2000 on 23 July the CO held his own O group. The same day an event occurred which looked as though it might be a good augury. A shell landed beside the pit of Capt Jock Grieves and buried him up to the neck. Fortunately the Novies were able to dig him out unscathed and ready for battle. Was fortune smiling on them?

Just after midnight on 24 July Lt Ward was ordered to take six other ranks and two Free French guides on a patrol along the D230 from Bourguebus towards Tilly. As they crept cautiously along in pitch darkness they could hear the enemy laughing and chatting on both sides of the road. It was clear that Tilly did have a German garrison. One of the Frenchmen was young Guy Merle who had already assisted the Canadians at the crossing of the River Orne. He gives an epic account of the patrol:

we were to avoid anything that would give away our presence . . . the observation should last about half an hour . . . we made ready by smearing our faces and hands with charcoal. Furtively, when night had almost fallen, we left Bourguebus, crossing gardens, climbing over walls, or going through holes made by bombardment. Here and there a head popped up. 'Good luck, friend!' Then nothing else, absolute stillness. Our footfalls, smooth and stealthy, seemed to slide over the grass. We reached the [Tilly] hedge. A relatively deep ditch ran parallel to the hedge. All six of us [sic] settled down, each one within reach of the other. Our eyes sought to see through the thick branches.

Our ears, not our eyes, finally gave us satisfaction. Two fellows walked by in a ditch parallel to ours on the other side of the hedge. They were conversing in barely hushed tones. They had no idea of our presence. I had no trouble in recognizing that they were Germans. They stopped approximately 60 metres from us, and the voices multiplied. We counted four. The two others were occupying a fixed position, without a doubt a machine-gun nest. We held our breath. A slight tickle in my throat gave me a chilly feeling. I wanted to cough. I swallowed saliva desperately.

The two walking Germans were farther away and talking to another two men. And then to another two. We were able to figure where the posts were. We touched each others' hands as a signal to depart. Then the two walkers came back and halted right by us, talking away. Four times they came and went while we held our breath and tried not to cough. At last they moved away. One by one we left the ditch and crawled for the first two hundred metres. 'Halt!' It was our own sentry. 'Daisy', I whispered the code word. 'OK. Come in', and people were slapping our backs and bombarding us with questions. But we knew we had to go out there again soon.[4]

The plan was to launch the attack at 0300 hours on 25 July, with Charlie and Dog companies of the Novies leading the way straight across the wheatfields to Tilly. Able company was in reserve. It was planned to provide some minimal illumination through 'Monty's Moonlight', shining searchlights on the clouds, yet not with sufficient illumination to provide the enemy with easy targets. The light would be sufficient to enable the men to keep station in relation to each other as they advanced. They were not yet aware that awaiting them in Tilly were veterans from the Russian Front, members of the 1st SS Panzer LAH. Untersturmfuhrer Gerhard Stiller commanded a platoon of four tanks in the village but with a total of twenty tanks within easy call.[5] While these were the long-serving Mk IV tank, smaller than Tigers or Panthers, they had an upgraded 75 mm gun, still more powerful than the normal Sherman 75 mm. With their low profiles the Mk IVs were lethal against infantry. Pits had been dug at strategic points in the rubble of Tilly so that the tanks could fire hull-down in the ground. They would be at a considerable advantage against high profile Shermans advancing across open ground. In support, infantry of 272nd Division were well sheltered in the machine-gun pits and cellars of Tilly.

Ross M. Brown suggests that the first move in the series of Tilly battles was made by the Germans. Ross was in his carrier in the North Novas' pioneer platoon, responsible for clearing mines. The carrier was one in a convoy line waiting to move up to Tilly. At that moment German planes came over and bombed the convoy. The Novies were surprised as the Luftwaffe was not supposed to do that. The Allies were supposed to have total control of the skies. Fortunately for Ross's platoon all the bombs went wide and did nothing more than make the men more dirty than they were before.[6] However, Dog company suffered about twenty casualties.

The Novies' war diary records that the attack started at 0300 and Merle remembers that it was shortly after H-hour when the men moved forward. This may be because they were looking for the searchlights to illuminate the clouds. Nothing happened. The artillery had already been firing for ten minutes and so Charlie company started walking in unrelieved darkness. Their route lay between the railway and the D230 road. Leading his platoon, Lt Don Learment found it chaotic in the total blackness. The 13, 14 and 15 Platoons were made up mainly of men from the former Cape Breton

Highlanders who came from a tough breed along the Nova Scotia shoreline. The absolute silence after the artillery barrage did little to encourage confidence but tended rather to engender fearful suspicion of what the enemy might be planning.[7]

Suddenly the Stygian night was transmuted into a ghostly radiance as the searchlights lit up belatedly, perhaps misled by delays in the H-hour elsewhere. A mist had arisen behind the Novies and the reflected light played on the mist as on a photographic reflector. The defenders were presented with a prime view of the advancing infantry. Every gun and mortar within the Tilly perimeter opened up at the grey figures on the luminescent horizon. Charlie company went to ground but continued edging forward. Some of them reached the edge of Tilly. They sent up green and white Very lights to signal their progress. Many Charlie men were already lying dead or wounded in the high corn.

Guy Merle and his comrades from the patrol were with Charlie company. Guy tells a grim story:[8]

When the men of the North Nova left Bourguebus squads assured a progression line approximately three hundred metres wide, with two similar lines making up the first and second reserves. Progress was slow through the dark fields where wheat and vegetation were tall at this season. We were still quite distant from the dark [objective] hedge when command started an 'artificial moonlight'. Between each shell burst the major's strident voice encouraged the men in their advance towards the enemy line. Shells exploded ten metres ahead of us, giving us the goose pimples. Then a moment of silence.

On the partly illuminated ground I saw on either side bent bodies holding their weapons in front of them. The major was soon to give the order to rush forward, but where were the enemy posts? Why was there no reaction? Had we made a mistake? No! Unfortunately! At the very moment I was asking myself those questions, enemy automatic weapons opened up on all sides. The Germans, in turn, shot flares which seemed to float in the sky and further showed up the lines of North Novas on the plain.

At the first bursts shouts rang out all over. The major was hit in both legs. Two Canadians and I tried to stop the blood which gushed out in red spurts. We tried in the uncertain light to apply a torniquet. He turned over on his back and, as though nothing had happened, shouted as loud as he could, 'Come on, boys!' Around us men fell with abominable shouts which mingled with the groans of those already wounded. The major's voice kept weakening.

While Lt Don Learment and other survivors dug their fingernails into the ground and crouched in the wheat under the tempest of fire, Dog company had moved to the left of the road. Maj Matson was leading his company. As the sudden, coordinated enemy fire rent the silence, Matson dashed forward, shouting his men on. In moments in the pulsating light they were literally falling into enemy trenches around the outlying barn of the Marie farm. The regimental historian describes:

The trenches were filled by shouting [Novie] survivors who shot and threw grenades like wild men. Soon the night was a bedlam of noise. Enemy guns began shooting from all angles. Dug-in tanks began shooting. Machine-gun fire came from emplacements concealed in haystacks, from the tin-roofed building, from the orchards, from everywhere. . . . The Germans shouted and yelled as if they were drunk or drugged and the North Novas pitched into them with bomb and butt and bayonet in one of the wildest melees ever staged.

Maj Matson was killed and Capt Nicholson took up the lead. The enemy abandoned those trenches. Capt Nicholson fell dead. Sgt O'Hanley and L/Cpl Capstick dashed on into M. Marie's orchard. They found themselves alone. On the other side of the road a German officer was screaming orders. Voices called for help. Bullets, grenades, mortar bombs were all whizzing and exploding almost indiscriminately. There were shouts of 'Surrender, Canada.' For what seemed hours, O'Hanley and Capstick held their ground under the apple trees. Nobody came, but German voices were all around. The two Novies began their long crawl back across the open wheatfields.

Baker company was directed to loop around Dog and deal with two German tanks identified by a patrol. They quickly knocked out one tank with a PIAT but the second tank deluged the area with 75 mm explosive and machine-gun bullets. The company commander was hit and the signaller killed in the first salvoes. Other men rushed on and found themselves in the same kind of situation as Dog in a maze of enemy defences. Firing was now so intense that anyone who stood up was cut down in a second or two. Men lay in the wheat and heard the almost ripe grain being scythed off the stalks by bullets. Ears of wheat fell on them as they realized there was no way forward in the open. Once again a slow, low crawl back was the only resort for rational humans on a night when irrational actions seemed to be achieving little.

The Novies were not easily dissuaded from their task. With Baker, Charlie and Dog all out of contact, Lt-Col Petch resolved on one last throw of the dice. Able moved in the footprints, and more often knee and chest prints of Charlie between the road and the railway. Charlie had held on to the line of the first Tilly hedge. Maj A.W. Jefferson took his men through mortaring and shelling and with some casualties found Charlie. Jefferson's left hand platoon, moving on the road, reached the big Marie barn as the light of day brought better visibility. The barn proved to be a hive of well-armed enemy soldiers. Both sides fired with total abandon and Canadians and Germans fell. They had virtually fought each other to a standstill.

The only company commander left, and with other officers lost, Maj Jefferson decided to patrol beyond Charlie himself, to see if there were any other Novies in the shambles of Tilly. With his 2 i.c. (second-in-command) and three signallers he probed forward. Inevitably they were spotted by the enemy and another torrent of fire greeted them. The 2 i.c. was killed, the signallers wounded and the wireless set smashed. There was nothing else Jefferson could do.

Many men were in the position which Guy Merle describes so well as he watched and worried over his profusely bleeding major:

Advance turned into retreat. The enemy redoubled his volume of fire. We soon had nothing but dead bodies around us. Each squad tried to drag off those who could be saved. Taking advantage of the tall grass, a remaining Canadian and I dragged the major. With the hope of reaching the shelter of the railway embankment, I led them towards the Falaise [Hubert Folie?] road. Bullets whizzed by our ears. The major no longer seemed to hear us, but he did not complain.

Finally we reached the bank and the rail tracks. The major was saved. Each of us in turn carried him on our backs. His bloody legs dangled, which must have aggravated his wounds, but what else could we do? By daylight we were exhausted when we arrived in view of the first ruins of Bourguebus. The men of the North Nova who had managed to escape had rejoined their foxholes and raised the alarm as soon as they caught sight of us. An ambulance arrived. The major was put on board.

The confusion in the dark and the intermingling of enemies had been astonishing. Later the bodies of about twenty Germans were found, apparently all killed by their own fire, as they were working around the back of the attacking North Novas. In Tilly, Nova Thomas Douglas fell dead at the feet of the panzer commander, Gerhard Stiller, who was so impressed that he took off Douglas's identity discs and gave them to his own Red Cross men with orders to ensure that Douglas's body be given an identifiable burial.

At dawn the Novies' carrier section was sent along the road to support the shattered companies. Three of the fast but frail carriers raced into the village. They almost collided with well-camouflaged panzers dug into the rubble. Bren gun bullets and hand grenades bounced off the front armour of the Mk IVs. The high velocity 75 mm guns opened up and reduced the carriers to twisted metal fragments. The first two carriers caught fire and continued to burn. The third one blew up. With light now increasing Lt-Col Petch appealed for the aid of tanks. (The infantry CO had no direct control over the Sherman tanks.)

The Fort Garry Horse (10 CAR) had the misfortune to be waiting to move with the Highland Light Infantry of Canada nearby. Their Baker squadron with some fifteen Shermans available was ordered up. When the squadron leader held his O group for tank commanders, including five officers, a mortar bomb fell on the group and three of the officers were put out of action. The Shermans, with three commanders instantly promoted, made three attempts to enter the open zone, le Clos Neuf in front of Tilly. That was the preserve of the 7 Panzer Company, Stiller's veterans of 1st SS. Eleven of the Fort Garry tanks were brewed up in the usual helpless confrontation of undergunned Sherman against upgunned panzer. Some of the Shermans blazed in a way which earned them the nicknames of Ronson Lighter or (as the Germans said) Tommy Cooker. Huge columns of flame rose to as much as thirty feet above the turrets. The surrounding wheat caught fire and wounded infantry, as well as frantically ejecting tank crews were killed or horribly roasted.

Accidents of that kind were as terrible as aimed fire. Even rushing across rough terrain in a carrier with quixotic gear and balance tendencies, men were at risk without coming under fire. Ross Brown's carrier was cresting the slope at speed, destined for the ill-fated dash into Tilly, when the driver, steering almost blind in the darkness, hit a steep bank and overturned the carrier. The three men in it were thrown out. Its tracks still milling and with the impetus of its onward rush, the carrier spun over and its steel bulk, fragile against panzers but formidable against human flesh, crashed down on the three. Ross played no further part in the battle around Tilly.[9]

Throughout all this the Germans in Tilly were suffering violent artillery bombardment as well as death and wounding in the mass of bullets and ricochets which congested Tilly's tiny central stronghold of farms and houses. While tank and infantry commanders yelled their orders and tank gunners and loaders concentrated on maintaining a mad rate of fire, tank drivers were sometimes subjected to simply sitting and waiting and imagining the most horrible of fates. As one driver observed:

Defending our strong-point in this little dot on the map was a new christening for us young German Spratts. Although young in Torso these Torsos held old men in them as far as war was concerned, or so we thought. Well, what was thrown at us from Land, Sea and Air AND all at the same time was just the beginning of a new lesson in Western Warfare to be learned. It was no longer as in Russia – Manpower with the odd War-weapon backing up. Now the roles were reversed. Now it was Machines in abundance – not that there was no Cannon-fodder. Our enemy was now three-fold. The losses too. Ours and theirs.[10]

At the time of worst confusion in and around Tilly the Canadian artillery had to stop firing because the troops of the two sides were so intermixed. In addition every wireless set had been damaged, its operator put out of action or its battery run down by about 0830 on 26 July. 'Runners', the usual replacement for unserviceable wireless sets, could not run but had to crawl with great difficulty back to uncertain locations. This was one reason for calling up the tanks who might be able to discern close targets and fire without jeopardy to friends. The infantry watched the advent and destruction of the tanks with both horror and disillusionment. The regimental historian again illustrates the Novies' truly worm's eye view, seeing a Sherman arrive:

It rolled close by their shell hole and the tank officer looked out and said they would pick up any wounded men, if they knew where to find them. Miller shouted at him than an 88 was trained on the spot and his only hope was to move fast and get back. The tank had barely started when a shell [or probably an armour piercing shot] took the turret off. Then the tank started running backward and came toward the shell hole, catching fire and burning. No one made any attempt to get out from it. A second tank came and Miller shouted warnings at it as he lay among the wheat. Before it could turn it, too, was hit. Three men climbed from it [probably of a crew of five] and one was badly wounded. A third tank arrived but Miller saw it hit before it reached them. It burned at once.

The North Shore regiment had been holding the base for the Nova Scotia withdrawal. The North Shore were D-Day veterans and were due for a rest. Another tired battalion was now alerted to be ready to attack alongside the Novies. This was the Stormont, Dundas and Glengarry Highlanders (the 'Glens') commanded by their revered CO Lt-Col G.H. (Chris) Christiansen, who had First World War experience. He was described as 'a big man physically but had a fatherly attitude. He led by example . . . he was able to create a unit who had great pride in themselves. He knew enough to "think two down", that is, to know and understand the capability of the troops who would have to carry out the orders.' He was also famous among his troops, although not necessarily adored, because, having 'laid down very strict orders about drinking on duty . . . he had his bodyguard turn his Bren gun on some fine vats of Calvados, for it would have been a disaster if our troops, or others, had been tempted to drink the stuff.'[11]

However the Glens' orders to attack were retracted that same afternoon, and the remnants of the Novies continued to crawl through the corn into the North Shore lines at Bourguebus. Five enemy tanks were reported still shooting at anything that moved. For some reason not known to the Canadians around Tilly, brigade HQ was unable to obtain more support from air, artillery or armour (probably due to excessive demand in other areas of Operation Spring). Petch summed up the German tactics (as witnessed by the puzzled Guy Merle in the silence before the storm) in the concise phrase 'he had opened the door, let them in and trapped them'.[12]

Although the Glens had been reprieved, Christiansen was so perturbed by higher decisions that he objected to the use of the battalion in the way it had been intended. He was partly responsible for sparking off one of the most controversial incidents in Canadian military history, involving the removal of three commanders, of whom at least two might have been considered to be among the most able of their rank.

Maj Reg R. Dixon was battalion intelligence officer to Christiansen at the time, often sharing the same pit, and therefore had a unique view of the traumas of the Glens and their CO:

I 'lived in his pocket', but often he would leave at all hours to visit the companies to be seen by his men and to keep his finger on the pulse. On 20 July we were told we had to occupy the village of Hubert Folie, just ahead on ground leading up to the high ground of Verrieres Ridge. We were told we only had to occupy the village and 'rest' as it had already been taken by a motorised infantry unit but they were not strong enough to hold it. . . . The area was dotted with burned out and smouldering tanks and the ground churned up by tank tracks. My half-track wheeled to the edge of the village. We went into the orchard and started to dig. The shelling unfortunately angered a hive of bees and the situation became untenable![13]

We began to think that this place was worse than Hell's Corners. We certainly experienced more shells, more mortar bombs, Moaning Minnies and more mud at this place. My log then recorded, '5pm – Susie 2 Observation Post hit. Some casualties. 6pm – being shelled. 6.20pm – being shelled. 7pm – being shelled. 7.20pm – being shelled. 8.50pm – being shelled. 10pm – being shelled.' Thus our 'rest' continued! 11.45pm the shelling continued. 1.40am a shell crashed through the barricaded window and stuck in the stone wall on the opposite side of the room. Chris and I and the others were numb, waiting for it to explode . . . fortunately it was a solid 88 mm anti-tank shot. Then the RSM's ammunition truck in the yard outside was hit and caught fire. The artillery observer was so tired he gave his own map reference as the target!

At 11.25am on 25 July the order came for the battalion to be on notice to move and attack to assist the North Novas. I wrote in the war diary: 'This is indeed a mental blow and is felt by all ranks. We need a rest and refit, having been in the line since D-Day.' The men and officers are looking worn out. . . . This [order into action] was especially a disappointment, for even the Germans, with their reported lack of divisions and manpower, have withdrawn divisions for rest and refit.

It was about this time that Chris, standing in our kitchen command post, said to me, 'Reg, this is beginning to look like the First World War.' I knew what was troubling him. He could see static trench warfare starting again. I think it was about this time that he wrote his report to the Brigadier setting out his concerns in terms which eventually sent him, a disillusioned exile, to live in Australia.

Meanwhile, the Regina Rifles had been assembled along the railway embankment with orders to be ready to attack La Hogue after the Novies had taken Tilly. They were sheltered from direct machine-gun or rifle fire by the embankment, but casualties resulted from the constant mortaring and shelling. They also had to endure another of those rare but dangerous Luftwaffe raids at midnight. As it became apparent that the Novas could not take possession of Tilly their survivors fell back through the Reginas as well as the North Shore Regiment. The Reginas were then told to prepare to attack. They waited, suffering more casualties, until 31 July when they were ordered back for rest. They were able to march at ease across a Class 40 bridge over the Orne at the place where Bergeron and Chatelain had climbed along the shattered girders of the old bridge under point blank fire.

There was a moment of black humour in the acres of fiendish battle around Tilly, but its object, young French guide, Guy Merle, was not amused. He recalls the frightening confusion:

When my wounded major was taken away in the ambulance I stood there dazed, utterly drained and morally devastated by everything I had just seen. I asked questions and was told that almost two hundred fellows had been left on the field. My battledress was covered with blood. Blood had mixed with charcoal and had turned into a gooey paste on my hands. Around me it was bedlam. Nobody understood what had taken place. All of a sudden about a dozen wild men rushed at me, shook me up roughly, shouting 'You're a spy, a German spy!'

My English with a French accent led them to think that I was in the enemy's pay and the root of their misfortunes. Nobody knew me except the major, but he was no longer there and, to make matters worse, in the rush of my assignment I had never had chance to learn his name. The frenzied survivors were shaking me, while I shouted 'I am a Free French.' They backed me up against a wall. On 7 July I had found myself buried waist-deep by a shell but with only a few scratches. This time, however, it was 'curtains'. All these backened faces with eyes popping out of their sockets.

My blurred vision noticed another soldier, running towards me, shouting at those who were threatening me with their weapons. His battle dress, like mine, was covered with blood, the same blood since it was the major's . . . my Canadian night companion! He shouted 'You are crazy. He is the one who saved the major'. The weapons were lowered. The wild men's faces decontracted. They rushed towards me again, but this time to apologize. They picked me off the ground and carried me around triumphantly.[14]

There was little enough to be triumphant about. The Novies' total casualties amounted to 196.[15] Major Don Ripley, a company commander, had been LOB (Left Out of Battle – each battalion left a survival cadre behind when attacking) and so survived. He was appalled by the battalion to which he now returned. He found that the 'original North Nova Scotia Highlanders had ceased to exist. Not more than 6 original officers [from D-Day] were still available for service; not more than 60 original other ranks were ready for battle. New inexperienced, incompletely trained reinforcements came. Few of them came with any battle experience'.[16] A day or two later a battalion officers mess was set up, not as a dining club but because few of the officers knew any other of the officers, such was the flow of new faces.

Don Ripley had been adjutant of the North Novas for two years and on D-Day + 1 became a company commander. So he had become, as he says, 'close friends with the CO', Charles Petch:

> I was able to see behind the strict, no-nonsense disciplinarian a compassionate man. Always, hidden perhaps, there was a genuine concern for his men. I could sense that he was aware of a reciprocal response from his soldiers. He did not want to lose that trust.

As Ripley further observes, the result of the Novies' attack on Tilly 'was a disaster . . . the casualties were heavy. The battle results were demoralizing. For those taking part in this battle this was complete chaos. It was a very nasty place to die.' Petch seemed to believe that the 'whole sorry mess was simply a sacrifice in some way made important by holding German forces to the Falaise axis so that Monty's grand plan could succeed'.

Ripley then quotes as most relevant a poem by Matthew Arnold which he himself was reading at the time, the closing lines of 'Dover Beach' which say: 'And we are here as on a darkling plain, swept with confused alarms of struggle and flight where ignorant armies clash by night.' All the poetry in the world could be of little help to a colonel who had trained a highly disciplined battalion, only to have to order it, company by company, to advance to certain death in the most forlorn of forlorn hopes. It is difficult to believe that Petch was relieved of his command for what some writers have described as failing to push his battalion hard enough.

Don Ripley testifies that, though discouraged, his CO was still 'ready to carry on'. When they had a moment to talk in the battle's aftermath, Petch made his feelings clear. He said:

So here we are, a remnant of a regiment, bloodied but still ready to carry on. We remain dedicated to the purpose of defeating the Germans but the sacrifice here at Tilly was in excess of the purpose. It may well have been a futile effort to attack at Tilly in the light of day as I myself had urged. But to do so in the night with uncertain light had no chance of success.[17]

At the time Petch had his conversation with Ripley, he also conferred with Lt-Col Christiansen and wrote a damning report to the brigadier, Ben Cunningham. The latter had himself been adversely assessed by his divisional commander, Keller, who in turn was in a last chance situation with the commanders above him. Corps commander Simonds was under tremendous pressure to press ahead although he himself was firmly in his seat with a growing reputation and a tight, if sometimes too rigid control.

Following the failure of the North Novas to take Tilly a board of inquiry was convened on 29 July at which Cunningham and Petch were required to defend their conduct of the battle. The outcome of the inquiry was that both officers were relieved of their commands and sent home to Canada. At the same time Christiansen decided he must make his opinion known to the divisional commander, Keller. Christiansen had not actually been ordered to take the Stormont, Dundas and Glengarry Highlanders into the attack but simply to assemble it in readiness. No operational blame could be attached to him. However, he made it clear that in certain situations similar to that encountered by Petch, he would refuse to commit his exhausted troops. It could well be that the final consideration in sacking both COs was reflected in the old military adage 'one is a complaint but two are a mutiny'. The vision of two lieutenant-colonels getting together to refuse orders, under a brigadier who would not overrule them, must have caused some trepidation in higher quarters. The two divisional commanders, Maj-Gen C. Foulkes (2nd Division) and Maj-Gen R.F. Keller (3rd Division) were also called to account for command failures over the preceding weeks.

Simonds' biographer cites Christiansen writing to Keller that, 'he had lost confidence in "leadership which kept every unit in action continuously in spite of severe casualties and culminated in the launching of worn-out and disorganized men into the attack on Tilly-la-Campagne on July 25,1944, when it was apparent that the North Novas could be written off. . . . Under the above circumstances, or similar ones, I would have, and will, refuse to put the SD & G Highlanders in." On receiving an adverse report on Christiansen from Keller, Simonds lamented that Christiansen "had the impression that battles can be fought on a limited liability basis" and had him repatriated to Canada. As for Foulkes, Simonds spared him, for he could hardly give Keller a second chance and not Foulkes.'[18] Simonds' biography is very aptly entitled *The Price of Command*!

Dixon remembers that as the Glens went out to the rest area during the night 'Chris was the last man out. . . . In war there is little or no time for mourning or tears. There was nobody like him. "Christy, you bastard" we sang, but we loved him.' Similarly most of the scattered remnants of the North Nova Scotia Highlanders, learning that Petch had been sent home, asked a simple question, 'Why?'

The curtain had come down at last on the tragedy of the Novies and their CO. But other Spring scenes were being played out around Verrieres and St Andre with similar sacrifices and frustration. And the curtain would rise again soon for another act in this tiny cockpit of Tilly and across the meagre expanse of fields which would hardly provide space sufficient for a major racecourse like the real Goodwood.

CHAPTER FIVE

Operation Spring – Unsprung!

To baffle the extraordinary bravery of our troops they resorted to all kinds of devices . . . they have extensive iron mines in their country and are thoroughly familiar with every kind of underground working . . . they made frequent sorties by day and night.

(Julius Caesar, 52 BC)

Lt Mishon of the Calgaries was deeply mystified. Something spooky was taking place near the churchyard of May-sur-Orne. In the first place, the landscape had changed subtly. And secondly, Germans kept appearing out of nowhere, out of places where they could not possibly be. It was like a ghostly haunting by panzer grenadiers killed in those fields.

Taking over Dog company when his company commander was killed, Lt Mishon led his reduced group through the night, in conditions described as 'cloudy and smoky and so thick we could not see anything', to his objective, the church of May-sur-Orne, as he thought. They cleared the area of an enemy force which proved to be mainly Russians and other non-Germans, and counted up some thirty prisoners. Suddenly and quietly the area was filled with more enemy infantry who had not come through the Calgaries' lines. After a brief spell of firing the enemy group surrendered and were counted up to about thirty prisoners. 'This could not happen twice', thought Mishon. But it was happening thrice. Another almost disembodied mass of darker human shades appeared within the nocturnal mists.

Again the Calgaries attacked, and the enemy surrendered, and were counted up as some thirty prisoners. Eventually daylight filtered through and dispelled the spectral emanations. The prisoners were real but hardly any of them spoke more than a word or two of English, leaving Mishon still unable to explain the mystery of the church at May that wasn't.[1]

The pilgrim wandering the Normandy battlefields finds that some villages, such as Tilly and May, more or less retain the shape and location familiar from maps and battle accounts. Other villages, like Cormelles and St Martin-St Andre, have developed into quite different urbanizations. The main road from Fleury to May runs between St Martin and St Andre. In 1944 those villages lay off the road and were small groups of dwellings near the respective churches, with few buildings on the main through road. Today the traveller on the main road goes through what looks like a village centre where the two villages meet and both communities have extended considerably. To the south of St Martin, consisting of just a few houses in 1944, a large field was interposed before the 'factory area'. Now all that space is taken up by a housing development called 'Cite de la Mine'.[2]

This dual Orne community, together with May, was a vital German bastion which would task the Canadian right flank for Operation Spring. On higher farming land between Troteval, Beauvoir and Verrieres the centre troops would march, while Tilly-la-Campagne formed the left flank of the attack. Troops were already in motion on 24 July, in preparation for night operations for, having seen the hundreds of tanks knocked out in daylight during Goodwood, Lt-Gen Simonds had vowed to attack at night.

The German front defences were held by the numerically strong but multi-national 272nd Infantry Division of Generalleutnant Schack. His 982 Grenadier Regiment (British/Canadian brigade strength) had dug-in from St Andre back to May. The 981 was defending St Martin and the farms to the east while 980 waited on reverse slopes towards Fontenay-le-Marmion. But the main instrument of German defence was fast counter-attack, with the 1st SS Panzer LAH on hand to reinforce the 272nd. Other elite units were near. General Heinrich von Luttwitz of the 2nd Panzer Division would say, 'When the Americans attacked on 25th, we had been fooled as to your intentions. By placing this large [German] armoured reserve south of Caen we wasted it.'[3]

Before the main attack, the Camerons, who had been tenaciously holding on to the outskirts of St Andre, were required to clear the village entirely. The situation was so confused that they had found a large enemy patrol to their rear on the morning of the 24th, but that intruding group was eliminated by the Toronto Scots with their medium machine-guns. In the centre, Troteval Farm had to be secured. Lt-Col Rockingham had suddenly been whisked from the austere silences of the Staff College into the maelstrom of Verrieres to command the Royal Hamilton Light Infantry (the 'Rileys'). He now went up in a spotter plane to survey the terrain.

Overnight on 24/25 July the Calgary Highlanders were moving up through darkness across formless terrain. The task was so difficult that one company got totally lost and had to return to the original departure area and start again. However Maj Campbell with Able company was able to advance along the side of the main road to the edge of May itself. The confused night had been an advantage. Daylight proved to be the reverse. From all sides Able company was pounded by fire from dominant positions and had to withdraw to defendable pits in the outskirts of St Martin. The company's wireless link had been destroyed with the result that the CO and brigadier thought that Able still held part of May.

As Baker company moved alongside Able, their commander, Maj Nixon, was killed. Two platoons were trapped by eight machine-guns firing from St Martin. Another platoon reached houses in May but encountered at least five panzers and a large infantry force. The Calgaries' platoon commander, Lt Moffat, considered that their twenty men and a single PIAT were insufficient to overpower such a huge enemy force and so they joined in the general withdrawal back to St Andre.

Charlie company, under Maj S. Robinson, advanced along the ditches beside the main road, and also reached the first houses in May where a signals sergeant was valiantly trying to lay a telephone cable through to Able. A change in the artillery programme, to support the Black Watch attack, now brought fire from both sides down on Charlie with such intensity that the men could do nothing but crouch deeper in the ditches.

It was at this time that Lt Mishon from the reserve company followed through the smoke and mists to his objective near the church in May. With no visible landmarks for orientation he was pleased to arrive at a church, only to discover some hours later that it was the church at St Martin not May. In the course of his odyssey he passed through what was marked on the maps as 'the Factory area' and had collected prisoners from the enemy who kept reappearing from nowhere. The 'nowhere' was the shaft of a large iron mine of which he had no prior warning.

It is relevant to pause and consider the 'mystery of the mine' which became so important in the next phases of battle. A number of sources confirm that on 24 July 1944 the attackers were not fully aware of the existence of a mine system with multiple entrances, nor of its value to the defenders. The war diary of 6th Infantry Brigade notes that after two days of fighting around the Factory area the brigadier (H.A. Young) 'began to suspect' that the area might include a mine shaft. Another commentator refers to 'a mine shaft running all the way back to Rocquancourt, undiscovered until days later, [that] let the Germans move in and out of the villages at will'.[4] Fred Pollak, an intelligence officer at corps HQ, remembers that when they received the first unclear messages about a 'mine problem' they thought it referred to anti-tank or anti-personnel mines.[5] This incredible failure in research and information must be blamed on earlier and higher authorities than Fred Pollak and his recently arrived colleagues.

The system of mines was producing in peacetime 500,000 tons of iron ore a year, much of which was exported to Britain. A special grader had been installed so that British customers could obtain the standard of ore they needed. The St Andre and May concessions stretched from the Orne to the the main Caen to Falaise road. The unique ore stratum averaged 7 metres in depth. At St Andre during the war the mine shafts went to a depth of 450 metres. Two cages enabled the descent of fifteen persons a journey. At May there was a walk-in entry with trains. St Martin's associate mayor, M. Andre Grard remembers that, as a seven-year-old, the first part of his evacuation journey was on one of the trains through the mine galleries. At another large access between Fontenay and Rocquancourt (the Taraud shaft) thirty refugees led by the chief engineer, M. Tesson, had entombed themselves for safety in a winch room 85 metres deep and safe from the hand grenades which SS men threw down the shafts.[6]

The railway which ran past Tilly had a loop to Rocquancourt from which ore went to the furnaces at Colombelles and the docks at Caen. The mining operation closed down in 1968, but in 1944 it presented the Germans with a ready-made Hindenburg Line at a vital location. It is a logical assumption that the pre-D-Day planners would have seen this area as the next bastion of enemy defence after the seizure of Caen and the crossing of the Orne. Either they then failed to identify this mining complex, so well known to British industry, or they failed to provide the attacking troops with clear indications of the lurking dangers of the deep diggings, around which the battle would swirl for days, causing unnecessary casualties.

It was in this same operation, to the left of the 'Factory area' where Lt Mishon and others had dug-in, that the Black Watch set out on the fatal march described in Chapter One. Guns from the mine buildings cut down numbers of the Black Watch, as did fire from at least three other enemy concentrations. From 0330 to 0400 hours on 25 July the Black Watch had been moving to the eastern edge of St Martin. There were high walls and hedges surrounding thick orchards, three or four k.o'd Panthers used as machine-gun posts; slits in walls, dug-outs and 'scurry holes' among the trees. All had to be taken out one by one in pitch blackness. 'We were fighting in the shadows against a good many Huns, probably about a company in strength. We lost at least one and a half hours. The fighting cost us three vital commanders, Col Cantlie and the two leading Coy Cdrs.'[7]

At 0530 Maj Griffin took over and held an O group in an orchard by the church. The battalion was extended but the companies were still intact and under good control. Light was breaking and they were under fire from the ridge. Contact was made with the armoured regiment which had lost two tanks in the village. 'Maj Griffin is a brilliant officer of absolutely outstanding courage and ability. His take-over in this strained and ticklish situation was superb.' As the companies advanced and were seen to be losing men, Capt E.R. Bennett of Dog company called carriers forward in support but, as with the tanks, the moment they showed themselves out of the orchards German anti-tank guns knocked them out.

There had been concern about the reported enemy Spandau in May. Bennett sent a scout patrol under Sgt Benson to May with orders to investigate and report to Maj Griffin. 'It is not likely that Griffin received report from Benson.' At about 1030 tanks pushed forward on the main road to May but met Sgt Benson who reported May in enemy hands. Bennett himself returned to where other tanks were still 'milling around' in the orchards. The squadron leader advised that even in the Factory area they were heavily hit by 88 mm fire and could not move out into the wide stretch of open ground. At that point Capt John Taylor of the Black Watch returned wounded and said 'Don't take men up there. The battalion is absolutely pinned down. As soon as they pushed over the crest they were pinned down by machine-guns and 88s.'

All the Black Watch 18 sets as well as the artillery wireless had now ceased to function, so Capt Bennett grabbed a motor bike and sped back to HQ to report what he knew. He then roared back to the front edge of St Martin, recruiting anyone he found along the way, including three CSMs, four CQMSs, drivers, cooks and stragglers to a total of about fifty men to hold a line of three gardens, an L-shaped house and two barns. This scratch force resisted enemy penetration all night and collected the few wounded, limping or crawling back from the slopes. It was at this time that the two cooks mentioned in

Chapter One, impressed as stretcher bearers, carried a wounded comrade out of the house to find themselves surrounded by Germans armed to the teeth. The enemy let them pass. (Capt E.R. Bennett was promoted to major, wrote his report on 1 August and was himself killed, in a situation of apparently lesser peril, on 5 August.)

Since the war criticism has been aimed at both Brig Megill and Maj Griffin for the Black Watch catastrophe. This ignores the confusion of ultimate battle and the sense of responsibility that good commanders felt for their men. A glimpse of that profound concern is provided by a mortar commander, George Cooper of the Reginas, who had been viewing the battlefield from on high:

Believing my mortar section had been wiped out while I, up in the church tower nearby, was ranging them on a defensive target, I stumbled down from my perch on the rotting boards thickly covered with pigeon droppings. I had heard this one cannon shot near the mortar pits and then the radio suddenly went dead. I stumbled down the narrow spiral staircase sobbing at the thought that the whole section had been wiped out. At the scene at the edge of the village I saw the abandoned mortars and no crews. A Panther tank had approached unnoticed by the crews I later found, and fired a solid which dinted the lip of a mortar but otherwise did no damage. The tank did not enter the village but apparently withdrew immediately to rejoin its main group which attacked with some force later in the night. I found the crew eventually, one or two of whom had gone to rescue a couple of carriers and bring them into the yard where Bn HQ was located. What a relief to find the fellows later unharmed and over their fright.[8]

In the central area of Spring the weakened battalion of Les Fusiliers Mont-Royal had been grimly holding on to the fields around Troteval farm. They were now ordered to retake the farm and their CO Lt-Col Gauvreau had to draw men from all companies to form a one company strength unit under Maj Jacques Dextraze. At 2000 on 24 July Les

Fusiliers expressed their frustration in a frenzied two-pronged attack. In the terms of the war diary, 'they were throwing grenades, jumping with agility through hedges, and finally closing in for the final assault with bayonets'. Within the hour the composite unit, aided by Sherbrooke tanks and artillery, had cleared the extensive farm buildings with their deep cellars.

The clearing of Troteval was the prelude to the next move on the military chessboard, which proved to be one of the finest feats of Canadian arms in the whole war. Studying such tactics at the peaceful Staff College was Lt-Col J.M. 'Rocky' Rockingham when he was urgently recalled to command the inexperienced Royal Hamilton Light Infantry (RHLI – the 'Rileys') before Verrieres village itself. What relevance Staff College studies might have for actual action, 'Rocky' was soon to find out.[9]

The Rileys' start line was to be the east–west road past Troteval and Beauvoir farms, though when the plan was made this was still held by the enemy. Rockingham wished to clear the road using his own troops but was refused on the grounds that the area would be cleared by dark on 24 July. At 2130 that evening he was assured that the way was open and sent his scout platoon ahead. One of that platoon, Cpl Doug Shaughnessy, remembers that moment all too well:

> After the bridgehead and the small fields these wide open spaces were scary for recce and patrolling. Around Verrieres the wheat was blackened by fire and the land was like the face of the moon. I was sent crawling towards Troteval in almost total blackness with Harry Green who was an unflappable character. Very reassuring. We were laying white tapes as we crawled, to guide the following troops. But as we neared the road we could hear German voices where the enemy was not supposed to be. We crawled even tighter into the charred crops.[10]

At 2330 the scout officer reported to Rockingham that the road to the side of Troteval was still not clear of enemy and there was at least one tank with the German infantry. The colonel decided to pass his reserve company through the front troops to establish control of the entire start line even though this meant missing the full support of the artillery barrage which could not be halted at that point. Forty minutes later than planned Doug Shaughnessy led Capt R. Hunter and Charlie company along the taped route to Verrieres.

Like Les Fusiliers, the Rileys attacked with considerable elan. 'Whooping like Indians' they fired at anything that loomed up in the darkness, still unaware that certain haystacks were well camouflaged enemy tanks. Resistance was fierce. The dug-in tanks and machine-guns opened a devastating fire. Capt Hunter fell and Cpl Harold Sawyer found himself in charge of the lead men. Having spotted the location of four machine-guns which were holding up the advance he selected three men and alternately wriggled and sprinted between the immense Tiger tanks. Although wounded he led his party round behind the machine-gun nests and successfully eliminated them one by one. (He was awarded the DCM.)

Majors Halladay and Stinson led the advance into the village from opposite flanks. Rockingham himself came forward to consult with Stinson and as they talked the major was shot and killed. But as dawn brought increased light several 17-pounder guns from an anti-tank battery had been brought forward and set up. They were powerful enough to knock out the forward German tanks while artillery dealt with other machine-gun posts. Troops were on all objectives although Dog company was now commanded by a corporal.

It was not to be expected that the proud 1st SS Panzer LAH would meekly accept this intrusion into one of the most vital villages of the entire Normandy front. LAH counter-attacked from the Rileys left while the 9th SS Panzer Division came in from the Rileys right. Corps commander Simonds pushed forward two British tank units on loan to him, squadrons from 4th County of London Yeomanry (CLY) and 1st Royal Tank Regiment (RTR). Rockingham was thankful for the support, but commented:

The artillery, mortar, bren, rifle and even sten, grenade and PIAT fire was just as responsible for repelling the enemy as were the tanks and Typhoons, which were, in any case, being directed by RHLI. It may be of interest . . . that one round of red smoke which fell short of the enemy tank it was intended to mark, landed on my HQ and caused three Typhoons to fire their rockets on us.[11]

Rockingham was a formidable character. An anti-tank gunner recalled that 'from what I saw of Rockingham he feared neither man nor devil, but I believe he put a lot of trust in God, because the rest of us did'. That night, the two armies were stalking each other around and through Verrieres village. One patrol, trapped behind the German lines during the day, came back with a prisoner whom they had caught reading a book. He was in a slit trench, popping up to observe and then popping down to read a few more lines. The Canadian patrol came from behind and captured both him and his book.[12] The title of the book is not recorded.

Doug Shaughnessy was patrolling cautiously between two CLY tanks and two Panthers when the CLY commander leaned out of his turret and yelled 'Stand aside!' Doug's eardrums almost burst as the two CLY tanks fired and knocked out the unsighted Panthers. Doug and others were utilizing German slit trenches, which was dangerous because enemy artillery and mortars quickly zeroed in on them as their infantry moved back. But even so it was more dangerous to stand around digging in front of Verrieres.

German reaction seemed well disciplined and clever. Doug reported in to the house which had been a German HQ in Verrieres. There was a Telefunken radio which was the centre of interest. People were fiddling with the unfamiliar knobs, but every time they did so a salvo of shells landed on or around the house. Doug pointed out that the radio must contain some kind of fixed two-way device linked to German artillery. Nobody could confirm his theory but they stopped twiddling the knobs and Doug moved on.

Perhaps the most astonishing escape was experienced by the colonel himself. 'Rocky' was sharing a Baker company trench when a German tank approached and halted, partly overhanging the trench. The Canadians could look up and see the protruding, high velocity gun but the tank crew could not look down into the trench. The men in the trench had time to prepare a PIAT bomb which they then fired at a few inches range, the tank flamed and the crew literally fell into Canadian hands. This kind of intimate fighting was described by German Werner Sternebeck as:

> The Canadian infantry stood even between our panzers . . . the enemy penetration meant that we had to abandon the company's position along the hedgerows. In just five minutes the company lost four or five Panzers and men from each crew. My own Panzer was crippled. During this attack the Canadians enabled us to take our wounded with us. They did not fire on us as we collected our comrades.[13]

In this battle the Germans used robot tanks from which the crew had ejected, leaving the tanks to roll on, aiming to blow up in the enemy lines, causing casualties. The defenders' guns destroyed all but one at a distance. Doug Shaughnessy watched one robot blow up with great interest until he was ordered to go out and examine it. He brought back a piece of track for expert examination. At that point prisoners from the German 272nd Infantry Division were wandering in, dazed by the tremendous Allied artillery fire. Doug collected one prisoner who kept repeating, in German, 'Damn the thunder. Damn the thunder.'

The Rileys had to hold on during a week of counter-attacks. The enemy were well aware that the Verrieres position offered a window on the countryside down to Rocquancourt. However, that countryside was still dominated by the German Spandaus and 88s, as the Royals, endeavouring to exploit the Rileys' success, were soon to discover. Indeed their diarist was to write of 'some of the fiercest fighting of the whole war'.

Platoon commander Bob Suckling described Verrieres Ridge as 'a blur of unbelievable exhaustion, lack of appetite, lice, dysentery, constant noise, dust, revolting odours and paralysing fear . . . and everywhere the all-pervasive smell of decaying flesh and other disgusting things'.[14] There was always the fear, dulling sometimes to numbness, engendered by seeing so many comrades fall in action. The Royals had a theoretical strength of 845. They had lost casualties in an accident before embarking for Normandy. After the Louvigny battle they received a draft of 6 officers and 74 ORs to make their strength up to 36 officers and 658 ORs. After Verrieres they would need another reinforcement including 280 ORs. The then Lt M.E. Berry recalls that 'I had 18 Platoon, D coy on 27 July, but only one man remained who had landed in early July. The rest were reinforcements. Those from the Rocky Mountain Rangers were well trained. 45 minutes after I took over the platoon my sergeant was badly wounded and I did not get another for two days.'[15]

Lt-Col J.C.H. Anderson had been confirmed as CO only on 22 July and now was directed to take the Royals through the Rileys in Verrieres and capture Rocquancourt. However, by 0730 the Rileys were still engaged in bitter street fighting in Verrieres and a large tank battle was developing around the village. So it was agreed that the Rileys would swing east of the village.

The signs and portents were not auspicious. It was like turning up a Tarot card with the figure of Death. They saw a squadron of Hussars tanks wiped out. They saw the emergence of the enemy super-tank called Elephant or Ferdinand, far larger and more powerful even than the dreaded Tiger. They saw the burning trooper fall from his tank and set the cornfield on fire. The diarist noted that 'the entire area looked like a charnel house with dead bodies and blazing vehicles everywhere'.[16]

If one could have ignored the battle it was a clear warm Tuesday morning and the golden wheat fields were waist high to the walking men. At first they were heartened by the action of Capt A.B. Conron of the 1st Hussars. As he advanced he saw eight Panthers which were not looking his way. Coolly he called up his other tanks on the wireless, arranged a fire plan – which Hussar tank to fire on which Panther – and on the order 'Fire!' the Hussars brewed up the entire enemy group with a few well aimed shots. But it was like pushing a stick into a wasps' nest. Field Marshal von Kluge, commanding all German forces in Normandy, had himself visited the area and ordered his operational reserve, the 9th SS Panzer Hohenstaufen to counter-attack.

Lt-Col Anderson sent his carrier platoon racing forward along the edge of the main Caen to Falaise road where they found a small quarry in which to set up their mortars. They were immediately counter-attacked but held off the attackers by machine-gun fire until the mortars could start firing. Nearest to Verrieres, Capt Singleton led Charlie company forward with Baker company (Maj Law) on their left. Up to the nearest crest all went well but beyond the crest they came under fire from numerous machine-guns and tanks hidden in the corn. Singleton used his 18 set to radio for tank support but when tanks appeared they were driven back by the virtually invisible Tigers dug deep into the ground among the wheat.

Charlie company pushed on bravely but found themselves in a kind of deep saucer of ground, Delle des Fourneaux, the perimeter of which was thick with enemy guns of all kinds. Charlie company soldiers fell dead or wounded and the remainder were driven to earth. Massed enemy infantry then arose from the wheat and surrounded the remnant of 13 and 15 Platoon, including Singleton, at their point of farthest advance about 350 metres south-east of Verrieres. Sgt Doug King rallied a few of 14 Platoon and brought back some eighteen men to the main body of the battalion. At the same time Maj Law had been wounded by friendly fire from a Typhoon aircraft, and Baker company survivors also withdrew.

Dog company, having moved up in support, found themselves in an impossible situation. They were amazed when a staff officer appeared and ordered them to keep on attacking against immeasurable odds. Lt Berry later heard, whether it was true or not, that 'another Coy commander refused to go forward when he realized what had happened to 'C' and said "we would only reinforce failure". I heard he was threatened with Court Martial but he was correct in his decision.' At the same time Berry found that, once in motion an infantry attack could be 'stimulating . . . in one very good attack I felt I could take my platoon all the way to Berlin by myself', although his NCOs 'were reluctant to go forward without me leading'.[17]

In a similar vein a Gordon Highlander recalled lying at the edge of a large field with enemy fire audible. The platoon was ordered 'fixed bayonets', which was the first time he had heard that order in action. Then the shout came 'Charge! Forward! Keep going!' A mass frenzy swept through the platoon and they charged at a full sprint across to the opposite hedge . . . where no enemy awaited! It had been a ploy by the officer to get them across a bullet-swept field and they had arrived without a single casualty.[18]

Intelligence Sgt W.R. Bennett remembers:

when 'C' Coy of the Royals was over-run by the enemy they had been in wireless silence for hours due to operators killed and wireless sets destroyed by enemy fire. 'A' and 'D' Coys were in a very fluid position trying to consolidate their positions. It was the Artillery and Typhoons who saved the day.[19]

In addition to the infantry losses tank numbers had also suffered. The Canadian Corps war diary shows that at the start of 24 July the strength of 6th Armoured Brigade was 160 Shermans but by the end of the day it had fallen to 122, losses of almost a quarter of its strength. The Royals' attack had broken down but it may have taken enough heat off the hard-pressed Rileys to enable them to maintain their finger hold on the stone walls and house of Verrieres. (The Royals' own losses over three days were 42 killed, 106 wounded and 10 POWs out of a Canadian total of 450 killed and 1,100 wounded.[20])

A sad footnote to the day's action was that one of the Royals taken prisoner, Pte G.E. Kennedy, died a month later after contracting diphtheria in the POW camp.

On 26 July Capt A. McMillan commanding Dog was ordered to move his men 300 yards forward behind an artillery barrage. This they did successfully, blissfully unaware that the artillery barrage had hit the 1st SS Panzer tanks as they were forming up for a counter attack which would have taken them straight into the ranks of Dog company. McMillan's men then occupied a useful hedgerow which the enemy had held by night but vacated in the daytime.

The Germans experienced just as much confusion as the Canadians in the ebb and flow of battle. At twilight the amazed Royals saw an SS officer and his NCO calmly climb out of a hide in the wheat and come strolling, the officer smoking a cigarette, towards the Royals' hedgerow. The Royals held their fire until the officer had jumped quite unconcerned into their slit trench. During the night more SS attacked on two occasions and during the second struggle SS soldiers tried to dig-in ten yards away from the hedgerow but were driven back. The defenders were saddened to find that among their dead lay CSM F. Ruggles who had won the MM during the abortive Dieppe raid two years before.

The situation was still confused and that night Lt-Col Anderson sent Sgt Bennett forward on his motor-bike:

> The CO asked me to locate our forward positions. At dusk I rode up to the Beauvoir-Troteval road on my Norton and left it there. I continued further towards Verrieres on foot. Suddenly our Sherman tanks, positioning themselves for the morrow, came under fire from entrenched German Tiger tanks and I was caught in the middle. But a lone infantryman was of no concern to them in their battle, and I withdrew as quickly as possible. I had not expected a tank battle at that time and in that light, and further, I had not found either 'A' or 'D' coys.

Bennett then had an object lesson in the waywardness of fate. His friend, B67498 Provost Sgt Art Harmand had carried more than his share of duty in directing traffic under constant enemy fire zeroed in on crossroads. Arriving late at the battalion Tac HQ Harmand begged the use of Bennett's slit trench while the latter rode off on his Norton. A rogue German self-propelled 88 mm gun (not normally a spearhead vehicle) suddenly appeared in the battalion lines and opened fire in all directions. A shell hit the Bennett slit trench and Art Hardman was killed, leaving two families fatherless, one legitimate family and one illegitimate.

Although the official Spring operation had ended nobody seemed to have informed the enemy who continued counter-attacking. The Rileys continued to grit their teeth and dig deeper into the ruins of Verrieres. The Royals continued to be exposed and on 31 July had a novel experience. They encountered for the first time German robot tanks. These were tracked vehicles filled with combustible fuel. About 150 yards from the Canadian defences the drivers jumped out and left the tanks running on towards the defenders. Fortunately their speed was low and anti-tank gunners knocked out the robots in 'huge sheets of flame and clouds of black smoke'.[21]

A brief element of humour was introduced into the grim proceedings when a stray German V1 flying bomb, obviously intended for London, flew over the Royals' trenches and descended on the enemy lines.

There was little humour elsewhere. On the Canadians' extreme right Le Regiment Maisonneuve was still finding it almost impossible to advance in the St Andre-sur-Orne area. In their defences west of the main road they were pinned down by accurate mortar and artillery fire coming from three sides, the enemy on both west and east sides having the advantage of quite high ground overlooking the St Andre positions. The troops had not eaten for twenty-four hours as all routes were cut off by the intense fire. Perhaps even more serious was the lack of water. Having been deluged into inactivity by waters a few days before, the troops now found the hot midsummer sun drying the roads into fine dust and any spare surface water was evaporating rapidly. In the dust and the dirt and the flames of continual explosions and the merciless rays of the sun, men were suffering from agonizing thirst and dehydration.

The next day when the Maisies company commanders were called to an O group at battalion HQ they could only go by crawling all the way. The battalion's jeep ambulance had disappeared, possibly through a succession of direct hits. Lt Hudson of 'D', who had been wounded in an attack, spent a night and a morning in the enemy lines before snaking his way slowly along ditches and the bases of hedges back to safety.

Lt Charlie Forbes was not sure what day it was but he was ordered to attack with his platoon of Maisies at 1400 hours. His recollections are very clear:

At St Andre I was ordered to clear 2 m-gs well dug in across a field to allow 'A' coy to go through on a planned attack. The men were totally exhausted, hungry and thirsty. There were only about a dozen left in the platoon. I lined them up. I told them there was only 50 yards to run. At 14.00 hours I got up and ran at the machine-guns. About half way across I flung myself flat ready for another dash. I looked around. I was all alone in the field. Nobody else, I thought, had moved. Then I saw Pte Kelly's head peeping from a crater nearby.

Suddenly Kelly shouted 'Follow me!' – which even in the heat of the moment I thought was humourous, the private calling the platoon commander to follow him – but Kelly was running forward. I went with him. We both ran and jumped into the first m-g pit. They were all dead from shelling. It was the second pit causing the problems. I ran on to the second pit firing the Bren. It knocked out the gunners.

It was a miracle that in a 50 yards dash and pause and dash again, with their machine-gun firing 1,200 bullets a minute, say 200 bullets in the time, at as little as one yard range and not a bullet hit either Kelly or me. Soon the Bren rounds were all used up. Once in the second pit I decided to use the German gun which was still working. I thought I would cover the support company as they came forward. But when they heard the unmistakable sound of the

Spandau – we all knew that sound only too well – they thought that the Spandau had not been taken out and that I was the Germans still firing it at them. So they waited with their heads down . . . until I ran out of Spandau bullets.[22]

So the attacks went remorselessly on and on, probing the enemy's front. On 26 July the Black Watch's senior remaining officer in the line, the adjutant, Capt C.L. Stuart was wounded becoming the twenty-eighth battalion officer killed or wounded during the week, leaving only six fit officers still operational.

St Martin-de-Fontenay church was still held by the enemy. At 2200 on 29 July, the Maisies' Maj J. Biseau of Able sent Capt A. Angers with forty-five men to attack the church. Charlie company secured the crossroads to the north. Angers' men advanced against the now customary defensive fire which one man described as 'like walking through thick hail but a bloody sight hotter'. By simply ignoring the casualties, the noise, the hot breath of explosions and the knowledge of danger two sections managed to infiltrate into the church. Enemy machine-guns and counter-attacking infantry built up an iron screen through which nobody, it seemed, could pass. But as it was clear that the church was untenable a few Maisies contrived to return. The next day the remainder of Able attacked at 0500. Fifteen men burst into the houses surrounding the church and sniped from there, but the church resisted and there was no way through to the church door or to gaps in the walls.

On 1 August, new month, old story! Les Fusiliers Mont-Royal were launched against St Martin church. German m-g fire again sent a blizzard of bullets down the open street. This was a crisis moment. Maj Jacques Dextraze faced up to that moment which comes to all infantry commanders at the arrow point of advance. An insane act was called for, but a fatal outcome was likely. Stepping out from the shelter of a wall, Dextraze calmly walked across the street where logic suggested that every cubic yard of air must be penetrated by several bullets a second. Surviving, he stood against the church wall, still a target for bullets and for grenades hurled over the wall. This inspired his men to charge cheering across the street and follow him as he vaulted over the church wall. The impetus carried them irresistibly into the church itself and the enemy infantry inside died or surrendered. There was no time for thoughts of sanctity or sanctuary. Dextraze was awarded the DSO for his bravery.

While death and ghastly wounding pursued their mission amid torrents of bullets outside St Martin church, danger was lurking at every corner of supposedly less perilous areas. CSM Charlie Martin and the Queen's Own Rifles of Canada knew this well enough, as Charlie recorded:

Lindy Lindenas and I were sharing a slit trench. We were in a holding position while the enemy kept us under steady fire. . . . Lindy had gone over to company headquarters and I was about ready to go for my regular check on the hot meal that the men had every day. Along came our company stretcher-bearer [Rfmn S.E. Armitage] up from battalion HQ. He was a very kind, gentle person and I guess maybe he'd had a lot to do that day. He said he was tired out, didn't know where to go under all the constant fire, so I said, 'Well, sure, use our slit trench. . . .' He was glad to stretch out. I had not gone farther than ten feet when an 88 shell landed right in our trench. He was killed instantly. The blast knocked me for quite a few yards.[23]

Operation Spring has been seen by some as a failed attempt to break through and over the Verrieres-Bourguebus feature. By others it has been justified as a holding operation to keep elite panzers away from the American 'Cobra' breakthrough. Its demise is best described by one commentator in the remark 'next morning in the ghastly grey wet dawn the Canadians beat off no less than four attacks. For the moment both sides had fought each other to a standstill.'[24] That could apply to either Atlantic or Spring. More specifically the same commentator states that the '116th GAF Division [Luftwaffe] had been practically destroyed and [that] the 21st Panzer Division [had been] reduced to the equivalent of a battalion and lost 109 tanks' (which were mainly irreplaceable) over the combined periods.

There is some debate about the worth of Spring as a holding operation because the German Supreme Command, under Hitler's direct instructions, was already moving armour from the area. However, on 25 July opposite the Americans there were still 'only 110 German tanks, most of them obsolete, and 9 divisions, some of them mere fragments'.[25]

According to his biographer, Simonds held that 'nothing is more dangerous than to sit down in front of the Boche and not know what he is up to'. Inaction against elite troops was not sensible. The biographer also states that 'Spring was the bloodiest single day [sic – 25 July] for Canadian arms except Dieppe. A holding operation, which Spring was without any doubt, is thankless, for there is usually no compensatory gain in territory. However, the pill was sugared by Spring being represented as a holding operation with a chance of gaining the high ground around Cintheaux . . . but a slim chance', which was not fully grasped.[26]

A more recent critic, himself a distinguished general, found the basic plan lacking. Maj-Gen Michael Reynolds makes the following points. 'Although the Canadian plan for SPRING looked on the face of it reasonably simple and logical, in reality it left a lot to be desired.' An example was in directing an infantry division towards Tilly but attacking with only one battalion. 'The 2nd Can Infantry Div's plan was quite the opposite, over complicated and seriously flawed. The Start-Line . . . was not even in Canadian hands; and then, almost as if to ensure that there would be chaos, the three Brigades of the Division were muddled up. The 6th Brigade lost two of its battalions to the other Brigades so that they could secure the Start-Line, but then each of those two Brigades lost one battalion to the 6th Brigade.'[27]

It must also be remembered that although German units were suffering from the battle of attrition, their morale generally was still high, even if some of them had already decided that the war was lost. Lt Fred Pollak was a signal's analyst with the special intelligence wireless unit listening to German wireless messages and interrogating prisoners. His impression was definitely not of a defeated or highly dispirited enemy at this time:

> my main duties were to analyse and interpret intercepted German traffic . . . and when something unusual occurred to go to Corps and tell them about it. I was also involved in interrogating captured signals personnel. . . . The usual questions: unit identification, call signs, frequencies, personalities, morale, casualties, etc. I remember little evidence that morale was suffering. The odd one volunteered 'we simply cannot take on the whole world'. Some intercepts suggested however that things were NOT good. When messages ended 'HH' (Heil Hitler) this often meant that they were either surrendering or getting out. Another indicator was exaggerated claims of enemy action such as 'we are surrounded by 200 allied tanks!' – which suggested that they were preparing to quit with a good reason.[28]

Although additional British armour was made available to Simonds in case a breakthrough around Verrieres became possible, it is a moot point as to whether this was ever likely at the time of Spring. Goodwood had shown how difficult it was for three armoured divisions to make progress against the more powerful German guns. During Spring not only did areas like the Delle des Fourneaux become killing grounds for any Allied tanks or infantry which appeared, but there were also reports of thirty or forty more panzers dug-in a little way further back towards the Rocquancourt-Fontenay road. That would have been a much stronger forward defence line than that which had awaited the first thrust of Goodwood.

The capture of the houses in Tilly-la-Campagne or May-sur-Orne would have facilitated Totalize a week or two later but would only have pushed the German FDLs back to the Cramesnil spur or at most the Soignolles positions. An immediate leap to Falaise was neither feasible nor necessary in terms of timing for a junction with the Americans at the River Seine, as was intended still.

It is possible to criticize some plans of the higher command and some actions of intermediate commanders, but the great majority of officers and men at the sharp end did their duty beyond the normal calls of that duty. They did not reach Cintheaux just then but hundreds of them were destined for Cintheaux as their last rest in a beautiful garden where doves abound.

CHAPTER SIX

Tilly – Encore plus!

Similar attacks followed day after day, and work had to be continued throughout the night, so that even the sick and the wounded could get no sleep.

(*Julius Caesar, 54 BC*)

'The moment of truth was at hand. This was clear on 31.7.' Thus thought Untersturmfuhrer (Ustuf) Gerhard Stiller, 2 Platoon commander in the 7th Panzer Regiment/1 in Tilly.

Whatever trepidation the Canadian infantry might have about launching another attack towards Tilly, Ustuf Stiller and his colleagues knew that the panzers' position was precarious. Only tanks 711 (Stiller's) and 712 were still operational. 713 and 715 had been damaged by artillery fire and were in the workshops about five miles away while 714 had been taken to base workshops near Paris. On 25 July the company had been able to employ four tanks forward in the hedges looking towards Bourguebus, two in Tilly streets, two in farms behind the church and another eight within easy call. The infantry company, which had been at about 75 per cent strength on 25 July, had also suffered. And every day under the incessant Allied bombardment, fresh casualties occurred and new damage was done.[1]

The overriding Allied preoccupation with keeping the elite panzers away from the American sector and the rapid break-out of Gen Patton's Third Army, meant that Simonds was under continual pressure to attack, attack, attack. What was not known at the time was that the German generals had come to look upon a huge air attack by several hundred heavy bombers as being the only accurate signal of an impending major attack. No matter how many infantry might die in desperate attacks on vital sites the German generals would not be impressed. They would accurately construe the next Tilly operations as being only of a holding nature.

The apparently more sheltered fields between Bourguebus and Tilly, with their hedges and orchards, having proved to be a killing ground, the next attack would be launched from another direction, the west, although that area appeared to be more open. By the main Caen to Falaise road there stood a small farm, le Noyer, with orchards, a small reservoir and a pump house. The Essex Scots were told to capture le Noyer so that the Calgary Highlanders would have a firm base for the planned attack on Tilly. After traumatic earlier experiences the Essex Scots were determined to prove their mettle. (Their adjutant, Capt Fred Tilston, would later win the VC.)

The attack force would consist of Dog company and one platoon of Charlie, a section of Bren gun carriers, a section of anti-tank guns, and also a troop of tanks giving supporting fire from hull-down positions. Under the command of Capt Telford 'Si' Steele, Dog company had been able to assemble only 300 yards from the objective on the afternoon of 29 July. From 1655 to 1708 a generally accurate barrage fell on le Noyer but some shells fell on the Essex assembly area, causing casualties. At 1708 Capt Steele gave the order to move quickly over the 300 yard gap. Immediately, heavy machine-gun fire flamed from the hedgerows of le Noyer.

The then Capt A.J. Hodges of Able company later wrote his account:

17 Platoon under Sgt Russ Burdick did a marvellous job, following close behind the bursting shells of the covering barrage on to its objective. No 18 Platoon (Lt C. Law) whooped successfully on to its designated position, but 16 Platoon, mowed down by intensive m-g fire, went to ground when its youthful officer, Lt W. Pope, was

wounded. Capt Steele . . . hurriedly marshalled men of coy HQ – runners, drivers, batmen, signallers – and led them in a wild and successful charge.

CSM Les Dixon, who would that day add a bar to the MM he won at Dieppe, with Sgt Charles Wold raged like wild men up and down the Hun defences, ignoring personal safety, dropping Mills grenades in enemy slits, wreaking terrific havoc. Lt-Col Jones in his carrier, saw his driver killed at his side by a sniper, but took the controls and drove on. Capt Steele was awarded the MC and Sgt Wold the Croix de Guerre.

Later Able coy saw a strange sight. Heading straight at Baker coy were robot driverless tanks – filled with high explosives set off by means of time devices. One by one they entered the confines of Baker coy, caving in slit trenches, the deadly blast killing, wounding, maiming. One courageous soldier fired his PIAT at point-blank range, destroying both the 'beetle' tank and himself. Among those killed was Pte Shawanda, a likeable Indian boy.[2]

During this Essex attack on le Noyer, the artillery FOO, Capt Stewart McLeod in his carrier was up with the advancing infantry. Suddenly his carrier was riddled with machine-gun bullets. The driver was killed instantly and Capt McCleod died from his wounds. The other two members of the forward observation crew were mentally shattered. 'Only nine days after seeing their previous captain almost cut in half by an 88 solid-shot [designed to stop a tank], and having had the sad task of removing the almost headless torso of their cherished buddy from their carrier . . . they witness the fatal wounding by machine-gun fire of another troop commander as he crosses through the wheat to contact the CO of the Essex.'[3]

The Calgary Highlanders had been withdrawn from the west flank battle at St Andre on 25 July and were now to attack in the Canadian eastern sector. On 31 July they marched from Fleury via Ifs to assemble on a line which was being held by the Royal Regiment of Canada. The prairie men were to attack at night from le Noyer, leaning into a considerable artillery bombardment and supported by tanks from the British Royal Scots Greys. At the same hour the Lincoln and Welland Regiment would make what was essentially a diversionary attack over the 'blasted heath' from Bourguebus.

Before the tragedy a moment of comedy intervened when the Royals, who were to mark paths for the Calgaries, discovered that a road marked on the map did not exist on the ground, 'as is common' commented the Royals' diarist! It was therefore necessary at short notice to mark out a special non-existing road for the attackers to follow. At the time the Calgaries did not find this to be worrying. All their company commanders had been able to recce towards Tilly and were satisfied with dispositions, saying 'everything points to a very successful attack early tomorrow morning'.[4]

Battalion HQ was located in the basement of the pump house. Up to 0230 when the artillery was due to fire, patrols had heard no movement around Tilly and discovered no mines. Confidence was high. At 0230 'all hell let loose and our artillery pounded the ground' but 'the Hun improved the din and clamour by laying down a terrific mortar barrage'. Confidence was still high as at 0232 Dog company crossed the 'blue' start line. Baker company moved only to find that their wireless failed immediately, so that they had to report by sending runners to HQ or to other companies. The men went calmly forward at a pace of 100 yards in three minutes. By 0253 Dog reported 'yellow' position which was 400 yards from the start.

'Bn HQ resembled a buzz saw, messages going hither and thither, runners coming and going and odd casualties being directed [into HQ] by mistake.' At that point the first serious qualms arose when the artillery barrage appeared to be constantly falling short on top of the Calgaries, as they followed at the pace of the barrage's movement. Complaints and curses were heard by HQ. Lt-Col McLauchlan immediately assumed that the Germans were firing into the barrage and dropping shells on the troops as though these were Canadian shells falling short. Forward troops were not convinced. McLauchlan asked for the barrage to be suspended. The 'short' shells continued to fall, proving it to be a clever enemy stroke to affect the morale of the attackers.

Confidence grew again as Baker company spotted two prowling enemy tanks, often at a disadvantage against infantry in the dark, and knocked them out with PIAT shots. The main body of Calgaries had braved the maelstrom of shot and shell and reached the railway line at the entrance to the village. At that point there were very low embankments of a foot or two, but they facilitated quick digging-in to reform. Three Shermans of the Scots Greys loomed up through the gloom. The Calgaries by the tiny station moved forward in front of the tanks into the street, still under a hail of fire. The Shermans approached the railway. The first bumped over the track and rolled towards what was the mayor's office, often grandly called 'the Town Hall'. At this point the Germans, masters at hiding their cards, boldly played a hand that looked like a loser's. The time was 0530.

Ustuf Stiller was watching the onward drive of the Calgaries, aware that in that stretch of street he was down to one tank, his own. He was also aware that the farms on the right of the street as the Calgaries approached it were empty of infantry. It is possible that the few available infantry had been drawn off by the 'Lincs and Welland' diversionary approach, coming as it did over the shattered battle ground towards Bourguebus. The Calgaries passed almost under the gun muzzle of Stiller's well-camouflaged Mk IV tank, invisible in the mayor's garden among its tangle of branches and hedge. The Calgaries were still moving in good order but cautiously as though fearing to tread on mines.

The first Sherman, towering over the Mk IV for height but with an inferior gun, moved along the grass beside the street. At thirty yards Stiller gave the order, 'Fire'. His gunner, Harald Pager, was actually a trained fighter pilot, sent like many Luftwaffe personnel as a reinforcement to the land forces. Almost instictively Pager fired twice and the two armour-piercing shots hit within 12 inches of each other, one in the turret and the other in the hull. The crew bailed out. Two minutes later the second Sherman approached the railway at about 150 yards. This time Pager fired as soon as the tank could be clearly discerned.[5]

Meanwhile the continuing salvoes of mortar fire had been joined by machine-gun tracer, sniper's bullets and hand grenades as infantry raced up to meet the isolated Calgaries who, having lost the support of the tanks, had to run for the shelter of the railway embankment as fast as they could. There they held on in a bitter exchange of fire until about 1000 when it was obvious that the position was untenable. More German tanks had rumbled into Tilly. There seemed to be no end to the Germans' supply of mortar bombs for the six-tube Moaning Minnies. The Calgaries withdrew to 'blue'.

It had been the battalion's misfortune to attack the proudest and most experienced soldiers of the German Army, heralded by many historians as the best fighting formation of modern times. The Leibstandarte Adolf Hitler was a rather battered but still dangerous panzer division commanded by the formidable Theodor 'Teddy' Wisch. His 5 Regiment (tanks and infantry) was disposed around Verrieres and the 7 Regiment around Tilly, under command of a man who was to become notorious far beyond his Fatherland, Jochen Peiper. In Tilly itself the under-strength infantry company was commanded by Obersturmfuhrer Tomhardt. The tank company was disposed around Tilly and in the thick woods near La Hogue, which would receive half of the bomb load of the tremendous RAF raid of 7 August. Panzer commander was Obersturmfuhrer Werner Wolff, another formidable personality who had four years battle experience and would fight on until killed on the Hungarian border in the last weeks of Hitler's Reich. During the Tilly battles two panzers got lost in the dark and found Canadian infantry all around them. They were startled by someone knocking on the turret. The tank commander cautiously opened the turret flap and pushed his gun into the face of Wolff who had come on foot to guide his two lost sheep back to the fold.

Both Canadians and Germans, and later Scottish Seaforths, were to reiterate that the fire holocaust of Tilly was unique. Ustuf Gerhard

Stiller has described the 'wall of fire' which crept towards his tank in the mayor's garden, passed over his head, and moved on down the street like a solid, flaming stream of molten steel pouring from a blast furnace and itself blasting off swarms of lethal, jagged coarse steel shards. The defenders were only able to survive by shutting down their tanks or lying under them, or, in the case of the infantry, hiding in deep cellars or withdrawing in front of this slow, deliberate embodiment of hell, and waiting for the barrage to cease.

Gerhardt Stiller himself had come up through the ranks, like so many SS officers, and had long experience at twenty-two years of age. He had been wounded twice on the Russian Front, precisely three years before the Tilly wall of fire, on 1 and 15 August 1941. While many Allied troops stood in awe of the German tanks, the panzer men themselves were not too happy about their equipment. Although many Allied infantrymen saw every enemy tank as being the fearsome Tiger, that 54 ton Mk VI tank with the 88 mm gun was very much in a minority. The most common panzers were the Mk V Panther – thought by some Allies to be the best panzer – and the smaller workhorse Mk IV. Wolff's company was equipped solely with the Mk IV. As that tank did not boast a name, the panzer crews invented their own. Having dubbed the Sherman the 'Tommy Cooker' because it so often flamed and grilled crew members, the German crews also picked on the weak spot of their own Mark IV: its relatively thin armour plating. They nicknamed it *Das Kochgeschirr*, the mess-tin.

One of the defending infantry, Rolf Ehrhardt, stated 'we dug ourselves into the ruins and looked for a place to shoot from. The walls of the town were centuries old and solid rock. They offered good cover against the shells. Probably better than our enemy wanted. Time and again they thought nothing could be alive in the rubble. Then a motor would howl, a track would turn, a gun would fire.'[6] Even so, digging was not easy in the rubble. Stiller found hard, rocky soil about 3 feet down. But 'mortal fear is the best driver for digging. "Sweat spares blood" is a special proverb of all old soldiers!!!' As an afterthought he admits the best diggers were the Russians.

The Lincoln and Welland Regiment had landed on 25 July and they were allocated the diversionary attack from Bourguebus as the Calgaries advanced from le Noyer. They had already suffered casualties in England. On 5 July a V1 'buzz bomb' had descended on 'B' Company cook-house while men were still sitting after their evening meal. Seven were killed and eighteen wounded of whom two later died. An equally dangerous moment with less serious outcome occurred during the first O group in Normandy. This was held in a large, well-lit 'chapel' tent housing the padre. As the officers listened to their orders a Luftwaffe air raid occurred and bombs began to drop. One of the officers instinctively looked up and saw in horror that there was no roof to the tent and the lights were shining high into the sky. Fortunately the 'hand of God' seemed to steer the bombs away.

Maj J.F. Swaze was ordered to take his 'D' Company towards Tilly as a diversion and also 'to assess the Calgary attack'. Promptly at 0100 hours he set out with 17 and 18 Platoon. Lt R.F. Dickie was sent through the wheatfields to work along the railway track. Lt R.M. Davis with his platoon and company HQ were left on the edge of Bourguebus as a firm base. Swaze himself set out with Sgt J. Connolly and ten men. In obscure conditions, they moved cautiously but 'demonstrating' to draw the enemy's fire. They reached a sandy path, point 63, some 500 yards along the road.

At this point the defenders replied with their customary zeal. Swaze saw it as a 'sea of fire' rushing through the darkness and thick fog. Machine-gun and mortar fire made further advance impossible. Swaze 'assessed' the firing in Tilly itself. It became apparent to both sight and hearing that the Calgary attacked had been rolled back. In his own blunt words Swaze decided the Calgaries' attack had failed, and, 'being paid to use my goddam common sense', sent his men back one at a time, before following them in. Dickie was not so fortunate for he had run into another sea of flame. The railway at that point ran along an embankment and the sandy path went under a tiny viaduct. Dickie and his men went to ground in this useful refuge. It is typical of the close, incessant warfare around Tilly that for twenty-four hours

Dickie's little force was trapped under the viaduct and cut off from all contact.

W.R. Bennett, intelligence sergeant of the Royals, had been speeding to and fro on his Norton motor-bike, guiding their reinforced Able company, under Maj Tom Whitley, up to code-sign 'blue' behind the Calgaries, ready to get involved in the battle if required. As they began to advance, company runner Pte Tom Dixon beside Maj Whitley was killed by a sniper. Then they saw the Calgaries pulling back 'in some disorder'. Whitley dug-in along the 'blue' line and the Calgaries went to earth in front of the Royals.[7]

Brig Megill visited the battle zone to see for himself. After discussion with Lt-Col McLaughlan he ordered another attempt to penetrate and hold Tilly. They had managed to get in among the houses once. The Germans must be even more battered and dismayed than the attackers. At 1430 the Calgaries, who were to become known as one of the finest battalions in later battles, lifted themselves from their dust scrapes and tried again. What was described as 'withering fire' hit them. By the time they had again crossed the 400 yards to 'yellow' so many men had fallen instantly killed, or doomed to prolonged agonies, that all ranks could see there was neither sense nor glory in continuing. Again the Calgaries scraped away the uneven surface, found themselves dips and mounds in the field and continued firing at the virtually invisible enemy in Tilly. Until 2230 hours. Then they were called back.

Next day they were still counting up the roll. Some missing men were still filtering in. The Calgaries experienced some sort of satisfaction at 1800 when Typhoon rocket bombers swooped in and 'Tilly went up and then down in a mess of stinking rubble'. The infantry had yellow smoke ready. Four bombs were dropped on them but the quick igniting of the yellow smoke warded off any further Typhoon error. Then the artillery again bombarded. The war diary continued, 'it is seemingly impossible for anyone to live under such fire but en. Mgs open up again. The Hun is like a rat and comes up for more no matter how hard we pound him.'

As the actual contact combat had ended a brief cease-fire was mutually agreed to recover dead and wounded of both sides. Manfred Thorn was still alive and took part in it:

And so we had a Fire-pause. From both sides, eager volunteers forgot their tiredness to give two willing hands to clear the field of wounded, dying and the dead. It had to be done and we did it as quickly as we could. One of my crew, looking at the bodies of so many young Canadian boys, whispered to me, 'Why didn't they stay at home?'

Stiller and radio operator Gerhard Teichert (four members of the crew were named Gerhard) climbed out of their tank as did Wolff and one of his crew. They heard 'help! help!' all around. First the panzer men picked or kicked all weapons out of the way. Then they began to carry or support the Calgary wounded into a reasonably safe room in the ruins of the town hall. The first knocked-out Sherman had not blazed. While medics began to attend the wounded, the tank crews climbed into the Sherman and helped themselves to what for them was a hoard of gold: cigarettes, cookies, chocolate, tins of fruit and jam. But fortune was not to smile on Stiller and his men. After the manner of tank crews they packed their booty on the back of the tank. That evening a heavy mortar shell blew the booty to smithereens and also cracked the rear deck armour of 711 so seriously as to need workshop attention.

As the cease-fire ended the Royals and Calgaries dug-in and held on doggedly to their FDLs. Sgt W.R. Benett noted 'As more wounded were taken out, the thought passed through my mind that "those of us that were left here at Verrieres Ridge would surely die here!" As dusk settled over the swirling dust and stench of the battlefields, huge swarms of Junebugs attacked us like the biblical locusts, to complete this viciously contested period of fighting.'

There was mutual understanding between the front line troops but not fraternization or even mercy at the height of battle. The remainder of the 'green' troops of the Lincoln and Welland were about to undergo the induction into war which Maj Swaze's platoons had already endured. Like the Black Watch, the L & W traced their history back to when demobbed soldiers of Butler's Rangers settled the almost desert 'Niagara frontier' in the 1780s. A muster of militia volunteers was first held in the two counties in 1788, and in the Anglo-American war of 1812 no less than five regiments of Lincoln militia saw action, often as boat parties raiding across the Niagara river border.

At times the personal antagonism, as distinct from the military enmity, of the front line troops was fuelled by stories, true or otherwise, about atrocities. These were publicized either as deliberate propaganda or casual rumours on both sides. SS mortar corporal Karl-Heinz Decker, who later settled in Wales, was told stories of Canadian atrocities by comrades who said they were eye-witnesses, but he had no way of checking that out.[8] J. Arkle Dunlop heard similar stories on the other side:

> I was a lieutenant in charge of 15 Platoon, L & W. We came up through Soliers. On the way through we were told that the German officer who fought at Soliers allowed his men to shoot 9 Canadians who had been captured and were being held in a cemetery behind a little church. On our arrival at Bourguebus I met an officer from the North Shore Regt who went in with the tanks on the original bash. He was completely exhausted and wanted to get out. We were being shelled intermittently from around La Hogue. In the early morning of July 31 I lost two of my guys, Papeneau and Swanson, who got a direct hit in a slit trench. They were the regiment's first two casualties in action.[9]

A number of witnesses confirm that a direct hit on a slit trench was perhaps the most horrific of occurrences. The explosive power of a mortar bomb dropping vertically was multiplied by its confinement in a very tiny space hewn in solid earth with most of the space packed by two frail human bodies. That perceptive Highland Division infantryman, Stan Whitehouse, described the hideousness of the fairly frequent happening:

> Our magnificent stretcher bearer Tom King . . . looking distraught, told us of his grisly ordeal in helping the battalion Red Cross empty the dugout after the Moaning Minnies had done their worst. 'I've never seen anything like it', he said, shaking his head. 'All the limbs were blasted out of their sockets. It was like trying to handle sacks of crimson jelly.' It was Tom who told me of the difficult choice he sometimes had to make when several wounded men needed attention at the same time. If one man was calling 'stretcher bearer' and another crying out for his mother, he invariably gave preference to the man asking for the stretcher bearer. Experience told him that a soldier calling for his mother was usually severely wounded and probably dying anyway. . . . I had heard badly wounded Germans calling out 'Mutter! Mutter!' and it was often the last word they ever uttered.[10]

On 1 August Montgomery called Crerar to demand that Simonds should push on with further attacks and pin the enemy down on the ridges. The idea at this time was not a breakthrough but a 'pinning down' by infantry. Every additional day that a German panzer unit was held south of Caen enabled the Americans to dash farther and farther around behind the German Seventh Army. The way was opening up for a possible encirclement. And every additional day Tilly became more important.

At 1800 on 1 August the L & W were ordered to attack Tilly in force that night. The axis of attack had switched back from the le Noyer road to the Bourguebus road. The regimental history suggests that the CO, Lt-Col McQueen 'received sketchy orders and received them late'. However, with H-hour at 2345 he was given longer notice than some other COs had received for attacks on a ridge position. Returning to his own HQ at Bourguebus he held his O group from

2000 to 2200. Five regiments of artillery were to support the battalion and armour would be supplied by the South Alberta Regiment (29 CRR), but only at first light. The Argyll and Sutherland Highlanders of Canada would form the firm base in Bourguebus. During 25 minutes of artillery fire against the enemy defences, 'A' and 'B' Companies would move between La Hogue and Tilly, armed with PIATs, to intercept any enemy armour counter-attack from that direction as had happened the previous night. 'D' Company would then move forward to take point 63, allowing 'C' to pass through them and take the village. The entire battalion would then garrison Tilly and to that end, rather than fighting light, they would all carry the full weight of impedimenta required for 'garrison' duty. For some the term impedimenta would so easily become impediment. The respective company commanders of 'A', 'B', 'C' and 'D' were majors A. Gillies, F. Fisher, R. Willson and J. Swayze.

After a meal of stew, 'B' Company set off in single file for about 500 yards. Then someone yelled 'Let's go'. The front men began to run. At that precise moment, as though triggered by the shout, a Very light shot up from Tilly. It was like the conductor's first beat to the percussion section of the orchestra. Machine-guns, mortars, tank high explosive, and grenades all strummed and beat their rhythms, creating again the 'sea of fire' effect to complement the thunderous noise. The machine-guns fired their tartan network through the tops of the wheat, defying anyone to find a square foot of empty air. Maj Fisher was one of the first hit, and went down. Pte Barton saw a friend fall dying and later reported, 'I can still see the tracer coming through the stubble and just drumming into him.'[11] Some 'B' Company men fired a few wild, desperate shots but were disorientated in the dark with lines of fire coming from several directions. 'B' began to fall back towards 'A' and move into a withdrawal mode. Lt John Martin saw it as accelerating into a disorganized dash for the shelter of Bourguebus's buildings.[12]

Platoon Sgt Percy Howse, like many others going into battle for the first time 'really had no idea what to expect'. His memory is that:

There was a railway track between Tilly and Bourguebus and beside it a very large field of wheat. The weather was very hot. The Germans had our approach covered by fixed machine-guns, mortar and artillery fire. They seemed to see every move we made although the attack went in at night and we could not see them. It was one hell of an introduction to battle.[13]

Like Howse, Cpl Charles Kipp, leading 9 Section of 9 Platoon, did not know what to expect but very soon learned the grim realities of war. He does not shirk the recall of moments of battle insanity:

Being green troops we had no idea of what was going to happen. But I did have a very deep suspicion that the going was to be hard. In this my first battle I learned that this was going to be dog eat dog, no quarter asked and no quarter given. This was going to be a case of extermination of one army or the other. And this set my attitude for the duration of the war . . . very aggressive, and kill or be killed . . . If they did not have their hands up when I got on top of them it was too late. The way I saw it, it was them or me, and I survived the war.[14]

'D' Company, under Maj Swayze, pushing down the main road had reached point 63 to which Swayze and a party had already penetrated once. They were isolated with a flank open to possible counter-attack from La Hogue. The brigadier thought it necessary to continue pressurizing the enemy and ordered that Maj Willson should take 'C' through 'D' as planned and try to enter Tilly. They advanced silently and reached a point 200 yards from the crucial first hedge guarding Tilly. Then again a concerted crashing of guns, as at another down beat from a conductor, drove them deep into the wheat. There existed a total prohibition zone, established by saturation firing across every foot of ground. There was nowhere to go forward. Willson drew his men back, taking advantage of any vegetation and ruts in the ground for cover.

This saga of death and defeat should not depict the battle as harming only one side. Throughout the seemingly hopeless infantry travail, the Allied artillery carried on its own war of attrition. Needing to surface sufficiently to fire their guns, the Germans had a tremendous respect for the Allied big guns. They were particularly impressed by the ranging and location ability of the Canadian and British artillery. Ustuf Stiller has recorded a good example of this. His companion panzer, 712, commanded by Ustuf Weiss, had been cleverly camouflaged at a bend in the thick hedge and had been undetected for some days. Then the *Werfer* (mortar) observer wished to use Weiss's radio to guide his mortars on to Allied artillery positions near the Caen to Falaise road. Weiss was worried about using his radio too frequently but had to cooperate with the observer. The radio messages went back from 712 to the mortar pits. Instantly Allied detectors fastened on to the signals. For about three hundred square metres the area was turned into an inferno of heavy exploding shells. Several shells hit 712, blasting away every fitting which was not solid armour plate welded on the tank. Weiss, who had stayed alone in the tank, bailed out and dashed into the town hall cellars. The defenders stated that they had seen shells exploding on hitting a twig of a tree, so sensitive were the fuses.

Back in the outskirts of Bourguebus the left hand companies of the L & W had been reorganized, Lt J.S.W. Burnett taking over Fisher's 'B' Company. The date had moved on to 2 August and the clock to about 0215 when 'A' and 'B' were ordered to attack Tilly again. The regimental history states that 'owing to the confusion, the change in plan did not become known to all the junior leaders'. One survivor translated that as 'the CO's dug-out was too far back'. Men were lying in scrapes and ditches over several hundred yards. It was still midnight dark. Orders went by word of mouth. More than one mouth in the line had been stopped for ever. In the event only 7 and 8 Platoon and some men from 9 got up and started along the terror trail to Tilly again.

Lt E.G. Phair was leading 7 Platoon in line ahead with Lt J.G. Martin and 8 following on and the few men of 9 (Lt Bill Armstrong) who linked up. All but the few front men were reluctant to fire for fear of hitting their own comrades. In the rough fields the line became more and more strung out. When the usual concerted German fire slammed down on the leaders it neatly cut off Ernie Phair and most of his men from John Martin and the rest behind. Very quickly men were hit and others dived to the ground. Those behind could not see whether those in front were still living and therefore slowed their move forward. John Martin tried to join up with the men in front. He noticed what appeared to be narrow lanes in the wheat. These had either been deliberately cut by the defenders or were the result of constant firing of machine-guns on fixed lines. Whichever was the cause, as the field was lit by flares the machine-gunners could see any movement across the lanes and fire their rapid Spandau bursts.

'We were green troops at night on unfamiliar ground with uncertain orders against well-prepared defences', admits Martin. The temptation was to break and run, but the enemy fire was so persistent and accurate that most attackers simply lay still. Phair and most of his men had disappeared (Phair was killed). Martin crawled among survivors and directed them back like field mice through the corn. When, at long last, their painful passage to safety brought them near to Bourguebus, a new hazard awaited. The Argylls on guard, believing there could be no more survivors, were about to fire on what they took to be an enemy patrol. A few well-known curses soon caused fingers to be taken from triggers.

The divisional commander had reported that the German tactic had been to open the door, let them in and then close the door. It was later learned that the lead platoon was cut up into small groups, some of whom were taken prisoner. Throughout much of the action J. Arkle Dunlop and his platoon had been lying in a potato field near the railway. Their mission was to wait and catch the Germans running away on that side of the village. No Germans ran away but for long enough incessant streams of machine-gun bullets hissed through the air inches above Dunlop's nose as he lay amid the potatoes.

1. The loneliness of battle: Pte H. Robichaud (FM-R) in May-sur-Orne, 9 August 1944. (Ken Bell/National Archives of Canada, PA-114507)

2. Pz-grenadier Göstl blinded, bleeding profusely and left for dead, continued firing towards the sound of enemy guns, Tilly, 5 August 1944. (G. Stiller)

3. Maj Philip Griffin, Canadian Black Watch, killed in action 25 July 1944, still lies among his comrades at Cintheaux 'that they might have life'. (Jai Tout)

4. Veterans: German prisoners near Tilly, July 1944, all holders of the Iron Cross and other awards. (Imperial War Museum B7928)

5. Maj, later Lt-Col, Jacques Ostiguy, DSO, of the Maisies, ready to go. (Ostiguy)

6. Jeeps wallow in floods and mud which washed out Operation Atlantic, July 1944. (Imperial War Museum B7859)

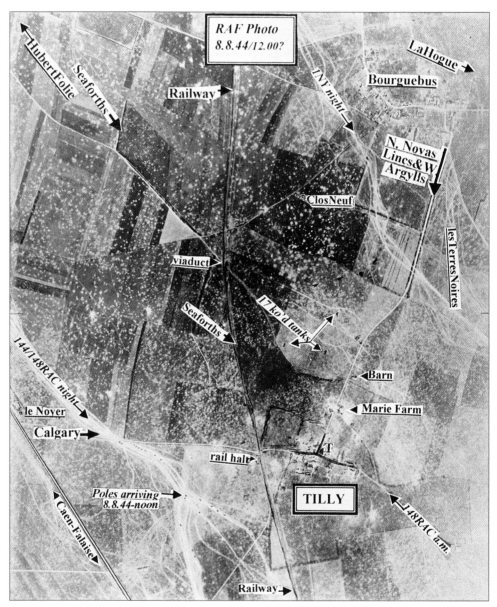

Labels on the aerial photograph:

RAF Photo
8.8.44/12.00?

HubertFolie
Seaforths
Railway
1NY night
La Hogue
Bourguebus
N. Novas
Lincs & W
Argylls
ClosNeuf
viaduct
les Terres Noires
Seaforths
17 ko'd tanks
144/148 RAC night
le Noyer
Barn
Marie Farm
Calgary
rail halt
T
Poles arriving
8.8.44-noon
TILLY
Caen-Falaise
148 RAC a.m.
Railway

7. Aerial photograph of Tilly, 8 August 1944. The untidy 'lanes' marked '*144/148 RAC night*' and '*1NY night*' are totally new 'highways' produced by the ploughing effect of hundreds of tracked vehicles moving in formation across open country during the Night March. The lanes did not exist at 23.30 hrs on 7 August. Follow-up troops then used these new highways and Polish tanks can be discerned on their way up to the Cramesnil spur. The fields are pockmarked by craters. (© Crown copyright – MOD)

8. Lt, later Maj, Don Learment, DSO, North Novas. (Learment)

9. Ustuf Gerhard Stiller, panzer troop commander, Tilly. (Stiller)

10. Tilly-la-Campagne, 1930s, looking from the Bourguebus end of the main street towards the church. The town hall (*mairie*) is arrowed. (M. Hue, Mayor)

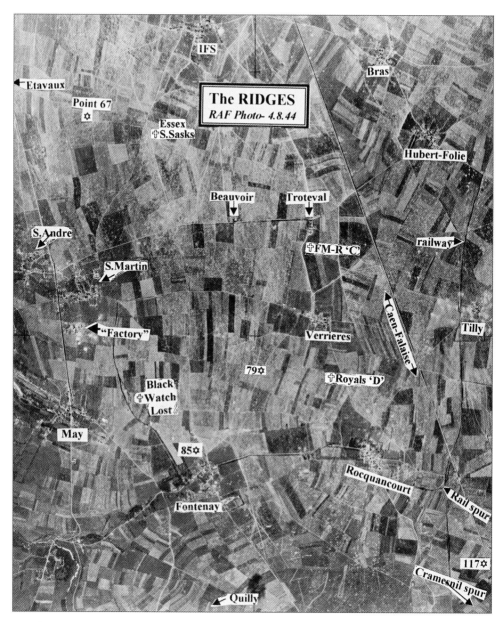

- IFS
- Bras
- Etavaux
- Point 67 ✿
- **The RIDGES** *RAF Photo- 4.8.44*
- Essex ✝S.Sasks
- Hubert-Folie
- Beauvoir
- Troteval
- S.Andre
- ✝FM-R 'C'
- railway
- S.Martin
- Tilly
- "Factory"
- Verrieres
- Caen-Falaise
- 79✿
- ✝Royals 'D'
- Black ✝Watch Lost
- May
- 85✿
- Rocquancourt
- Rail spur
- Fontenay
- 117✿
- Cramesnil spur
- Quilly

11. Aerial photograph of The Ridges. The gradual increase in height is revealed by the altitude points marked (67, 79, 85, 117 metres) while Bras lies at only 43 metres. In places, as between May and Fontenay, the steepest slopes are revealed by the curved formation of fields. (© Crown copyright – MOD)

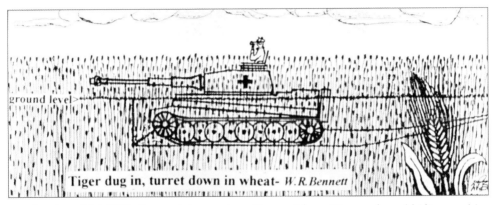

ground level>

Tiger dug in, turret down in wheat- *W.R.Bennett*

12. Sgt, later Maj, W.R. Bennett's impression of how a 54-ton Tiger tank could 'disappear' in, and fire through, a cornfield. (W.R. Bennett)

13. From the ruined outskirts of May, looking back across open fields to the pithead at St Martin with St Martin church, right. (Canadian Forces Photographic Unit PMR90-412)

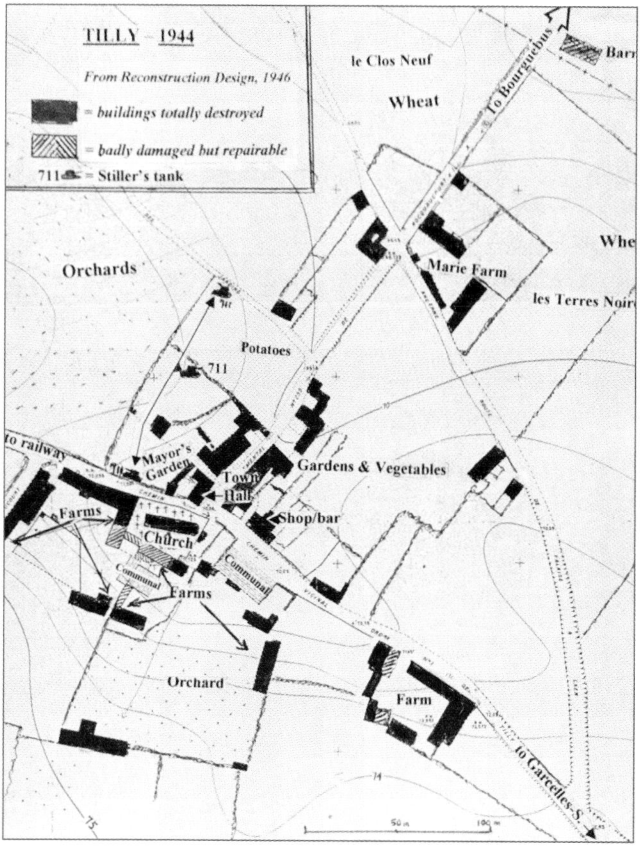
TILLY – 1944
From Reconstruction Design, 1946
= buildings totally destroyed
= badly damaged but repairable
711 = Stiller's tank
le Clos Neuf
Wheat
To Bourguebus
Orchards
Marie Farm
Potatoes
711
to railway
Mayor's Garden
Town Hall
Gardens & Vegetables
Farms
Church
Shop/bar
Communal
Communal
Farms
Orchard
Farm
to Garcelles-S.

14. Sketch plan of Tilly, 1944.

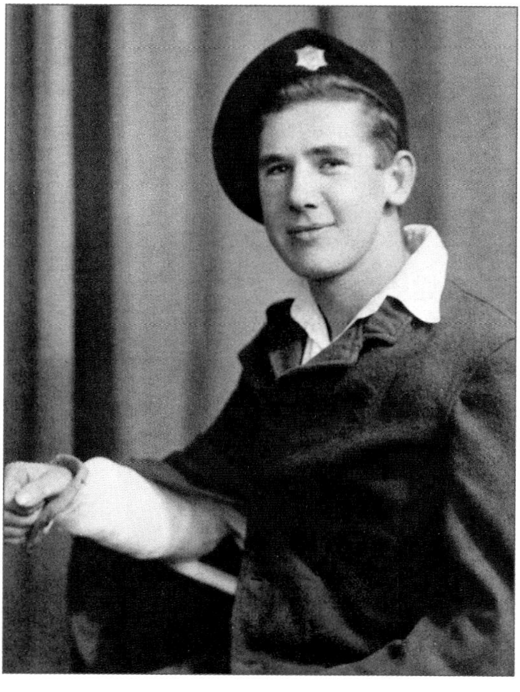

15. Cpl Cliff Brown, Lincoln and Welland, aged twenty, in England, December 1944, recuperating from wounds. (Brown)

16. *Top:* At the level crossing Tilly Deputy Mayor M. Samson shows the author the railway track and bank where machine-guns dug in. Caen buildings are visible on the horizon to the left. *Above:* Le Clos Neuf's fatal fields lead to Bourguebus, its church visible along the road. (Jai Tout)

17. Manfred Thorn, tank driver, aged nineteen, at Tilly. (Toon-Thorn)

18. Brig H.B. 'Black Harry' Scott, DSO, commander of the successful left flank armoured night march, 7/8 August 1944. (M. Scott)

19. Sherbrookes, left to right: Capt D. Bradley, adjutant; Lt C. Thompson, killed in action, Verrieres; Maj S.V. 'Rad' Radley-Walters, DSO, 'A' Squadron commander. (S.V. Radley-Walters)

20. Mines hold up an attack? Send for the engineers – in this case Sgt J. Hickman, 6th Field Company. (Michael M. Dean/National Archives of Canada PA-132918)

21. Lt-Generals Guy G. Simonds (left) and Dempsey point out the ridges to Churchill and Montgomery, 22 July 1944. (Imperial War Museum B7877)

22. A sight no infantryman wanted to see as he crouched in the ditch beside the road. Stiller's MkIV later k.o'd in the Falaise Pocket. (Stiller)

23. Military police, like L/Cpl P. Chimilar here, kept traffic moving at the most dangerous places on the roads. (Lt D.I. Grant/ National Archives of Canada PA-131267)

24. Simonds' idea: the first kangaroo. When under fire, the infantrymen would duck down inside the hull. (Imperial War Museum B8806)

25. Checking one of the iron ore mine shafts near St Martin are Sgt R. Therrien and L/Cpl
T. Notman (FM-R). (Ken Bell/ National Archives of Canada PA-131353)

26. The bane of Allied infantrymen, its siren bombs screaming down in batches, but this Nebelwurfer had moaned its last. (Imperial War Museum B7783)

27. Lt-Col, later Brig, G.L.W. Andrews, DSO, commanded 2 Seaforths in the last and successful assault on Tilly-la-Campagne. (The Highlanders Museum)

28. Artillery support was magnificent. Gunners of 9 Canadian Infantry Brigade fusing shells, a tough task. (Ken Bell/National Archives of Canada PA-131413)

29. Cautious infantry in a wheatfield which could so easily hide tanks, machine-guns or snipers. (Imperial War Museum B8557)

30. Canadian army band plays for French civilians in a liberated village. Theirs was no easy lot: the bandsmen were trained stretcher-bearers and saw some of the most gruesome aspects of war. (Imperial War Museum B8098)

31. Ghent, 1945: Don Learment marries Lt (Nursing Services) Cecelia McDonald, 16 Canadian General Hospital, who had served in Italy and Holland, one of the many women who were there under fire. (Learment)

32. Cintheaux, 1994. Left to right: Manfred Thorn, Colin Nelson (North Novas) and Gerhard Stiller at the grave of Thomas Douglas whose identity tags Stiller saved at Tilly. (Toon-Thorn)

Cpl Charlie Kipp never minced his words in commenting on what happened:

It was just plain murder. This was a very ill conceived attack. Very sketchy orders to a very incompetent senior officer. This wasn't a battle, just sheer murder. We were supposed to attack with both tank and artillery support. We went to our start position. And then received orders, 'Don't wait for our support. Attack now!' We didn't have a chance. We were driven back in complete confusion and the loss of half the company. My company. A terrible beating. My section was swept away and lost in the dark. I was last man back in. I was mad and very disgusted over it all. Now all alone and no idea where my men were. I never had a chance to fire my sten gun at a target. I was exhausted. I went into an open field behind the church and fell asleep on the ground. What hurt was the beating.

Ustuf Stiller recalled that the defenders' orders were always to hold their fire until the ultimate moment of crisis:

Our orders were 'let them get closer' . . . finally, the white flare went up. 'Fire at will!' The tracer trajectories shot out of our ambush positions. Shell after shell flew out of our barrels and more panzers raced up to join us. Five minutes of that punishment and the Tommies stopped in their tracks. Behind us there was a thundering – the heavy *Nebelwerfers*. For five hundred metres in front of us the terrain turned into hell. One of their tanks must have taken a direct hit. It simply disappeared. Others stopped and smoke began to rise . . .

The Germans were proud of the description of them as 'rats' who always came up for more. They lived like rats in the ruins and waited for the occasional 'calm at the centre of the whirlwind' of artillery fire in order to find food. Manfred Thorn, driving panzer 734, had to make 'a cumbersome trip across the rubble to the field kitchen' dug deep into rubble. Cook Heinz Wolfel had a captured British lorry in which he brought up the food every day from Garcelles-Sequeville. On one occasion a moment of calm had allowed Thorn and loader Pieper to go running to the kitchen. As they scrambled back with mess tins full of welcome food their commander, Rattke, shouted 'Where have you been? There are three Canadian panzers out there – 30 metres away.' Driver Thorn was needed as in a few yards time the three Shermans would have spotted the Mk IV and probably knocked it out. Thorn jumped into the driver's seat and reversed behind a wall. Later the three Shermans were outflanked and knocked out.[15]

As was the case with the Germans, numbers of Canadian front line infantrymen were only nineteen years of age and some were even younger. One of the Lincs and Welland survivors aged nineteen was already a corporal in charge of a section and his experience adds to the story of the L & W tragedy in front of Tilly. He was Cpl Cliff Brown, youngest of a family of fourteen, of which the two eldest brothers had fought at Vimy Ridge in 1917. Cliff was now on another French ridge which was to be as costly to his platoon and company as any at Vimy. He had experienced some problems in England when he was promoted to command men up to ten years older than himself. These difficulties tended to disappear as the battalion drew near to the scene of action. He tells of Tilly:[16]

Coming up the slopes towards Bourguebus it was impossible to stay out in the open because of enemy mortar fire. The moment we stopped we had to dig in. It was necessary to dig three or four new slits, preferably six feet deep, every day on the move. Before the battle I was sent out with a small group of men on patrol. We heard German voices and saw a dug-in tank in the dark. But we were confident because we had been promised artillery, tanks and Typhoons in support. We were to attack as three sections in 7 Platoon under Lt Phair. My section consisted of seven riflemen, one Bren gunner and two loaders. All of us, except the Bren gunner, carried a rifle, 150 rounds of rifle ammo in two cloth bandoliers and four machine-gun magazines, plus a 2 inch mortar bomb, grenades, small pack, water bottle and a spade. (We never carried a gas mask.) We were obviously not going to run very fast either way.

We advanced close to the railway. We saw some tanks blown up. The Germans seemed to ignore our barrage. We saw no Typhoons. The Germans allowed us to get right into the wheatfield then blazed away with many machine-guns, mortars and tank HE. Men fell all around, some dead, some groaning with wounds, others trying to dig into the earth. I tried to encourage riflemen to fire at the enemy, tried a shot myself, but they would not because first it meant raising up a little into the path of the bullets and also it would give away our position to what seemed dozens of machine-guns on all sides.

We lay listening to the weird sound of machine-gun bullets cutting through the heads of the corn, crackling and whizzing and hissing. Eventually as fire lessened a bit we crawled back on our bellies, not lifting a head. But of the thirty men in 7 Platoon only myself and Pte Bill Chowdrun survived. Phair died of his wounds.

Was I safe in Bourguebus? No. I was still not finished. Maj Swayze sent for me and said 'I want you to go out to that k.o'd Bren carrier out there and recover the 18 set. It is the only working wireless set we have left. It is invaluable.' Another crawl and I managed it. Then, looking at all the bodies and remembering the boys of my platoon still missing and who we could not yet go and find, I took off my stripes, went to Maj Swayze and said 'I'm sorry, sir. I can no longer give orders to kill.' I expected to be shot at dawn but Maj Swayze was a wonderful soldier and leader. He sat and talked and reasoned with me for ages, and said he himself had to give orders against his wishes. Then suddenly he said, 'Right! You've got half an hour to stitch those stripes back on.' I did.

I was not happy with some things. We were loaded down as we were supposed to be going to stay in Tilly. All of us. So nobody was lightly equipped like a fighting soldier in the front rank. And when we had to go to ground we were hampered by all that stuff. I was not happy with the sten gun. Once it failed to fire when I was taking prisoners who had been firing from a barn. But fortunately the prisoners did not know. I just kept waving the sten at them. Another man, sitting down tired, dropped the sten between his knees, the butt hit the ground, the sten fired and shot the man through the brain.

It is a matter of record that so much equipment was lost by the Lincs in their overloaded advance that a court of enquiry was held to find the reason. At a decent interval of days the CO moved on and Maj W.T. Cromb, Jnr, took over, soon establishing an excellent reputation as the colonel.

Although the L & W attack had been beaten back there was little opportunity for the panzer troops to make any inroads into the Bourguebus defences, even had they wanted to. The battalion of Argylls holding the firm base line was supported by tanks of the South Albertas. Here also the New Brunswick Rangers, one of the unheralded machine-gun battalions, came into their own. With their heavier Vickers machine-guns and mortars they put down a defensive screen sufficient to discourage any panzer grenadier commander from contemplating forays into the regrouping survivors of the battle. The L & W then moved to hold Bras where the Manitoba Dragoons, an armoured car regiment, had dug-in.

Before the battalion withdrew from Bourguebus a number of their frustrated foot soldiers decided to start a private war. Inevitably Charlie Kipp was involved:

I was mad over the whole show. I decided they [the enemy] could not do that to me and get away with it. I would go and get me a German. I got me a Bren gun and stuck my head up through a hole in a ruined wall. It seemed a freight train came through the hole over my head. German bullets! I had found my German. I kept popping up and firing and popping down. His bullets were hitting a stone house behind me so I could more or less calculate the direction. Suddenly a noise of movement behind me! Only Cpl Fred Storey, 8 Platoon, heard I was missing. Heard firing. Thought it was me. Came to help. He had a pair of binoculars, so crawled out past the wall and out in the field. I got the German firing again. Fred soon said 'I see him, laying out in the open field.' He directed my shots. 'Getting close. Up a bit!' I gave a good burst. Fred shouted, 'He's down'. I had got my German and had never even seen him. Fred said the few survivors of our company were gathered on the other side of town, so we went and joined them. We were lucky to get away with it. Later in the war I took a German prisoner. He asked me if I had fought at Tilly. I said yes and he said that was the worst fighting they were ever in.[17]

With the perspicuity of the front line soldier, Kipp comments, 'Our senior officers did not seem to grasp that this was actually the last stand for the Germans in France. If they lost Tilly and that area they lost the war. Our officers could not get hold of the idea that this position was NOT a company objective. Too many men were sacrificed before they learned that Tilly was a MAJOR objective. And the Germans were the toughest enemy one would ever want to meet.'

No doubt Charlie Kipp, if asked, would have advised the responsible officer on 4 August that there was no need to send out a patrol to see if Tilly was still held by the enemy. Charlie would have assured that officer that the panzer grenadiers would still be there. In fact at that moment 1st SS Panzer Leibstandarte Adolf Hitler were being given marching orders to rush south and counter-attack the Americans. In their place a full strength but novice infantry division, the 89, were on their way through France. The responsible officer persisted in ordering 'B' company of the L & W to send a sergeant and three men into Tilly to check. When they confirmed that Tilly still had a garrison, senior command decided that the Argyll and Sutherland Highlanders of Canada (Princess Louise's) would be the next battalion to suffer the traumas of Tilly.

As Manfred Thorn drove his battered 'mess tin' (both man and machine miraculously surviving) away from Tilly with 1st SS Panzer moving to fight the Americans, and to be caught in the eventual encirclement which Tilly had delayed, and to find a way out back to Germany, and to fight again there, he noted, 'As we finally left Tilly on the 4th August there was nothing, but nothing left of Tilly. Tilly had died. Our replacements held Tilly just for a further two days. With some it may be a melody that awakes a vivid memory, or a smile, or that whiff of perfume, but I – I only have to hear the name: Tilly!'

The Argylls had some cleaning up to do before any attack. As soon as they took over ready to advance they were troubled by snipers firing from haystacks. Lt Johnson was called forward with his Scout Platoon and ordered to use his initiative 'to rid us of this nuisance'. Johnson roared across the field in his carrier and calmly set fire to each of the haystacks. Exeunt snipers!

Aware of considerable movement in the German lines, Lt-Col J.D. Stewart ordered a stronger Argyll patrol to test the Tilly defences, on 5 August. A platoon from Baker company under Sgt McClaren advanced towards the village during the afternoon. Strangely enough McClaren had been ordered to 'occupy Tilly'. Typically, the platoon was allowed to trespass across the cornfields and almost up to the first farm before enemy guns opened up and reaffirmed the prohibition zone. The patrol fought back but, having achieved their main purposes, they retreated quickly and efficiently with twenty-three of their men unscathed. One reason for this successful withdrawal was the action of one of their number who continued on his own, walking up the Tilly street towards the church, firing his Bren gun from the hip. In an extraordinary act of recognition of bravery, the defenders let him come on and, when he had run out of ammunition, simply took him prisoner. His name was Pte Ed Purchase. Not so fortunate was Lt E. Dillon patrolling with two men along the railway. Dillon rose to take a brief look over the railway embankment and was shot and killed instantly.

There had been sensitivity about the danger of flank counter-attacks from La Hogue so, before the Argylls attacked, a diversionary strike would be made towards the panzer roost in La Hogue. This was to be undertaken by two motorized platoons of the Lake Superior Regiment, with a squadron of tanks of the Canadian Grenadier Guards (22 CAR). The resistance at La Hogue proved as stern as in Tilly, and the attack as costly, but it may have held troops in that village from reinforcing Tilly.

At 1900 Brig Jefferson ordered a two company attack. Charlie and Dog of the Argylls moved across le Clos Neuf, supported by Shermans of the South Albertas. Forward elements reached the first houses but again were deluged with concerted fire. Lt G. Sloane spotted an 88 mm gun position and desperately tried to charge it single-handed. He was killed. Twenty-four other Argylls had fallen. Behind them four of the Shermans were on fire. Again there was an impenetrable barrier of death across the Argylls' path. The Germans might permit one brave man totally alone to walk up to their pits, but not a company or even a section. Survivors would again recount a similar story to those of the battalions who had preceded them.[18]

Joe Carlton wrote home in a graphic letter, 'I managed to get out of the slit trench once in a while but I never got too far from it. It reminds me of ground hogs – they bask in the sun and whenever there is any danger they dive into their holes. I think I have all ground hogs beat for speed.' Pte Whit Smelser was alongside the colonel and remembered:

It's a sort of flat piece of ground almost like a billiard table. You're just sending a bunch of people across an open field, and they're standing over on the edge popping them off . . . He [the colonel] said, 'This is sheer slaughter. What's the matter with the people back there, telling me to send these guys in?' I felt sorry for him – but he was all man, that fellow.

Capt Bill Whiteside noticed the same tactical ruse which John Martin had observed and suffered from a short while earlier:

What Jerry had done was really very clever. Because between Bourguebus and Tilly it was a sort of dip, like a saucer almost. And there was a road that ran through it. And particularly on the west side was a wheat field . . . And they [the enemy] had cut narrow tracks through the wheat and they would site a machine-gun down there. And anybody who wanted to cross, of course, got himself knocked off.

Capt Ernest Sirluck, intelligence officer with 4 Canadian Armoured Division summed up the situation quite aptly:

By this time the corps and army commanders had realized that putting fresh Canadian division in against these seasoned troops fighting from fortified positions with completely calculated fields of fire and target ranges, was very tricky. Looking back on it, I think the worst difficulty the Canadian corps had was that almost all of its personnel were new to battle.

'These seasoned troops' included one particular man of heroic stature, a panzer grenadier named Gostl. Armed with a machine-gun, Gostl fired at the Argylls as they approached. The Germans were also suffering casualties and one by one the men of Gostl's section fell until he was left alone. He had been hit in the right eye which had been destroyed. He continued firing as the Argylls came nearer. He was hit in the face again and lost the sight of the other eye. He was able to hear the Argylls firing and he continued firing back at them although he could no longer see. This was indeed a brave new version of the term 'firing blind'. At last a direct hit on his gun smashed it and wounded his hand. He collapsed. At that moment more panzer grenadiers mounted a small counter-attack and rescued what they thought was his body. The doctors were able to save his life. He regained some sight in one eye and eventually became a Doctor of Law. He was rewarded for his bravery by the exceptional award of the Knight's Cross, the only panzer grenadier of the entire Waffen-SS to receive that medal.

Yes, the Germans still had a garrison in Tilly and the saga would go to yet another chapter. The Argyll's CO, Dave Stewart, had a last comment on Tilly: 'battle is disorganised, complete disorganisation'. Ustuf Stiller in 711 hurrying south would write a poem about Tilly. Remembering a panzer crew member hiding, like himself, under the tank from the stupendous Allied bombardment, he saw that 'Death is his terror, yet hope plagues his heart.'[19]

CHAPTER SEVEN

Operation Totalize – Eating Dust

Our countrymen faced this enemy in our fathers' time, by which the whole army earned as much glory as its commander. They faced them again more recently in Italy.

(Julius Caesar, 58 BC)

'I have no doubt' (said Crerar) 'that we shall make the 8th of August 1944 an even blacker day for the German armies than is recorded against that same date twenty-six years ago.'

Night. Midnight. Black dark. Then bleeding green and red. A desecrated land. Littered with defunct bodies, animal, human and mechanical. Stench of putrefaction, human and animal; of burning rubber, scorched steel, reeking explosives. Noise: monstrous, inhuman drumsticks beating on eardrums. Motion: constant, juddering, sickening. One night. Unique. 7/8 August, 1944.

The night was terrifying enough for tank crews, trained to grapple with the fear of being trapped inside a travelling incinerator. It was worse for . . . those driving cumbersome 'Crabs', lumbering tanks festooned with jibs, rotors and weighted chains to flail the ground for mines. . . . But it was probably worst for the infantry. Many of them were not walking but had been piled suddenly into open-topped armoured vehicles which would be called Kangaroos. . . . There, cramped in groups of ten they were made to ride through the night . . . knowing the rapidity with which such vehicles could catch fire. "All the ingredients of a Horror film", thought one.[1]

This grand march was supported by attacks by heavy bombers designed to obliterate the towns that eluded capture during Atlantic and Spring. Totalize was an extraordinary offensive, of such Cecil B. DeMille proportions that it overwhelmed senior officers in briefings.[2]

We were formed up in dead ground just south of Caen by 2210 hrs on the 7th August. It was a perfect summer's evening and the tightly packed column looked as though it was drawn up for a ceremonial parade. We crossed the Start Line at 2330 hrs. . . . All went well for the first mile, but, as soon as the barrage started, the column was immediately enveloped in a dense cloud of dust which made it impossible even to see the tail light of the tank in front. The Regimental Navigator had so far not heard a sound from his beam wireless and his compass started swinging wildly in all directions. He could see nothing in the thick haze and his light tank very shortly ditched itself in a bomb crater about ten feet deep.[3]

I was rolling along in formation, watching the ranks of tanks ahead when they hit a very bad patch of mist. I was astounded when the four vehicles ahead, being very confused, divided themselves conveniently to the four winds, N, S, E and W, and were never seen again. . . . Two flail tanks had collided, with booms interlinked, like two fighting elephants with their tusks jammed together.[4]

The tank commander in front and someone in the slit trench have thrown grenades at each other. No more movement down there. Commander in front points energetically down right. I traverse swiftly. Through periscope see . . . in trench, feet away, wearing familiar coal-scuttle helmet, a German, pale face turned upwards towards us, a kid, staring in frozen, paralysed horror. He does not move. Neither do I. Our tank rumbles past, almost shaving his grey chin. I realize what we look like to him: thirty tons of crushing steel, fifty feet of churning iron track swaying towards him like a diabolic mincing machine. . . . Had I fired the gun our shell would have screamed over his head. Already the memory of that pale, paralysed face is imprinted for ever on my mind's eye.[5]

The present author has dealt with Operation Totalize in his book *A Fine Night for Tanks* which concentrates on the first 24 hours of the operation from an armoured point of view. However, in following the fates of those battalions which have walked up the Verrieres-Bourguebus ridge from the crossing of the Orne, it is necessary to detail their eventual success in occupying Tilly-la-Campagne, May-sur-Orne and Fontenay-le-Marmion. As that success came during and because of Totalize this chapter will paint in the entire picture of that unique operation so that the difficult role of the unfortunate 'walking infantry' can be fully understood in context. The word 'unfortunate' is used because it will be seen that the men riding in the new armoured carriers suffered amazingly light casualties in comparison to the walking battalions.

Another word which may need to be justified is that much-abused term 'unique'. Simonds' biographer quotes a staff officer as remembering:

I well recall his 'O' Group before Totalize when the several div commanders sat in a circle under the pine trees (all being much older than GGS [Simonds] and some with desert sand in their ears) to whom he opened, 'Gentleman, we will do this attack at night, with armour.' Their jaws dropped noticeably.[6]

Another commentator, himself an expert in armoured warfare, says:

There were no doctrinal precedents. . . . It was Simonds' masterpiece and it had everything, from flame-breathing Crocodiles to electronic warfare . . . Totalize was a grand corps battle, as II Canadian Corps controlled almost every resource available to First Canadian Army.

. . . He decided that the Germans were not going to be surprised as to the location and direction of the offensive, but he was capable of perplexing them 'in respect to time and method'.[7]

'Succinctly put, "Totalize" was a massive armoured fist that would punch a hole through the strongpoints that had frustrated the Canadians since they had reached Verrieres Ridge.'[8] Who then was this Simonds? Although a Canadian general, he was born in England on 24 April 1903, making him a very youthful lieutenant general at the time of the Normandy campaign. His family moved to Canada where he was educated. He attended the Royal Military College and graduated top of his class in 1925. By the outbreak of war in 1939 he was a major and was appointed to 1st Canadian Infantry Division HQ.

Not long afterwards he was a lieutenant colonel commanding a battalion. By 1943 he was a brigadier and as such was a Canadian observer of the attack on the Mareth Line in North Africa, one of Montgomery's triumphs. He was impressed by a New Zealand attack at el Hamma when the problem of crossing open ground was solved by a clever use of a combination of smoke and dust to confuse the defenders. Still in 1943 he was appointed to the command of the 1st Canadian Infantry Division and fought with that formation first in Sicily and then on the mainland of Italy. On the arrival of the 5th Canadian Armoured Division in Italy he moved to command it, thus accumulating valuable experience with tanks. D-Day was being planned and Simonds was called back to Britain, with promotion to lieutenant general, to take command of II Canadian Corps for the D-Day landings. Young though he was, he had more experience of battle command in the field than a number of other Canadian and American generals.

It is not possible to judge the effectiveness of Operation Totalize without taking into account Simonds' intentions. These are clearly set out in his own 'Appreciation by Corps Commander', dated 1 August 1944 and for restricted circulation. He wrote:

1. *Object* – To break through the German positions astride the road CAEN-FALAISE.

[2. Location of objectives]

3. The positions are manned by as good troops as the German Army possesses. The area is the pivot which, from the German point of view must be held. . . . Each division has one infantry regiment forward, supported by all the tanks and SPs [self-propelled guns], while the other infantry regiment works on the rear position and is able to form the nucleus of a defence in the event of a 'break-in' forward. The Germans apparently rely on being able to get tanks and SPs back, but ensure that some infantry will be available in the rearward positions from the outset, in the event of forward positions being over-run. Two 'break-in' operations are required to penetrate the German defence. . .

4. The ground is ideally suited to full exploitation by the enemy of the characteristics of his weapons. It is open, giving little cover to either infantry or tanks and the long range of his anti-tank guns and mortars, firing from carefully concealed positions, provides a strong defence in depth. This defence will be most handicapped in bad visibility – smoke, fog or darkness, when the advantage of long range is minimized. The attack should therefore be made under such conditions.

5. During the last few days we have attacked and done everything possible to indicate that we intend to continue attacking, the positions opposite to us. Tactical surprise in respect to objectives or direction of attack is therefore impossible. Tactical surprise is still possible in respect to time and method, but very heavy fighting must be expected.

6. . . . If the first 'break-in' is based upon limited air support (heavy night bombers), all available gun support and novelty of method, then the heavy day bombers and medium bombers will be available for the second 'break-in' at a time when gun support begins to decrease [due to distance advanced by forward troops] . . .

7. In essence, the problem is how to get the armour through the enemy gun screen to sufficient depth to disrupt the German

anti-tank gun and mortar defence, in country highly suited to the tactics of the latter combination. It can be done by:–

a) Overwhelming air support to destroy or neutralize enemy tanks, anti-tank guns and mortars.

b) Infiltrating through the screen in bad visibility to a sufficient depth to disrupt the anti-tank and mortar defence.

It was soon apparent that the available Canadian troops on their own would be insufficient to the task. There were two infantry divisions, 2 (Foulkes) and 3 (Keller) with 2nd Canadian Armoured Brigade (Wyman) already well inducted into the realties of battle. The 4th Canadian Armoured Division (Kitching) was arriving on the beaches. Also crossing the Channel was the Polish Armoured Division (Maczek). Montgomery therefore loaned the Poles to Simonds for Totalize together with the British 51st Highland Division (Rennie) and the 33rd Armoured Brigade (Scott). To the Canadian army group of artillery were added three British artillery groups, together with supporting arms. This might appear to be an overwhelming force to launch at the Germans' newly arrived 89th Infantry Division and the battered 272, supported (as was supposed) by 1st SS Panzer LAH with 12th SS Panzer Hitlerjugend on call. But what must be taken into consideration, in addition to the strength of the defence positions, was the doctrine that the attackers needed a superiority of at least three to one. Also it was widely believed that it required the loss of five or more Shermans for every Tiger or Panther knocked out, yet the Sherbookes were already claiming parity with the Panthers as the new Sherman Firefly with its 17-pounder gun was proving its worth.

To reduce a most complicated operation to easily comprehensible terms the general plan was this:

In phase 1 after night bombing along the flanks armoured columns would drive straight through the German front lines at night, debus in the rear and set up a firm base for phase 2. The armoured columns would include infantry in carriers. Meantime 'walking infantry' would 'eat the dust' of the tanks and clear out the villages bypassed by the tanks, most notably, Tilly, May and Fontenay. This would all be carried out by 2 Cdn and 51(H) infantry divisions with the two independent armoured brigades – 2 CAB and 33. There would be full artillery support, including the firing of tracer overhead from Bofors guns to indicate the direction of march. It was planned again to use 'Monty's Moonlight' in spite of the devastating experience of the North Nova Scotia Highlanders when they were silhouetted.

Phase 2 would see the fresh armoured divisions, 4 Cdn and 1 Polish pass through the night marchers' firm base from St-Aignan-de-Cramesnil to the Betteville-sur-Laize area, and break through the next anticipated line of defences and open the road to Falaise. The Americans, who had broken out in a wide sweep from the St Lo area, were now sending a corps swinging north to effect a junction with the Canadians in the hope of cutting off a large German pocket and effectively ending the Normandy campaign with an advance to the Seine and Paris.

Several innovations were included in the plan, such as using radio beams to guide tanks on compass bearings across country in the dark. However, one of the innovations will be sufficient to illustrate both Simonds' innovative genius and his grim determination. This was the planning and production in a period of just over a week of seventy-two massive armoured carriers adapted from 'Priest' self-propelled guns by removing the guns and patching up holes. Brig M.C. Grant, the Canadians mechanical engineer (DDME), was instructed on 31 July to have these ready for use on 7 August. In so short a time Simonds and Grant resolved a problem which had been exercising military minds for decades. On 23 July 1947, Simonds gave a lecture in Normandy which gave the following insight.

Before the war there was a school of thought which considered that infantry were not really necessary and that, given reasonable going, tanks could motor along by themselves at 25 mph and capture an objective. Events soon proved this conception to be false, and that the infantry soldier was required as much as ever when it came to taking and holding ground. Various methods had been tried of moving the infantry forward with the tanks and at tank speed, but none had been really successful. Gen Simonds stated that he had given the subject a good deal of thought and efforts had been made to get a special vehicle, but the trouble was to find a suitable one, as no one at that stage of the war was inclined to produce a new one. Just at this period when he was studying the problem, the field regiments which had taken part in the assault landing [on D-Day] had started to exchange their American Priest 105 mm SP guns for either SP or tractor-drawn 25-pounders. The former were on loan from the Americans and, by previous agreement, would be handed back as soon as the corps was settled in the bridgehead. General Simonds continued:

> I was one day watching some of these vehicles and it occurred to me that, if the equipment was stripped, they would be sufficiently roomy and have adequate protection to provide the sort of vehicle I had in mind. I therefore asked General Crerar if he would intervene with the Americans to allow us to strip the equipments and use them for this particular operation.[9]

Simonds was aware that for the previous exposure of infantry along these ridges during Goodwood, Lt-Gen Sir Richard O'Connor (corps commander) had wanted to ferry infantry in self-propelled gun carriers of the artillery. 'There were predictable howls of outrage at this temerity to violate the hidebound organizational structure of the army,' and Gen Dempsey, O'Connors' superior, vetoed the idea. In fact the tactic had a pedigree. As far back as 1917 Britain designed the Mark IX tank 'to meet the requirements for carrying infantry . . . in an enclosed armoured vehicle'. The Americans had used sleds towed by tanks at Anzio. Simonds himself used towed knock-out armoured vehicles to carry infantry in Italy.[10]

The Totalize vehicles, nicknamed 'Unfrocked Priests', or more properly 'Kangaroos' would eventually lead to the formation of a properly constituted battalion of armoured personnel carriers (APCs) before 1944 was out. In the meantime, Grant and his men had recourse to many novel ideas in their pressing task. The removal of the guns left gaps which had to be covered up. No suitably thick armour plate was available. The mechanics therefore devised what might be called 'steel sandbags' or maybe 'sand sandwiches'. They used two thinner pieces of armour plating and packed them with sand to give the requisite thickness and protection.

Further credit goes to the determined Simonds. O'Connor, together with Roberts, the lead armoured division commander in Goodwood, wanted APCs for that attack but were vetoed without good operational reasons by Dempsey. Simonds decided that his infantry needed the protection of APCs and so he had them made. His instructions were given to Grant before permission was given for the APCs and before Montgomery had officially approved the Totalize plan. Perhaps some hundreds of infantry lives were saved as a result.

The story is resumed in Simonds' 1947 lecture. Time was getting short and it was not until about a week before the operation that American authorization was received; the workshops had, however, already been warned and the work was rushed ahead. Having got the equipment the next problem was to sell the idea to the troops. General Simonds explained:

It was obviously going to be quite useless to mount the infantry if they felt like a lot of sardines in a tin and had no confidence in the likelihood of the operation succeeding. So I quickly suggested to 2 Cdn Div that we might be able to produce some form of Armoured Personnel Carrier in order to get them thinking about the possibilities. As soon as the operation began to harden and I had received definite orders, I at once asked that my second infantry division should be detailed. The Highland Division was nominated and I was a bit worried as to how the Scots would like it, because they had the reputation of being rather canny and having their own ideas about things. General Rennie, who was unfortunately later killed at the Rhine crossing, came over to see me as soon as they had been nominated and I had a talk with him. He was very taken with the idea and I knew from that first talk that I had his support one hundred per cent and subsequently 51 (H) Div took to it with great enthusiasm.

In the command structure of the day British and Canadian infantry did not have regular tank support. Often infantry were allocated an independent tank brigade or regiment on an ad hoc *pro tem* basis which contrasted badly with the German battle group system. The 33rd Armoured Brigade was allocated to 51st Highland Division. Rennie was happy to know that the 33rd were commanded by a desert veteran, Brig H.B. 'Black Harry' Scott, who was later described as a man after the Highlanders' own hearts, with an outstanding appreciation of the issues of cooperation between tanks and infantry.[11] This was essential, as the two armoured brigadiers (Scott and Wyman) were to command the two flanks of armoured columns on the Night March, with the infantry commanders taking over after debussing on the objectives.

Simonds' greatest worry concerned timing. The last Kangaroos were not delivered until the day which Montgomery insisted should be D-Day for Totalize. Simonds had postulated more time for preparation and training, and would later be seen to be justified in that view. However, Montgomery was under pressure from all sides to move more quickly. Also, always aware of the publicity angle, he was anxious that the breakout should be associated with one of the great dates of the First World War, the battle of Amiens on 8 August 1918. Montgomery's idea was illustrated in Crerar's pre-battle message, already quoted, that 8 August 1944 should be 'an even blacker day for the German armies' than 8 August 1918, and a similar prelude to the last acts of the conflict. This might frustrate Simonds and it might be totally meaningless to the troops themselves, but others had the same thought. In the Canadian 6th Infantry Brigade war diary the brigadier, H.A. Young, wrote:

8th August: This appeared a historical day and one's thoughts went back to 8th August 1918. It is hoped by all that this day will prove the final turning point as it did in 1918!

Certainly in one Sherman tank waiting to go there was no thought of 8 August as significant, unless because it had been Bank Holiday weekend at home, the traditional seaside time for many British families. Thoughts were much more restricted to munching a final bully beef sandwich of hard biscuits, checking that trigger mechanisms were working properly, giving the engine a last smooth rev up and seeing that the red light was shining at the rear of one's own tank and at the rear of the tank ahead. Yet the massed procession of up to 200 vehicles around the tank brought thoughts that at last we might be going to achieve something worthwhile.

In dead ground south of Caen, the attackers formed up, by 2300 hours on 7 August, with their vehicles in fours like the old infantry marching formation. Shermans and flail tanks preceded the first company of infantry in their new Kangaroos. More Shermans protected the remainder of an infantry battalion in lighter armoured carriers. Various other useful vehicles, like bulldozers and ambulances, were guarded at the rear by more Shermans, a total of about 200 vehicles per armoured regiment.

From left to right the formations were as follows. Extreme left flank next to woods being bombed by the RAF, was 1st Northamptonshire Yeomanry (1NY) with its column commanded by Lt-Col D. Forster, with one Sherman out in front as the navigating tank (Capt T. Boardman), and a second navigator in front of the serried ranks of fours, including 1 Black Watch. They would circle Soliers and Bourguebus before heading across country to St Aignan. Next to 1NY was a double column under command of Lt-Col A. Jolly of 144 RAC, with 5 Argylls in carriers, followed by 148 RAC and 7 Black Watch.

Like 1NY they would have to find their way over or through the iron ore railway in the dark and then, skirting Tilly, head for Cramesnil. The 148 RAC (Cracroft) would turn off short of Cramesnil to occupy the woods of Garcelles-Secqueville. Brig Scott was in overall charge of three columns on the left of the main road heading towards Falaise. Flails of the XXII Dragoons would travel with all three British columns.

Brig Wyman's Canadian plan was a little more complicated. The 8th Canadian Recce Regiment (14th Hussars) under Lt-Col B.M. Alway, with two troops of Fort Garry tanks, was to trek along the right edge of the main road and cross the road just before the highest ground of the Cramesnil spur, alongside 144 RAC. Farther to the right, and crossing the fateful contested high ground around Verrieres, the main mass of Wyman's tanks would advance, also in three columns with similar components to Scott's but with a somewhat different line up.

Instead of there being a tank regiment to each column, the Canadian tank regiments were spread across the three columns. First there was a 'Gapping Force' of Sherbrooke tanks (M. Gordon) and Lothian and Border flails leading each column. From left to right the infantry were the Royals, the Rileys and the Essex Scots. The infantry constituted the 'Assault Force'. More Fort Garry tanks (R. Morton) rode along at the rear of each infantry battalion as a 'Fortress Force' to confirm a stable base on the objectives. The 1st Hussars (R. Colwell) were moving behind independently.

As the armoured columns, moving up from their dead ground assembly areas, crossed the actual start line and drove through enemy positions, the walking infantry stood up and trudged into the dust and noise on what was hoped to be a fairly simple clearing up of disoriented and stranded enemy remnants. The artillery would provide support with a barrage moving slowly forward, but would not be able to move their guns forward until the walking infantry had completed their tasks. At the tank objectives, once the farthest forward areas had been stabilized during the morning of 8 August, the phase 2 armour would move up and, in lieu of the normal artillery barrage, would advance following a huge daylight bombing attack by the USAAF.

Such was the plan. Its intentions and achievements have been criticized but it has to be said that the phase 1 armoured columns all reached their objectives, some on time and others with some delay, but with only relatively minor catastrophes. Of course there was confusion. Nobody had experience of the confusion which this type of operation would generate. Had there been such experience it could have been stated that confusion is normal, endemic, inevitable in night marches across country by massed columns of tanks. Confusion in itself caused some casualties. In some tanks moving mid-column some members of crews dozed. Many crews and infantry in their carriers were not involved in action on the move. The author's most hurtful moment was when he was stung by an angry wasp which, as the saying goes, must have wanted to get in on the act!

While the British troops on the left were amazed by the accuracy of the RAF bombing along woods just 1,000 yards away from the tanks, the Canadians found that the air targets were insufficiently dealt with due to smoke and mist obscuring bomb aimers' sights. While the British routes were fairly well spaced as between 1NY and 144 RAC, the Canadian columns were hemmed in in very restricted space so that any failure of direction in one column could affect the others. At the assembly point Sherbrooke squadron leader 'Rad' Radley-Walters was able to walk down his column on the tank decks, jumping from tank to tank.

One Lothian and Border tank sergeant paid an unusual tribute. The military police were not usually the most popular of soldiers. In battle they had to stand fast at crossroads well registered by the enemy, in order to direct traffic. Sgt D. Eason in his flail tank recorded 'a journey excellently policed by Canadian CMP for some miles during which we crossed the Orne'.[12] In a typical wartime encounter, the British colonel of military police proved to be the former Chief Constable of Northamptonshire who was delighted to wave his county Yeomanry on their way.

Also of note was the work of the engineers who rode with the columns. As training and experiment time had been so short it had not been possible to make an accurate measurement of the space needed by the clumsy Crab and other speciality tanks in passing through embankments and into sunken roads. Holes had been blown in obstacles, but in the darkness, punctuated incessantly by blinding light of various colours – mainly red and green – proficient drivers could err a foot or two and find themselves wedged into a sunken track. The engineers were on call all the way.

The confusion was created by the tanks and carriers themselves, who knew more or less what was happening. It was anticipated that the enemy in their FDLs, tiny slit trenches, would be bewildered and demoralized by the mighty armada of vehicles passing over and by them. The men chosen to suffer such torture were the 89th Infantry Division under Lt-Gen Konrad Heinrichs. The 89 was known as the *Hufeisen* (Horseshoe) Division from its badge. It had been in its forward slits only two days and was looking forward to its first night of decent sleep. 1st SS Panzer had been pulled out on Hitler's direct orders to face the Americans and 12th SS Panzer had also been ordered back, but were still standing just beyond the phase 2 objectives of Totalize.

As the Horseshoe men were roused by the first tremendous explosions from the RAF bombs on the right, and saw the inferno of flame take hold, the tanks churned into motion. Lt-Col Jolly started the journey behind his lead squadron, having elected to put his navigators into the light Stuart tanks, known to their crews as Honeys. When the small tanks fell into great craters and Maj Lovibond, the 2 i.c. was killed, Jolly found himself at the column's head, navigating and commanding. He wrote:

The Regimental Navigator . . . could see nothing in the thick haze and his light tank very soon ditched itself in a bomb crater. The two reserve navigators, following behind him, tried to avoid this crater and went into another. Not a very encouraging start. From this point, the column disintegrated. All one saw were the shadowy outlines of tanks as they loomed up out of the fog, asked who you were and disappeared again into the gloom. The confusion was indescribable.[13]

Nevertheless, Jolly led his column to its objective, the Argylls liberated Cramesnil and 148 RAC with 7 Black Watch cleared the nearby woods. RAF photographs taken that same day reveal clearly marked dust tracks through the cornfields which are evidence of the continuing cohesion of the columns in all the confusion.

The 1NY left column had to cross the railway and sunken lanes while working around Soliers and Bourguebus. Its route lay across le Clos Neuf and les Terres Noires where a score of brewed up Shermans from the Tilly battles made the narrow passage even more difficult. But before 0300 the regiment was on target. As the infantry CO (Hopwood) took over from the armoured colonel it was seen that the Kangaroos could be used to drive the Black Watch up to the very cottages of St Aignan, while the tanks blasted walls and orchards. The result was the capture of that strongpoint with a roll of casualties which was regarded as extremely light.

The Canadian columns were also finding that a straight compass route across unknown country was impossible. And radio beams which might have helped a plane coming in to land, only complicated matters as the lead tank swung to round a orchard wall, or find a better way over a sunken road, or to take evasive action as enemy guns opened up, fortunately firing blind. Again, the artificial moonlight on moving clouds and the coloured Bofors shells giving guidance (red for the Canadians and green for the British) and Very lights fired by commanders and the constant flashing and flaming of high explosive and the shrouding of mist and smoke, tended to leave drivers unable to discern any objects other than other equally erratic tanks, while commanders checked and rechecked and, when possible, dismounted to confer and ask the way of equally disoriented colleagues. But all the time the trend was southwards and the objective of a disused airfield sufficiently broad to allow most tanks to come home to roost somewhere along the line.

The sights and sensations of the night were common throughout the columns of tanks and carriers, except that on the extreme left fires still burned brightly after the bombing of the nearby woods, while on the right the smoke was blown across the columns to mingle with dust and mist:

Above us the searchlights' artificial moonlight and the green Bofors tracer constantly change colour in mad variations on the theme of fire. In front of us the blurred outlines of the four juddering, swaying Shermans are scarcely discernible in the shifting patterns of haze. Over on our left the other three tanks of our Troop are mis-shapen black beetles swimming in a cauldron of fire. . . . Warm, evil-smelling air rushes and rips about us, lashing us in the face and tearing at our collars. A spray blows in our eyes, not the clean salt spray of the ocean but a dead, burning spray of dust and filth.[14]

Over to the right it was a much darker stage:

A thousand vehicles raised a cloud of dust in the darkness. . . . At the same moment a smokescreen rose above the lines of the 89th Division of the Wehrmacht. Navigators were blinded. Drivers strained their eyes to make out the faint light of the vehicle ahead. . . . There were some spectacular collisions, lamentable errors of range, tanks firing against friendly tanks, while the blazing hulks provided a magnet for the German guns and mortars.[15]

Inevitably, the exuberant impetus of the first mile has been lost and a column capable of 25 mph slows to the speed anticipated in planning:

Once again we have fallen into the pattern of stopping and starting, crawling forward slowly over the shattered fields. The famous formation of fours has now completely broken up. We push on in random groups. The barrage still continues overhead but there is an increasing network of blazing tracer bullets criss-crossing our front, coming mainly from the flanks. Much of it seems aimless and partly spent . . . 'Hullo, all stations William! Hullo, all stations William! Our friends on the right have been held up. Message from Supreme Sunray [Montgomery] asking us to keep moving at all costs. I'm relying on you all to keep moving, keep pushing on, whatever happens.'[16]

'What a night! The most trying in my life time', observed Sgt W.E. Kitching fifty-five years later. 'Our Troop was lined up in order: Troop Officer, 1st Sergeant, an Artillery officer, myself and Sgt Munn. After crawling along for a couple of hours our line was broken for the Artillery officer in front of me had lost contact with the tank ahead. He stopped and came to me and said that it was too dangerous for him to be in the lead. He asked me to take the lead and he fell in behind Sgt Munn. In a short time we lost him. Don't know to this day where he got to!' It was to be a bewildering night for Sgt Kitching of the Fort Garry Horse. He continues:

About this time the trouble started. A tank was hit and took fire. Three of the crew got out. I saw one of the crew running around like a wild man in the dark. I found out it was our Troop Officer's tank that was hit. Confusion set in. The Troop Officer gone. The Troop Sergeant somewhere away in the dark. Sgt Munn and me alone on our own. Not another soul to be seen.

What a night and dark! After crawling a long, long way for what seemed hours I spotted the silhouette of a tank on my left. It was a Sherman. I stopped my tank, ran over and climbed on the other Sherman. I asked the commander what outfit he was with. I still remember his English accent. This was a long time ago but I still remember him shouting 'Yeomanry', not the rest of the regimental name. He asked if he could help. I said 'No' because I now knew

I was too far to the left. I took off again and later ran into Sqdn HQ. I started the night drive as the junior sgt. Next morning I was in charge of the Troop, reorganizing. All the other commanders lost.[17]

[Lothian and Border Yeomanry were giving flail support but Sgt Kitching is clear that the Englishman was in a Sherman. It could have been Sgt George Duff of 1NY who had himself drifted too far to his right and ended the attack with 144 RAC. A number of such involuntary transfers occurred before dawn and the Rileys acquired 'B' Company of the Royals in this manner en route.]

Simonds has been criticized for pacing the Night March at the speed at which Crabs would be flailing for anti-tank mines. It has been said that there were, in fact, no mines and that Simonds had an obsession about them. The Lothian and Border reports show that some Canadian vehicles were blown up by mines and that just beyond the start line the L & B were sweeping the ground for mines along the route and for fifty yards to each side of the Canadian columns. 1NY reported 'no vehicles were lost on mines although it was found later that the column had been within a few yards of a minefield for a considerable distance'. Another tank man agreed, describing La Hogue, 'complete and utter devastation everywhere and horrible smell of burning and rubble. Lots of mines about and plenty of odd shells fall'. He went on to illustrate the humanity of many soldiers against all the odds:

out of the rubble came a distressed tiny black and white kitten. We took it on board. It was too weak to take any solid food and had to be given liquid through a rubber tube. Consequently it was named 'Titti La Hogue' and signed on as spare crew. The kitten had also been deafened by explosions.[18]

Perhaps the most incredible adventure of the night was that of Capt Leonard Harvey, an artilleryman with the Royals, riding in a Bren gun carrier, not the largest of vehicles. As the Canadian columns had edged mutually in the direction of the main road to their left, the centre column had found itself driving through Rocquancourt instead of round the outside. It was even darker in the narrow streets. Harvey suddenly sensed a wall on his left and yelled 'Keep right! You're going to hit the wall on your left.' The driver yelled back. 'We can't be scraping the wall on our left because we're already scraping the wall on our right.' Confused in the obscurity Harvey put out his hand as though to fend off the wall. Astonished he felt 'not cold, rough stone but warm, smooth metal, vibrating under his hand'. His astonishment turned to horror as brief light from a shell flash focused on the regulation German cross insignia on the side of a big panzer. And he was patting it with his outstretched hand! Obviously the Germans were in no better state of awareness than Harvey. A frantic stamp on the accelerator took the mobile carrier swiftly away into the safety of outer darkness.[19]

The column which suffered most disintegration was the one on the extreme right containing the Essex Scots. Their war diary highlights that the weather was very dry and the top soil very light. As penetration into enemy territory deepened, dirt and fog were augmented by smoke. At H-hour plus 120 'A' Company reported visibility virtually nil. The infantry carriers became separated from the tanks as obstacles were negotiated. Several tanks were knocked out. Others disappeared into the void of night.

Capt A.J. Hodges, newly promoted 2 i.c. of 'A', recorded the events. His company commander, Maj Stewart Bull got out of his vehicle in a gallant attempt to restore order, was hit in the face by a shell fragment and temporarily blinded but managed to regain his vehicle. The CO, Lt-Col Tom Jones, ran into a group of Germans and was shot. Capt Bob Bradley trying to attend to the CO was also shot. Maj Jack Burgess, a quiet but determined man, was acting battalion 2 i.c. riding at the rear. Hearing nothing from the CO, he assumed command and somehow worked his way up the chaotic column in the dark. He ordered the regiment to debus, deploy and dig defensive shell scrapes.

At dawn Burgess himself went to a nearby village where he learned from the South Saskatchewans that it was Rocquancourt and also that Lt-Col Jones had been evacuated. Returning he began regrouping the column. Then leading it in a half-track he circled Rocquancourt, heading for the objective, Caillouet. Half a mile away he grouped the battalion into assault formation. At 1130 the Essex Scottish attack went in. The half-tracks bore the infantry speedily across the open ground, weathering a storm of small arms and mortar fire. The village was taken.

It was with great glee that the anti-tank platoon overran a Moaning Minnie position and captured two of the pestilential six barrelled mortars. Total casualties were relatively light but 'A' CSM Russ Case and other HQ personnel were very badly burned when their carrier was engulfed in flames. In the lottery of 'involuntary transfers' already mentioned, the Essex Scots had acquired most strays, including a platoon each of Royals, Rileys, and Toronto Scots machine-gunners, a mortar section and a Recce squadron![20]

If this description of confusion seems too critical of Simonds' plan it must be remembered that the confusion for the enemy was even worse, as it was planned to be, although it was not yet total. An 89 Division report suggests that 'the psychological effect of the extraordinary bombardment on the personnel was comparatively quickly overcome'. The worst effect was a condition of almost physical disablement and catalepsy of the brain 'through the detonations, the near misses, air pressure blasts, as well as the grit and dust, as well as direct hits affecting sight and movement, which caused military disruption as troops were unable to respond in a truly fit condition.

By 0900 the Canadian penetration was such that division HQ was referring to the remaining fighting groups as islands in what had been the division territory. At that time the army commander, Gen Eberbach, arrived himself to see what could be done, perhaps not realizing that the nearest Allied tanks were little more than a mile away (well within Firefly gun range). The 89th Division commander, Lt-Gen Konrad Heinrichs, 'betook himself urgently to the right hand

Regiment at the front to lead the right wing of the Division amid the heavy pressure. Similarly the div adjutant went to alert the reserve battalion of fusiliers.' A month or so later Heinrichs was to be killed in the same sort of situation, at the front of his men, rallying heavily pressed troops in a street battle.[21] Except ominously in Tilly, May and Fontenay, the 89th Division was beginning to break up.

The surviving Sherbrooke tanks which had reached their objectives now looked forward, as did 33 Armoured Brigade, on what appeared to be the wide open spaces of a tank commander's dreams. The author recalls sitting in a Sherman beyond St Aignan-de-Cramesnil and joining in a crew discussion on the theme 'Why are we waiting?' On a lovely summer's morning, silence in the immediate surroundings, and nothing stirring on the green Normandy panorama, it seemed that we could now drive all the way to Paris. Or Berlin if we so wished.

Sherbrooke CO Mel Gordon did more than discuss. As he and Maj Radley-Walters contemplated the open road to Falaise, Gordon requested permission to continue to advance. It was refused. Gordon repeated his request. Brig Wyman came forward to survey the land. Gordon pointed to the open road ahead but Wyman stated that his clear orders were to establish a firm base for phase 2. Then a sniper shot and wounded Wyman. Gordon could do nothing but wait. But his men waited to good effect. Four enemy tanks (not Tigers) drove down the main road, shooting up Bren gun carriers and lighter vehicles. Guided by an artillery observer the Sherbrookes knocked out the first four of many counter-attacking tanks.[22]

At this point most of the phase 1 spearheads were on their objectives and digging-in, or their tanks snuggling into woods and orchards. Two fresh armoured divisions rumbled along, stretched out from the beaches to the Orne, and coming up to form the phase 2 attack. But behind the spearheads the walking infantry had advanced. The Scottish 2 Seaforths had moved in some jeopardy. Aerial photos taken at the time clearly show that the lanes of the 1NY and 144 RAC columns were at one point near Tilly only some 900 yards apart. Into that narrow front walked the Seaforths in the brutal darkness, thickened by the dust thrown up by hundreds of tracked vehicles: a situation always worse at ground level than in a tank turret. It was the Seaforths' task to make the final assault on Tilly in between the armoured thrusts. They and the Canadian battalions with similar roles fought through the night to end the seemingly invincible German resistance in the Tilly, May and Fontenay areas. A new and terrible saga was being played out in each of those villages, each meriting individual study. But before returning to those now familiar sites it is instructive to see how the phase 2 operation developed and how the Germans sought to frustrate it.

Simonds has reasoned correctly that until the intervening villages had been mopped up his major artillery force would not be able to move forward to lay another barrage for phase 2. Indeed the battery which was to shoot coloured marker bursts to guide the air strike was in place only moments before the aeroplanes began to arrive. He therefore negotiated through the complicated, and sometimes complacent, command structure for use of a major group of American heavy bombers to put down a midday barrage prior to phase 2.

The fact that when the bombers arrived some of them accidentally bombed Allied troops was not highly significant. Many of the losses were in troops not committed to the attack or in back areas of attacking troops. It probably amounted to no more than the weight of an enemy barrage. The most significant factor of the USAAF bombing was that it necessarily caused delay, and that a lacuna occurred in the swift flow of Totalize.

The USAAF performance has been criticized and contrasted with the extraordinarily accurate night bombing by RAF Lancasters along the left flank of the Night March. It is therefore of interest to look for a moment at the daylight raid. On 8 August 1st Bomber Division and 3rd Bomber Division of the USAAF dispatched 681 Flying Fortresses (B-17s) to Normandy. Of these, 231 hit Totalize targets in Cauvincourt, 99 each hit Bretteville-sur-Laize and St Sylvain though only 1 found Gouvix, again probably due to the ground cumulus of smoke, mist and dust. Some 67 aircraft unloaded on 'target of opportunity' with 184 aborting. This aborting total was not exceptional as on the same day 414 planes sent to Northern France recorded 359 as 'effective' while the previous day only 132 out of 333 recorded 'effective', or bombs released over identified target.

On 8 August the lead bomber of 351 Bomber Group was hit by flak and the bomb release activated. According to the USAAF system at the time, when the lead bomber dropped its bombs all the other planes of the group followed suit. The bombs fell on Allied troops killing some 65 and wounding 250, and destroying 55 vehicles. The Americans did not emerge unscathed: 7 planes were lost over target, 4 crashed in England, 43 crew were killed or missing and a massive 294 planes were damaged by anti-aircraft fire.[23]

The Allied losses, though unfortunate, did not radically affect the first line troops at that precise minute, but the massive USAAF raid had to be timed in such a way that the impatient Sherbrookes and Yeomanry would seem to be waiting an inordinate length of time before the phase 2 troops came through. The opposing general Kurt 'Panzer' Meyer also thought the phase 2 armour should have attacked sooner and his remarks are now enshrined in Totalize mythology. In fact some sources, such as 'B' Squadron, 1NY's rearguard, suggest that the Poles, who had hurried from the beaches after recent landing, could not have attacked earlier. The Poles themselves have been irritated for decades over the German general's remarks that they did not attack earlier because they were having their breakfast. Of such comments is history misshapen. Be that as it may, Meyer of 12th SS Panzer Hitlerjugend brought all his phenomenal energy and personality to bear on the task of restoring a defence line.

As Meyer stood and looked down the long panorama which every German defender enjoyed, and as he contemplated the masses of Allied armour already visible, he saw a single Flying Fortress pass across from east to west just in front of him. He immediately assumed that it was a master bomber and that it presaged an imminent heavy raid on his head. His reaction was to order any available Hitlerjugend troops at hand to rush through the area which would be bombed and attack the forward Allied lines. Available to him were some eight or nine Tigers from the independent 101 Heavy Tank Regiment under the command of the tank ace, Haupsturmfuhrer Michael Wittmann.

Unknown to Allied tank crews at that time, but famous in the German Army and Press, Wittmann was credited with having destroyed some 270 enemy vehicles. When cited for the award of Oak Leaves with Sword on 14 June 1944 his score was put at 138 enemy tanks and 132 anti-tank guns (in Greece, Russia and Europe). He was accorded the kind of adulation given in the First World War to the flying aces like the Red Baron, von Richtofen. Wittmann was the prototype tank ace. It was German battle doctrine to counter-attack an enemy breakthrough immediately, irrespective of the ratio of numbers engaged. Often these tactics had proved successful. In this case, in spite of myths to the contrary, they were disastrous.

It had already been clearly demonstrated that, in the case of guns of equal power, the hidden defender had great advantage over the exposed attacker. Wittmann had four Tigers ready near Cintheaux and probed forward towards La Jalousie. In a shallow 'U' shape in front of him were the Sherbrookes, 144 RAC and 1NY, with a force of about thirty-two or thirty-three of the new 17-pounder Fireflys, with guns slightly superior to the 88 mm. Wittmann was traversing open ground, while the Allies had had time to go into hides in woods and hedges.

The first contact may have been with guns of the Sherbrookes, for Wittmann's four tanks were all traversed in that direction. At the other side of the 'U', a Firefly of 1NY with Trooper (Tpr) Joe Ekins as gunner had a clear view of the Tigers 'with their backs turned'. Capt Tom Boardman (1NY) and Maj Radley-Walters (Sherbrookes) had quite fortuitously achieved a trap which proved fatal to Wittmann. Joe Ekins' gun was recorded as hitting three of the Tigers in a few minutes while the Sherbrookes also claimed hits. The elite troop was destroyed and Wittmann killed.[24]

Shortly afterward a Hitlerjugend battle group under Maj Waldmuller also counter-attacked, mainly against the lines of 1NY and 1 Black Watch and were halted without reaching the Black Watch FDLs, a roughly equal loss of armour being suffered on each side (about twenty tanks or SPs). This is the succession of events at which the author was present. The Polish advance armour now came around the 1NY positions to the horror of Capt Boardman (right flank) and Lt Tony Faulkner (left) of 1NY who tried to warn the Poles that they would be terribly exposed. There was no adequate means of communication and, if there had been, it is doubtful if the language problem would have allowed urgent variation of action. The Poles even had different code words for the same locations, e.g. the Canadians and British referring to cinema names like 'Barrymore' and 'Valentino' while the Poles used names like 'Ygrek' and 'Markiza'.

The Poles' front tanks ran into Waldmuller's remaining guns which were now under cover. So many Polish tanks were lost that the advance from St Aignan could not be continued that day. The Canadians on the right moved forward with more caution but with gradual success during the day. That night a Canadian battle group called Worthington Force was sent on a smaller repeat Night March but lost its way, was surrounded and wiped out. The remainder of the road to Falaise was not easy country over which to advance, and Simonds saw that rather than indulge in more costly minor advances under the guns of Hitlerjugend, a further major operation (named Tractable) would be required a few days later. So Totalize ended, but not before the Argyll and Sutherland Highlanders of Canada had carried out one of the most brilliant infantry operations of the entire war, a silent, night infiltration up the steep slopes, and occupation of the dominating feature which Worthington had been intended to reach the previous night.

This is the general situation which required the walking infantry to clear the vital road junctions at which sat the villages now so notorious. Other writers have treated the evidence of Totalize in different ways, even as a victory for the Germans. A justification of this present account must find a place on another page. However, one remark is perhaps relevant at this point. The lack of training in dealing with confusion, the fallibility of some apparatus, the waywardness of Worthington, the problem of the bombing pause, and the small number of the efficacious Kangaroos available are all in some measure due to one root cause: lack of time.

Simonds planned for more time and argued for more time. It was largely Montgomery's insistence that he attack overnight on 7/8 August. Two more days of preparation could have seen better training, more experiment with technology, a better understanding of the chaos of night marching, more personnel carriers adapted, and, under Hitler's orders, Hitlerjugend might have been farther away from Cintheaux.

In terms of previous Anglo-Canadian advances in Normandy, Operation Totalize was a very substantial leap forward and proof that those forces could penetrate the strongest of German positions. Simonds' ideas and his ability to at least translate some of those ideas into action are of the highest merit. But perhaps the most significant lesson of Totalize was the disparity between the casualties suffered by the Kangaroo infantry and the walking infantry. Bearing in mind the number of casualties needed to capture a fortified village, 7 Black Watch took Garcelles-Sequeville with only fifty-two casualties and 1 Black Watch captured St Aignan, riding their Kangaroos almost into the streets, with sixty-nine casualties, of which eleven were fatal, which the infantry commanders considered minimal in the extreme.

Verdicts on Totalize, together with Atlantic and Spring were mixed, at the time and subsequently. The Germans that day had no doubt that something fateful had happened; as their overall commander von Kluge commented to Gen Hauser, 'A breakthrough has occurred near Caen the like of which we have never seen.'[25]

CHAPTER EIGHT

May – Tilly's Murderous Sister

On the seventh day of the siege they began hurling incendiary darts. . . .
The huts quickly caught fire, and the strong wind spread the flames.

(*Julius Caesar, 54 BC*)

'"Yea, though I walk through the Valley of the Shadow of Death", the Padre read out, "yet will I fear no evil." And, OK, that's alright for you,' thought the corporal, 'all you have to do is come and bury our bodies when we've passed through the Shadow!'

'But I know where the Valley of the Shadow of Death really is! It's that bloody open road from St Andre to May-sur-Orne, and I've walked it twice both ways, all the time doing it in my trousers. And as for My God – will He be with me? My God is sitting back there in a big chateau, with major-general's tinsel on his tunic. And will He be with me? Not on your Foulkes-ing life!'[1]

If the men between St Andre and May were reading the latest newspapers from home they would find that, 'in spite of enemy resistance with armour and infantry the advance has been maintained . . . battle-zone reports quoted the troops as saying the fighting was the fiercest yet known in France. . . . The enemy still has the advantage of the ridges . . . he had such a strong position established today on the ground between Fontenay-le-Marmion and Roquancourt. A slightly weaker [!] but still difficult line held the Canadian infantry up at May-sur-Orne . . . in his [Canadian] division four out of the twelve chaplains have already been killed', said a padre.[2] Even if some

HQ were sending out rather over-optimistic bulletins at times, and suggesting that the war might be over in three weeks or even before Christmas,[3] the newspaper editors recognized that the Normandy campaign was at a climactic point of decision. So did the Maisies and Les Fusiliers.

The fairly flat, straight road from St Andre to May had so far resisted all attempts to traverse and secure it. German guns of all calibre looked down from the rim of Verrieres Ridge on the left and from the Feuguerolles-Bully heights across the river. In St Martin itself the enemy had found vantage points and strongholds in St Martin church and the St Martin pit-head which dominated the main road. On 1 August Maj Dextraze's bold attack had captured the church. But the mine area with its high cage tower remained a problem. Linking into other underground systems from St Andre to Rocquancourt, the pit entrances and ventilation shafts seemed, to the despairing infantry attacking them, like a rabbit warren into which the field-grey human prey bolted, only to emerge at some other unexpected exit.

Brig Young, unaware at first of the 'Factory area's' true nature, had now flown over it and considered that the next step should be to eliminate the tower of the cage shaft. The capture of the church would enable the Queen's Own Camerons to set up a raid on the mine area. On 2 August two companies of the Camerons were suddenly accorded the privilege of visiting a mobile bath-house, the first time many of them had undressed since 17 July. The next day at 1700, army commander Lt-Gen Crerar visited brigade HQ 'informally'. What the war diary meant by 'informally' is not explained. However, a number of writers have commented on the way that senior German generals were often to be found within rifle shot of the enemy, whereas many Allied commanders remained rooted in remote HQ. It is likely that while Crerar was drinking his whisky or chlorinated tea he would have impressed on the brigadier Montgomery's almost daily orders to keep moving, keep pressurizing, keep the Hun on the run.

Brig Young had already alerted the Camerons to their task and the CO, Lt-Col J. Runcie, selected Maj McManus's Baker company to move out at 0035 on 4 August, from the vicinity of St Martin church. They were joined by a small group of Royal Canadian Engineers, equipped to blow up the tower and main mine entrance. Moving stealthily across the then open space and then attacking swiftly through the ancillary buildings of the mine, McManus and his men established themselves in a tight defensive block on the site by 0135, after precisely one hour. The engineers would now have to do some difficult climbing. Normally there was access by a trolley track and ladders to the open metal-work tower which rose well above a three-storey-high building. In the tower was the cage shaft through which the engineers would enter to fix their explosive charges. The Germans had dynamited the track and ladders, so that the engineers had first to climb about 40 feet up on the outside before entering.

Roused by the Camerons' attack, German infantry tried to retaliate while McManus and his men used the buildings and spoil heaps to defend their position. By now the night was alight with flares. The enemy could not move the Camerons, so they turned their snipers and mortar crews on to the engineers who were, one by one, climbing slowly up the edifice. And, one by one, the engineers fell from their perches, some killed, some wounded and some injured. McManus was left without skilled people to set the charges. It would have been equally disastrous to call for infantry volunteers to essay the same climb. Reluctantly McManus called his men together and carried out a fighting withdrawal, guarding the wounded engineers. After a perilous adventure the Camerons suffered less casualties in total than the luckless engineers.[4]

So the next probe would again have to be down the main road. As already indicated, in 1944 the twin villages of St Andre and St Martin lay snugly and privately away on either side of the main through road, the D562. Looking towards May down that road there was an open, fairly level area about 700 yards square and consisting of three large fields either side of the road. On the left edge of the area the slope of the ridge became ever more steep. On the right edge of the area the ground fell away rapidly towards the Orne. Just one large hedgerow part way along on the right blocked the enemy's field of fire.

If Tilly was 'T'-shaped, May was largely 'Y'-shaped. The tail of the Y pointed back towards St Martin. The left stroke of the Y was a main road running off to Fontenay and Rocquancourt. The right stroke was a fairly straight continuation of the D562. The church and Mairie stood at the intersection. A few houses lay to the right of the D562. With a population of about 1,000 May was much larger than Tilly, but still of village proportions. An attack along the bank of the Orne was impracticable, firstly because there were large buildings, quarries and mine outlets easy to defend, and secondly because of the proximity of German guns on the other bank of the river. So the way lay across those several hundred yards of utmost peril.

Reinforcements were landing in considerable numbers on the beaches, and after their tragic experience in the attack led by Maj Griffin, the Black Watch were back up to strength with Lt-Col F.M. Mitchell, formerly 2 i.c and LOB in the Griffin battle, now in command. It is generally recognized that some of the Black Watch blamed Brig Megill for not overruling the Griffin attack. Also there was little empathy between Megill and Mitchell, so that the latter viewed the brigadier's decisions with some reserve.[5] Perhaps that is why it was the divisional commander, Foulkes, who appeared at the Black Watch HQ on 5 August to spur them on with the erroneous advice that 'apparently the enemy is withdrawing his depleted forces and we MUST keep contact with him'.[6] It was true that 1st SS Panzer LAH were moving south but still waiting in the wings were those other storm troopers whom one would least like to meet on a dark night, 12th SS Panzer Hitlerjugend.

Aware of the dangerous nature of the main road, Lt-Col Mitchell ordered a cautious advance led by Able company. This was commanded by Maj Tom Anyon, a highly regarded officer who had arrived with reinforcements as recently as 27 July. Dog company followed in support. About fifty men went into action with each company. Again the Germans watched and waited until the lead infantry had reached the outskirts of May and the two companies were committed along the road. Then it was a case of trying to find superlatives, for 'all Hell broke loose'.

There were ditches on either side of the road. Many men threw themselves into the perceived shelter of the ditches. The enemy fire neatly boxed off the lead company. From May there rumbled a panzer which rolled up and down the road, firing into the ditches. Anyon and a platoon commander and others were killed. Dog company began to withdraw but some of the front men of Able were made prisoners. As often happened, it was no safer in the rear, for battalion HQ was doused with mortar bombs which killed the colonel's signaller. The hero of the Griffin attack, Maj Edwin Bennett, also fell dead. He it was who had gathered cooks, drivers and others to form a defensive perimeter as Griffin's few survivors fell back.

Although such casualties were a shock to the entire battalion, they still had a care for others in distress. The war diary recorded 'a pall of sadness over the Bn having seen a Typhoon shot down. The pilot emerged from the falling plane but his parachute failed to open.' In the midst of their own death pangs the battalion could mourn an unknown pilot.

Le Regiment Maisonneuve had been instructed to hold two companies in support of the Black Watch. The O group for the Maisies at 1600 had advised them that the enemy had withdrawn from May. Their Baker and Charlie companies were to occupy St Martin and, if May was indeed clear, the two companies were to march through, on the left hand stroke of the Y, to Fontenay-le-Marmion. This plan could be described as excessively hopeful. In the event brigade HQ had to advise them that May was not clear but that the Black Watch were holding the 'Coaliary' – presumably the 'Factory' area by yet another name. Baker and Charlie therefore to take May as 'only a few dug in en. tanks'.[7] Hope was indeed springing eternal!

When moving in support of the Black Watch the two companies had been made up to about 80 per cent of normal strength by borrowing personnel from the other two companies. The strength of the company rolls at this time was Able 40, Baker 60, Charlie 40, Dog 60. As the battalion lined up in St Martin it was decided that it would be Able and Charlie companies which would carry out the attack. Able with an artillery FOO would leave from the orchard south-west of the village and Charlie on the left of the main road from the south-east. A squadron of tanks was to give supporting fire east of the 'Factory' on Charlie's left. The code word for the Factory was 'blue' and for May 'gold'.

H-hour was scheduled for 2045, and by 2055 both companies had reported on the move. Signals came in for a while.

22.15: 'Peter 1 [Able] – Blue!'
22.17: 'Peter 3 [Charlie] – Blue!'
22.20: 'Peter 1 – 200 yards beyond Blue.'
22.21: 'Peter 3 – enemy tanks at 100 yards!'
22.30: Communication difficult as several nets on same frequency and there seems to be all kinds of jamming in the air.

Apart from spotting enemy tanks, Maj Jacques Ostiguy commanding Charlie had another nasty surprise. He had been told that friendly tanks would be waiting near the mine area to support him. As he led his company along he was glad to see several tanks where they were supposed to be. He could not, however, understand why nobody was moving. On several tanks men in tank suits were leaning on the turret of the tank or draped over it. They seemed to be totally unconcerned about any possible danger. Then as Ostiguy came nearer he realized that all the tanks had been knocked out. All the men on the turret were crew members who had been shot by machine-guns while trying to bale out and escape.

By now Ostiguy was not surprised that his men were allowed to progress almost to the edge of May before the enemy opened up in full pandemonium of noise and fire. Charlie company made a dash for the first houses and found shelter there while the Able company commander was badly wounded and his men (only forty of them when they started out) sought refuge short of the houses. Any movement then brought down further deliveries of fiery hate. The survivors gritted their teeth and fired back, keeping the enemy at a distance. Ostiguy tried to coordinate the remnants of the two companies and reported that he could hold on.

In the light of burning vehicles and buildings both sides were able to deny each other a close approach. Confused fighting continued all night. Enemy tanks were firing but, as always, tank guns were blind at night and not able to target precisely. Ostiguy remembers especially, 'Germans still popping out of all those damn holes in the ground' – the various orifices of the mine. At 0700 hours on 6 August battalion HQ reported Charlie still probing. 'Recce patrols do not draw fire but any attempt to push a fighting force into May is met with heavy fire.'

At midday a headquarters decision was taken not to continue with the Maisies attack on May and the Charlie/Able survivors were ordered to pull back. Ostiguy was 'bloody mad'. Although his men could not move any distance forward, they were well settled in strong stone cottages and believed they could stay there indefinitely. Ostiguy now believes that the decision to withdraw his men from a lodgement in May prompted the corps commander, Guy Simonds, to issue an order forbidding any further withdrawal from a position which had been firmly occupied in this way.[8]

Casualties were suffered during the night but astonishingly a higher Maisies mortality occurred in an unfortunate incident at midday. A queue of hungry men from the carrier and mortar platoons was forming at the support company kitchen in the open air. As the cooks started serving, two 88 mm shells homed in on the queue and exploded into instant butchery. When the shambles could be sorted out, no less than thirteen men were found to be dead and twenty-two wounded, most of them badly. In modern news phraseology it was 'an accident waiting to happen', assembling men in that fashion under fire.

In view of the events described, when the plans for Totalize were settled it became necessary for walking infantry to be launched into a final attack on May. Whereas the armoured columns would bypass Tilly and Rocquancourt, and possibly confuse the defenders, May would be least affected by the passage of the several hundred tanks. Les Fusiliers Mont-Royal, commanded by Lt-Col J.G. Gauvreau, were allotted the task of finally clearing May. Although the Fusiliers were not in the mainstream of tanks, they would be included in the grand bombardment plan of the RAF at 2300 hours on 7 August, when May would receive its share of aerial wrath.

The RAF bomber chief, Sir Arthur Harris, was greatly perturbed by Simonds' plan to have RAF Lancasters dropping bombs in the dark at no more than 1,000 yards from the nearest friendly forces. He was inclined to veto the plan until a practice run by RAF Pathfinders and master bombers proved the Lancasters capable of hitting the targets. The FDLs of the Fusiliers in front of May were too near the aerial strike area so Gauvreau was told to move his men back to St Andre.

An unsung German colonel now made a decision as acute as Panzermeyer's decision to push tanks through the anticipated bombing zone when he saw the USAAF pathfinder crossing the Cramesnil front. Observing the approach of the Lancaster group attacking May, and calculating that a major attack was about to be made on that village, the German commander correctly calculated that the attackers would have been pulled back to St Andre. He ordered his artillery and heavy mortars to put down a devastating barrage which landed precisely on the assembly area of the Fusiliers. It caused consternation, casualties and delay, although not sufficient to hold off the attack altogether. A number of men were wounded by the speeding ricochets of shrapnel shooting off the solid stone walls of cottages in St Andre, a phenomenon which had also been noted in Verrieres and elsewhere. For want of a positive identification, the credit for this swift anticipatory barrage should, perhaps, be given to Col Roesler.

As the weary soldiers of 1st SS Panzer LAH withdrew from the Tilly-Verrieres lines and headed for another distant confrontation, they were replaced by a fresh, full strength if novice division, the 'unlucky Horseshoe' (*Hufeisen*) 89th Infantry Division. Formed on the Bergen, Norway, manoeuvre area in February 1944 from various scratch units, the division's two founder regimental commanders were Col Rossman of 1055 Regiment and Col Roesler of 1056. The story goes that, as both names sounded like 'Ross', meaning a steed or a horse, the division took the emblem and name of the Horseshoe, no doubt hoping for good luck. The division, led by Lt-Gen Heinrichs, still relied on horse transport and had no tanks or SPs of its own. It was classified as 'for defence missions' only.[9] It had no battle experience but it did have the regulation numbers of personnel. As the division moved in, Heinrichs directed Rossman's 1055 to the Tilly area and Roesler's 1056 to Rocquancourt and May. There was to be no good luck for them in either area.

On the extreme left flank of the Totalize Night March, 1st Northamptonshire Yeomanry had been amazed by the incredible accuracy of the RAF bombing so close to the columns of tanks. On the right flank Brig Young was not so impressed. Because of smoke and dust reducing visibility the Lancasters had to abandon the May attack early, rather than risk the ground troops suffering from 'friendly fire'. Also a number of the bombs which were dropped fell harmlessly in the fields surrounding the enemy defences. The Fusiliers might be forgiven for feeling that the initial auguries of the night were not favourable.

Undeterred, the infantry lined up on the east to west road through St Andre. 'B' Company, which was only forty strong, was to advance on the right of the main road to May, with 'C' on the left of the road. 'A' and 'C' were to follow 500 yards behind with a total anticipated advance of 2,000 yards.[10] It was noted that this night attack was 'conducted under very difficult conditions of visibility for the clearness of the night had been changed completely by the movement of armour over dry ground, by arty fire, and by enemy smoke. These conditions permitted silent infiltration but made for poor control.' An extract from the participants' own report may convey something of the flavour of the action:

'B' Coy, 40 men strong, advanced, and along the route got separated considerably by shelling. The coy reached the village with about 20 men who were split into two gps by the coy comd. The first gp went into the town and the coy cmd, a Bren gunner, and batman, were killed when about 50 yds past the first house in the main street. The remainder withdrew in disorder. Meanwhile the other gp of 'B' coy was pinned down by fire about 20 yds short of the first house on the right-hand side of the rd in the village. The offr and his men were held down in a shell hole until about 0530 hrs by MG fire. At that time the offr was wounded, but managed to bring his men out. Behind 'B' coy 'A' Coy waited for a success sig. They waited [in the fields] about 200 yds NORTH of the first house in the village under MG fire, but no success sig came.

It was the same old story of May: partial success achieved with elan but not enough success for the signal to be given to the follow-up troops. On the other side of the road 'C' were hit by another cleverly placed enemy barrage just after crossing the start line. An officer and a number of NCOs were killed or wounded. The attack continued but the barrage and machine-gun firing from in front caused straggling, until the number of men in a coherent group had dwindled and there was no realistic chance of reaching the houses and mounting an attack. 'D' company also waited for the success signal which never came.

After rapid reorganization a new approach was tried. 'A' and 'B' would advance down the road as though renewing the direct attack. At the same time 'C' and 'D' would move quietly, without firing and without fire support, around the right flank and try to penetrate into the village via the quarries. There was some wooded cover on the slope towards the river, as well as quarries and a ravine through which they might enter the houses. At 0430 hours they could hope to escape observation from the overlooking enemy on the other bank of the river, who were able to enfilade daylight attacks. 'C' had about thirty-five men available for this detour. For a while it looked as though the tactic would bring the desired result. Then a German officer was observed hurrying around his posts and physically shaking men awake. The rudely awakened Germans were in time to greet the infiltrating Fusiliers with the usual intense point-blank fire and a number of casualties again caused a withdrawal. All companies went back to their former FDLs. The entire action had been dogged by drastic, and usually inconvenient, changes of visibility. The dust cloud from the bombing was blown away by the wind at the wrong time, fog descended at the wrong time, dawn broke at the right time but with unforeseen mists, and these dissipated when the gods of war again disowned the Fusiliers.

At 1100 hours on 8 August Brig Young called Lt-Col Gauvreau back to brigade HQ for consultation. The brigadier was in the middle of a communications crisis with the Queen's Own Camerons around Fontenay and did not want to leave HQ. He advised Gauvreau to use quantities of smoke to confuse the enemy. Before the CO could return and implement the advice it was overtaken by the availability of another and more deadly type of smoke. Four troops of Crocodiles, Churchill tanks fitted with flame-throwers, were being sent to the Fusiliers, and a squadron of the 1st Hussars tanks was escorting the Crocodiles, dangerous to their crews if attacked by enemy tanks, across the Verrieres Ridge and down into St Martin. These rather clumsy vehicles would need close infantry support as they would be vulnerable to close attack by enemy on foot. It was perhaps typical of pre-invasion planning that the infantry battalion had received no training in cooperation with Crocodiles, which were a unit of the specialist 79th Armoured Division. Instructions had to be given and introductions made in the brief period before H-hour at 1545. Although May was not on an arterial highway central to the Totalize front, every possible north to south road was needed for the mass of traffic now on the move. No delay could be tolerated in opening up the way through May. There was no time to refine the plan for the Crocodile attack, accompanied by the very depleted battalion of Fusiliers.

In order to mount the attack and use the Crocodile force (of 141 RAC) effectively it was necessary to mobilize the entire battalion

Mont-Royal, except for the carrier platoon which, with one troop of Crocodiles, formed a reserve in the Factory area. 'C' and 'D' companies working as one could assemble only sixty effectives. They would walk down the right hand side of the main road with one troop of flame-throwers. 'A' and 'B' mustered ninety rifles and they would take the left hand side with two troops of tanks. The Y shape of May meant that one of the 'A' and 'B' troops of Crocodiles could take the left fork if they reached it.

Although the Crocodiles still had the normal Churchill equipment of big gun and co-axial machine-gun, they would be vulnerable in the open moving at the slow infantry pace. The Churchill was not a fast tank if forced to withdraw in reverse. Les Fusiliers were able to reassure the tank men that there was little danger from land mines or anti-tank guns and the tankies subsequently 'performed very aggressively'. At 1545 all arms moved forward from the front area of the Factory. A brief but intensive barrage of smoke had been laid in front of May, blinding the defenders. The procedure which had been agreed was described in the subsequent report:[11]

The Crocodiles would open fire with all guns as soon as the march commenced, hitting the houses which were visible in the village to keep the enemy's heads down. The Fusiliers would walk a few yards behind the tanks which were in open line abreast. Nearing the houses the tanks' high explosive shells would break holes in buildings or enlarge windows as possible. Each tank would release a jet of flame into a house and set the interior on fire.

The infantry force was split into two small sections for each Crocodile and they followed close to the trailer which carried the inflammable mixture behind the tank itself. As a tank squirted its flame in through the hole in the wall and the interior of the house caught fire, a section of Fusiliers would dash into the house through the door and clear out any lurking enemy. Meanwhile the tank would move to the next house, repeating the process with the second section of infantrymen.

This may appear to be a horrific and dangerous process with men untrained for the purpose. It was pointed out to the Fusiliers, as they expressed some reasonable fears about it, that the task was not as dangerous as it sounded. The fire which was lit inside the house was a normal fire which would take time to spread through the building and it would be possible to spend enough time inside to flush out any enemy. The grave danger lay in the jet of flame from the thrower, for the flaming mixture attached itself to any object in its path and continued burning that object, much in the way of the napalm bombs which would become notorious in later years. The Fusiliers would not approach the doorway until the jet from the thrower's nozzle had been cut off. Inside the house enemy soldiers, if there were any, would be either in a state of psychological shock or actually physically on fire until oxygen was cut off from the flames. There were no reports of serious burns to any of the Fusiliers involved.

The right flank troop moved steadily towards the houses, firing as it went. As they approached the first houses, they left the main road, which had been such an excellent field of fire for defenders in previous attacks. They drove down the backs of the houses, spacing out so that while one tank set fire to the first two houses, the others stood guard ready to respond to any enemy action. Other sections of infantry followed some way behind this operation and, as it became possible to enter the houses, they began to set up defences in the area cleared of enemy.

It was an extremely well considered plan, normal practice to the men of the 79th but novel to the infantry. And for once the plan worked well. In quick time the right flank flamer group had reached the back of the church at the centre of the village. On the way the Crocodiles had also given the fire treatment to any suspicious-looking roosting places for machine-guns or snipers, such as hedges, clumps of trees, sheds or deep ditches. As the infantry advanced it became evident that the enemy was not staying to face the flames. By the time the church had been reached it was agreed to switch off the fire jets. The Crocodiles in the role of normal tanks than rolled on south-west to the end of the built-up area, followed by some of their attendant walkers. The rest of the right hand composite company consolidated for the first and final time around the church and Mairie at the Y junction.

The left flank advance took a rather wider sweep, a kind of vengeance mission, for they set fire to the bushes, hedges and undergrowth on the lower slopes of the ridge from which the enemy had so often been able to enfilade the main road. The second troop on the left moved nearer to the houses and did a similar job in orchards which had also proved centres of resistance. That troop then reverted to a similar role to the right flank troop in driving along the backs of the houses and setting them on fire. The Fontenay road to the left or south-east was an obvious escape route for the retreating enemy. While the right flank group was able to switch off its jets at the church, the left hand group still had to flame and clear the houses which were strung along the Fontenay road for some 200 yards or more. 'A' company men then had to clear two quarries and a block house but the defenders put up only a token show of resistance. Consequently all the houses in the village had to be flamed except those south and south-west of the church. Having said that it will be understood that after several fierce battles the majority of houses were already ruined, but still afforded excellent machine-gun nests and eyries for snipers. Only a jet of flame could adequately penetrate some of the mounds of house rubble which were used as strongpoints.

Among the equipment abandoned by the enemy were five mortars, one 88 mm dual purpose gun, one field gun and an entire telephone system. The infantry of the green 89th Division had fought grimly throughout the night and early morning. However, by the time the Crocodiles arrived, the spearheads of Totalize had been established in locations threatening German communications with May. It is possible that the last defenders of the village were under notice to be ready to retreat in good order but that the flame throwers precipitated that departure.

The infantry reporter was most complimentary to the men of the Crocodile troops:

The infantry had nothing but praise for the flame throwing tks used during this attack. They were impressed greatly by the aggressive and bold attitude displayed by the tank crews who rarely, if ever, hesitated before taking on any job asked of them. The inf were not disturbed by the problem of having to clear houses ablaze, but were very glad to have such effective sp[support] even at the cost of a lot of extra sweat.

The attack also indicated that the enemy posns were very accurately pin-pointed by air phs[photos]. The . . . prints indicated every posn exactly as it was found to be on the ground with the single exception that a small cemetery to the north of rd junction 0124592 was incorrectly labelled as an entrance to the quarry directly south of it.[12]

In many of the houses the fires raged throughout that night and in some houses they were still burning well into the next day. The depleted attackers had no resources to attempt a fire brigade operation, nor would such an action have been totally safe. May village itself had been rid of the enemy, but on the next day, 9 August, pioneers were still searching the mine shaft and galleries for any lurking enemy. German infantry units were famous for their doctrine of staying behind and then hitting the advanced troops from the rear. On this occasion the few soldiers routed out of the mine were only in the mood for surrender.

It has been noted that the use of the new Kangaroo armoured personnel carriers saved many lives in the armoured columns in which they travelled. Although Les Fusiliers Mont-Royal had the support of Crocodiles they still had to walk dangerously, there not being enough Kangaroos for all battalions. The Fusiliers brigade, the 6th, all walking infantry, lost 54 killed and 155 wounded. The Kangaroo-borne brigade lost 7 killed and 56 wounded and penetrated three miles and more through the German defences.[13] This again reflects badly on commanders and planners of high rank who had rejected the 'Kangaroo' response since it was first seen as necessary in the First World War.

May was free, and thus the liberty of St Andre and St Martin was also assured, but at a sorry cost to the inhabitants. Over the decades they would rarely complain about their liberators but for two years the agony of living in the villages was almost unbearable as the region of ruins was afflicted by two of the worst winters in living memory. Official surveys revealed the buildings of May 94 per cent 'sinistres' – destroyed, St Martin 90 per cent, Rocquancourt 90 per cent and St Andre 80 per cent. Mine damage was estimated at 75 per cent with the majority of the galleries flooded or choked.

A graphic description of the desolation of May has been left by a priest, Dom G. Aubourg, in a speech at the laying of the first stone of rebuilding on 14 May 1950. For two days after the battle civilians had tried to enter the burning village and were turned back by either flames or smoke and toxic gasses. Then on 10 August the priest and a friend walked through the ruins:

Everything was burning still: crushed furniture, collapsed beams, the very stones themselves. A few Canadian soldiers, grey with dust and soot, wandered from house to house, from cellar to cellar, driven by thirst. All around there was the silence of death: no people. Three white goats, lost, maddened, running away. The recent traces of the enemy seen everywhere: their arms, their grenades, their provisions and their bodies already stinking the air. It was the worst of days. War . . . monstrous crime . . . without discernment . . . as though all were accomplices! We were destroyed by our friends, our liberators . . . they triumphed amid our own ruins.[14]

For two years the survivors struggled to patch up the ruins without electricity or phones, little available employment and rationing of food. Trees and hedges were virtually non-existent so there was no easy source of fuel. It was precisely two years after the battle, 10 August 1946, that some prefabricated barrack huts arrived, donated by Sweden. The reconstruction, with full electric, telephone and drinking water facilities, repaired roads and basic housing was not completed until eight years after Liberation.

The main source of employment, the iron ore mines, took some years to reach post-war production. Modernization in the early 1960s was offset by competition from Brazil, Mauritius and Sweden, all with better stocks and offering lower prices. British buyers switched their custom to other sources of supply. In 1968 the mines closed down, and the iron ore railway past Rocquancourt and Tilly ceased to function. Civilian engineers, without threat of snipers, brought their explosive charges and levelled the mine towers which had dominated the landscape and which Maj McManus and his group of engineers had failed to destroy.[15]

Pertinent words of the priest, Dom Aubourg: 'Sombre revelation of Man, made in order to create and construct, and who yet persists in demolishing both his works and himself.'[16]

CHAPTER NINE

Fontenay – Fatal for Officers

Our troops attacked with such vigour when the signal was given. The Germans' left was thus routed, but their right began to press our troops hard by weight of numbers.

(*Julius Caesar, 58 BC*)

The commanding officer falls in battle. Another one takes his place. He, too, falls in battle (as do his adjutant, HQ company commander and artillery FOO). Another takes his place. He, too, falls in battle. Two majors take his place, neither of them knowing where the other is. Nor if the battalion still exists. The company sergeant-major takes command of the company and then takes command of the battalion's last attack. Then a new CO is appointed. If this all sounds confusing it is because it was confusing. It was the extraordinary chaos of Fontenay-le-Marmion. And perhaps the most extraordinary thing about it all is that the Queen's Own Cameron Highlanders of Canada then contrived to win the battle. Totalize, 8 August 1944.

As the armoured columns of Operation Totalize rolled forward, the walking infantry of the 6th Canadian Infantry Brigade, the 'Iron Brigade', were ordered finally to clear May, Rocquancourt and Fontenay, until now virtually mirages on the Canadian horizon. Having sent Les Fusiliers Mont-Royal off to deal with May, Brig Young allocated Rocquancourt to the South Saskatchewans and directed the Queen's Own Camerons on to Fontenay. These three mining villages lay on a road off the main Caen to Falaise route and effectively blocked major traffic movements on the west of the main road. Rocquancourt lay nearest to the Falaise road. Between the village and the road there was a spur of the iron ore railway which ran past Tilly, and around the spur were railway sidings and the most easterly access to the complex of iron mines.

Les Fusiliers and the Camerons were unleashed wide of the armoured column routes and were spared some of the immediate confusion and obscurity. The South Saskatchewans were right in the middle of the right flank columns which were supposed to pass on either side of Rocquancourt, so they endured the worst of the dust eating in the immediate rear of the tanks. As the columns deviated from their precise routes in the darkness and conflicting light, one of the columns passed right through the village and some of the South Sasks were at times in mortal peril of being mashed under the tracks of the blind, churning monsters.

On the positive side the battalion was able to take advantage of the confusion around them, the serried columns of armour, the dust, the artillery barrage, the startled enemy. They dashed forward from the start line around Troteval Farm and entered Rocquancourt with unexpectedly low casualties. According to their 'A' Company commander, Maj Courtenay, they achieved this by walking dangerously in the wake of the exploding artillery shells. This tactic was not always successful and at times infantry and barrage could become separated, either by miscalculation of speed or reluctance to come too close to the area of shells. But the South Sasks appear to have got it right, as the major reported:[1]

Walking with the barrage, 'A' coy hit the village right on the nose, touching at the NW corner of the orchard which left room for manoeuvre. A lot of prisoners were taken in the orchard along the central wall. The orchard had been used as a mortar position and the mortars and crews were captured complete. Lesson – one must hug one's own arty shells, ignoring m.g. fire unless it is very close – grenades and bursts of m.g. fire were sufficient to quieten most of the enemy who seemed still absolutely dizzy and stunned from the barrage.

The traumatic effect of artillery barrage, even on its own side, is well illustrated in the words of a gunner, George Blackburn. His gunnery training group was made to advance behind a training barrage in England (under the eyes of none other than Gen Crerar), in order to etch on the brain the need for total accuracy as to both location and timing of shelling, so that the infantry might have a clear passage. Blackburn did not enjoy the experience:

Every man . . . will run up a grassy slope . . . 'leaning into the barrage'. While common sense tells you that those crashing orange-and-black flashes – causing the ground to shudder beneath your running feet – are a safe distance ahead, it seems as though you are running right at them as you feel their hot breath and are enveloped in a continuous reverberating roar. After the briefest pause between lifts – lying prone on your stomach in the grass, with much heavy breathing and the sour taste of the drifting acrid fumes in your dry mouth – the muffled *crumping* begins behind and the vicious sizzling and cracking overhead as the earth before you again flashes and spouts with furious overlapping thunderbolts . . . you are passing over shell-pitted ground so close behind the crashing, threshing storm, you are leaping over gashes in the earth still steaming and smoking from the explosions that gouged them. Unscathed but totally subdued by the awesome experience, you find yourselves wondering how the infantry can be expected to engage the enemy in combat with any vigour . . . having suffered the full force of that horrific maelstrom.[2]

The main difference between George Blackburn's training experience of leaning into a barrage and the real thing is that the infantry would not be running, but walking steadily, often hampered by an excess of gear, for a longer distance with even more time to suffer all the pangs of terror. Having achieved the feat the South Sasks dug-in at Rocquancourt and thought their major task was over. Their CO, Lt-Col Clift had been wounded but was able to carry on after attention. For about six hours a few individual Germans stayed on in hiding, coming out to do some sniping and then disappearing again, until they were hunted down. But it was over to their right, where the Camerons were advancing into another hell-hole, that some of the South Sasks would be called into action later that day.

Throughout the morning there was massive traffic on either side of Rocquancourt. Some stragglers from the Night March were still trying to find their way back to their units. Ambulances were returning from the front lines with the wounded. The first artillery battery was moving up to fire marker flares for the next air bombardment. Then the entire force of the 4th Armoured Division was moving into position for the second leap of Totalize. On the other side of the main Falaise road the Polish armoured division was also moving up. It was like London's Piccadilly Circus or New York's Times Square suddenly magnified to one mile wide by four miles long and crowded with traffic hardly able to move, while shells dropped into the chaos and mortar bombs came whining down and machine-gun bullets spat their fire. While all troops were under the most urgent orders to press on!

It had been intended that the Camerons would have been next to the main Falaise road in the thick of the traffic. The first plan had them clearing the railway spur and sidings. Indeed it looked as though the Canadian Camerons would hold hands with the Scottish Camerons who would be on their left. The Scots Brig Cassells suggested that the two COs, Runcie and Lang, should meet and liaise. Derek Lang has no recollection of such a meeting – possibly because the Canadian cousins were switched at a late moment to the Fontenay task.[3] The withdrawal of 1st SS Panzers LAH had persuaded Simonds that he could capture the entire May to Rocquancourt spur area with one brigade instead of the two originally planned.

So in conditions of relatively lesser chaos the Camerons set off on a rather lonely cross country trek between Les Fusiliers and the South

Sasks. Starting also at 2330 on 7 August, they would walk through an almost featureless countryside for some 3,000 yards, with hardly any buildings and certainly no church spires to navigate on. The centre line was a minor road lined with poplars which guided some of the advancing troops in the darkness and eventual fog. But the majority had a thankless quest over hedges, through similar fields and patches of trees. Just short of Fontenay, as the Camerons came in from the north, there was a substantial quarry which would be an obvious hazard. The village itself lay on a reverse slope of the kind which the Germans so expertly used to punish attackers coming over the skyline. It was a very sharp slope. At the northern fringe of the houses there was a trig point at 85 metres altitude. The church in the centre of Fontenay, a mere 800 metres away, lay at only 53 metres. In fact the houses straddled what might be termed a one-sided ravine with more open country and amenable contours to the south.

While the Camerons could listen in to the diabolical orchestras of guns strumming their barrage ahead of the armoured columns, they themselves would have no artillery support over those first 3,000 yards. The Toronto Scottish with their heavy mortars and medium machine-guns would do their best to simulate a barrage from the start line. However, as the Camerons waited impatiently at that start line they could see that, on their behalf, the RAF was sending in hundreds of heavy bombers to pound Fontenay and May into the ground. The soldiers were not to know that because of the vast pall of smoke and dust engendered by bombs and churning tracks, the RAF master bombers would have to halt the Fontenay raid with about a third of the bombs still wombed up in the Lancasters' bomb racks. There would be bomb damage on Fontenay's steep slope but not total devastation. The Hun who was a rat coming out of the ruins at Tilly would be a barely chastised wolf in the streets and gardens of Fontenay. And while some inconsiderate words of Panzermeyer, accusing some men of running away up the Falaise road, have maligned the 89th Horseshoe Division at the judgement bar of history, Col Roesler's men around Fontenay knew nothing of this.

Many hundreds of them waited in slits and ditches, behind hedges and walls, out in the featureless countryside, along the poplar-lined road, among the houses and down the mine shafts, green troops anxious to prove their mettle in their first 'show'.

Prompt at 2330 hours, the Queen's Own Cameron Highlanders of Canada, spread across the western area of Verrieres Ridge, stepped out on a slow climb, a walk along the summit and then the quick dash down to the objective.[4] Dog company (Maj J.T.D. Gagnon) led on the left and Charlie (Maj Ted Talbor) on the right. Baker (Maj J.E.E. McManus) in the centre was close in contact with the lead companies, while Able (Maj A.C. Kavanagh, MC) followed in reserve. The carriers, mortars and anti-tank guns of the battalion had no easy access road forward and would not be available until dawn.

Trouble struck after a gentle walk of about 1,000 yards. Trouble struck twice in perhaps the two worst possible ways. The wireless sets of the lead company ceased to function, not due to enemy action. And the reliable CO, Lt-Col Runcie was badly wounded and out of action. No sooner had this happened than the friendly guidance of the poplar-fringed lane became a trap. It ran towards Fontenay with hardly a bend and permitted enemy machine-guns and 88 mm guns to set up fixed lines of fire from a distance. Land mines were discovered on the road and in the verges at the roadside. Engineers were called forward to deal with this blockage while infantry tried to probe on either sides. Platoons further out on the flanks were becoming isolated from the centre. The CO at forward HQ was being removed to an aid post while the 2 i.c. was, as normal, LOB in the rear area. The ingredients for a disaster menu were being mixed.

Lt N.J. Burnside found the enemy adopting harassing tactics from the flanks, throwing hand grenades and firing sporadically. Then out of the darkness came a solid enemy charge right out of the First World War manuals. The Camerons responded and halted the enemy at about 20 yards range, before hand-to-hand contact but near enough to cause casualties.[5] Dog company HQ found itself surrounded with the major, a lieutenant and a dozen others being called upon to surrender.

'Kamerad! Surrender, Tommy!' The isolated Camerons merged into the darkness and slithered silently out between the loudly shouting attackers. On the other flank the 'Horseshoe' men let 14 and 15 Platoon pass by, then poured fire into 15 Platoon and company HQ from several directions. Maj Talbor fell grievously wounded as did several other ranks.[6]

It was Baker company, following up, which hit a large quarry with a number of machine-guns well sited in the rim. A problem for the enemy was the uncertain loyalty of foreign conscripts. Capt W.S. Watt saw a Polish conscript jump up and start shouting directions as to where the machine-guns were located. Lt Burnside accepted the surrender of two more Poles. Maj McManus used a German-speaking Pole to shout an surrender invitation to the defenders of the quarry, others of whom were non-German. There was no response so McManus quickly reorganized the company and made a swift attack, which caused the defenders more casualties than the attackers and also opened the way into Fontenay from that route.

By 0100 hours Gagnon's Dog company, with a platoon of Charlie which had become attached, hit their target among the first houses and, when the flickering wireless set permitted, sent the code message for success, which was 'Garbo!' (All Totalize codes for report lines were names of Hollywood film stars.) It was ironic that Dog should report 'Garbo!' whose well-known watchword was 'I want to be alone'. Dog and the Charlie platoon were alone at that point as the advance had fractured. Gagnon was not to know that he had bypassed some hundreds of enemy scattered across the ridges to the north and so at first light he was virtually surrounded. In fact the situation at that time was of two enemies each surrounding the other, like coiled snakes.

The 6th Brigade HQ was reporting confusion, with messages, when able to be transmitted, differing from one sender to another, the attack bifurcated, Maj Kavanagh acting as OC in one sector and Maj Gagnon OC in another sector and, due to signals problems, neither knowing where the other was or who was in charge. At this point

Brig Young told his brigade major, a former Cameron 2 i.c., C.W. Ferguson, to go up and take over.

Here the historian finds himself in as much confusion as Kavanagh, Gagnon, Ferguson *et al*. One authority reports that Ferguson arrived one hour after Runcie was wounded and 'in the darkness . . . he had done remarkably well'.[7] The Camerons' own diary has Ferguson arriving at first light, while the brigade clocked the event between 0630 and 0900 amid 'confusion'. Be that as it may, Ferguson, an outstanding officer, was most unlucky. Trying to stabilize the situation at about 0900 hours he held an O group in a farmyard. A shell fell into the group of officers, fatally wounding Ferguson, and taking out also the artillery FOO, the adjutant, HQ company commander and the intelligence officer. On hearing this McManus took command and his company sergeant-major, Arbour, took command of Baker.

At first light the battalion strength remaining was about 150. Burnside reported 88 mm fire from the north-east, behind the Camerons. Thick fog hindered the enemy artillery and mortars as groups of Camerons filtered through the houses. At 0900 a strong counter-attack was mounted, supported, according to reports, by twelve 'Tigers'. The Germans would have been very glad to have twelve Tigers available at that place and time, as they struggled to send four against the main armoured spearhead near La Jalousie at midday. But it has been said that to the man in the front line 'one tank was a Tiger and one infantryman was a sniper'. The tanks were in fact Mk IVs but still formidable.

Maj Kavanagh commanding Able reported on 10 August 1944:

08.00 (8 August) established in a rectangular block of buildings south of the village. 50 men to hold half mile of line. Enemy infiltrating between A and village centre. Attacked all morning. Heard that Bn HQ was KO'd. Spotted an 88 mm. Asked for troop of tanks. Tantalizing to see 4 Armd Div. going by scarcely a mile away with Jerry a thousand yds away, watching it go by and not molesting the armour but shooting at us.

What Kavanagh could see was the 200 or more tanks of 4th Armoured, with their motor and recce regiments and three infantry battalions and machine-gun company and all their attendant satellite formations moving up to become the second wave of Totalize. Understandably the 'Fontenay Jerries' were not going to attack that vast force but would consider Kavanagh's fifty men fair game. However, Lt John Graham was not too impressed by some of the German attackers commenting that when the 'very heavy counter-attack' came in 'we were pitiably weak in manpower but fortunately for us the inf. did not have the guts enough to follow up the tank attack.'

Fate had not yet completed its fell purpose for the Camerons. Maj McManus, MC, in command after Ferguson's death, was making the rounds of his men, aiming to reinforce their morale when he was shot by a sniper. Gagnon took command of the battalion. In the chaos of the farmyard headquarters, an artillery bombardier had taken charge, moving the artillery wireless set into a solid building, directing very accurate artillery shoots and linking to brigade HQ as there was no certain road link. Along that road, inevitably a well ranged target for enemy guns and mortars, Lt R.R. Counsell and his carriers risked death time and time again, availing themselves of their only protection, the very high speed of their vehicles, to bring supplies of ammo, food, water and a few very valuable reinforcements. Arriving at Ferguson's farmyard HQ just after the shelling at 0900, Counsell helped to clear up the shambles and then raced off on his mission of sustenance.

At 1000 hours a battalion request for armour had been passed on but there was, as yet, no armour available, for some of the first phase of Totalize armour was either assisting infantry to root out stubborn defenders around the axis roads or reorganizing after the involuntary transfers of the night. The Camerons' lines had just held firm and the battalion had taken 207 prisoners. While some enemy had fought determinedly, others were either too inexperienced or were uncommitted conscripts from vassal states. Capt Watt thought that the battle could well have been lost:

Enemy troops (89th inf. div.) were very poorly led. A determined counter attack a.m. on 8.8.44 could have taken the Cam's mortar positions. Also poor shots. Fired 6 2 88 mm at stationery anti-tank vehicles at less than 600 yards and only hit 3. But their positions well camouflaged.

About noon, as the first phase of Totalize was consolidated and the baton was handed on to 4th Armoured and the Poles, it was decided that the South Sasks should come to the aid of the Camerons. Lt-Col Clift stated that he could release two companies and at 1315 he held an O group. Nearby the Shermans from 'C' Squadron of Lt-Col A.D.A. Marks' 1st Hussars (6 CAR) had been sitting in reserve. Things began to happen very fast. Lt-Col Marks later described the action:

Major George HEES, 6 CIB BM [brigade major] drove up in a scout car. He said that the Cdr, 2CID [Foulkes] ordered that 'the first armour he met was to be taken off whatever job they were doing and, together with S. Sask R., were to relieve the pressure on the Camerons'. Lt-Col Clift said all he could spare was 2 coys. He wanted to drive direct to Fontenay-le-Marmion but information was that there was an anti-tank gun there.

Marks had already detached some of his Hussars' tanks to escort the Crocodiles from 141 RAC to May for the final act of that battle. So he ordered two troops of 'C' Squadron to link up with the two companies of South Sasks plus the infantry's carrier platoon. At 1430 they set off from Rocquancourt. There is a good road direct between the two villages but because of the likely presence of an anti-tank gun with a long field of fire, Marks and Clift agreed on a northwards loop out into the countryside, up the ridge of le Grand Clos and then westwards out of sight of the main road. There is almost a thrill of relief in the Camerons' diary entry that the 'S. Sasks were heard advancing', although it is more likely that it was the 1st Hussars Shermans which made the happy noise.

As the relief force bore southwards over the crest, Clift, undeterred by his wound, was sitting on Marks's tank. Clift spotted Germans dug-in at between 600 and 800 yards. The tank colonel recalled:

I moved the tank forward and fired the two Brownings [one in the turret and the other in the co-driver's seat 'downstairs']. Germans kept popping up to surrender all over the place. We left the POWs with inf. and started off again. One tank troop dealt with the anti-tank gun while the remainder swung north. Then it was pretty well clear sailing. 80 POWs were taken.[8]

Some of 141 RAC Crocodiles had also been available as at May, but unlike the May operation it does not appear that the flame-throwers were needed in a major role in Fontenay. Also hearing the relief force coming, Cameron L/Cpl Middleton was guarding a prisoner. He took the prisoner with him towards the enemy pits in front of them and 'persuaded' 150 more to lay down their arms. They may have heard not only the South Sasks arriving but the full might of the 4th Armoured Division now well behind their backs. The USAAF had also mounted a major attack of nearly 500 planes, which became notorious for hitting friendly troops, but must have been frightening and disheartening to the novice 89th men isolated on the wrong side of the bomb line.

At 1800 hours the Camerons' war diary recorded the take over by another CO, Maj E.P. Thompson, former 2 i.c., although on 9 August Maj Gagnon was promoted lieutenant-colonel and commanded the Camerons onwards in Normandy. The casualty roll of the battalion was high. 'It had the heaviest casualties (thirty killed and ninety wounded) of all units attacking during the first phase of "Totalize".'[9] There were numbers of German troops still occupying the hospital about fifty yards away from the nearest Cameron positions, but as the enemy were now completely cut off (with Canadian armour some miles beyond Fontenay) it was decided to let the battered forward troops rest and attend to the hospital garrison on the morrow. The main confusion now arose as to numbers of prisoners. South Sasks were claiming about 250, added to the 200 and more taken in the advance plus L/Cpl Middleton's 150. There were smaller groups still surrendering in the evening.

The saga of Fontenay extended over to 9 August when, at 1100 hours, 'B' company headed the battalion attack on the hospital area, this time with plenty of tank and artillery support. The attack was commanded by CSM Arbour, still going strong and about to be awarded the exceptional distinction of the Military Cross, normally reserved for officers. Other Camerons were checking out the mine at the same time. In view of general criticism of the 89th Division it is worth noting that some were still being flushed out of the mine on 9 August as were those down the mine at Fontenay, while their snipers had caused the South Sask six hours of searching in Rocquancourt after the village had been captured. It is probable, although unproven, that the toughest resistance came from German nationals, with many foreign conscripts taking the first opportunity to surrender.

A postcript to the brigade's actions to-date came the same day, 9 August, when Maj Edmondson revisited the battlefield of 20 July. He found bodies still lying there including Maj Matthews and five other officers whom he could identify. They had been hidden in wheatfields, hedges and craters for almost three weeks. The next day, 10 August, the South Sasks Padre, H/Capt R.L. Taylor and Edmondson took a burial party to the site and honoured their comrades with the last rites.[10]

It is not recorded how many of the 6th Brigade suffered from battle exhaustion during the chaotic battles at Fontenay, May and Rocquancourt. Most human beings have a threshold of tolerance beyond which they cannot endure, and it is the fortune of war which indicates who shall pass into the abyss of psychological collapse and who shall successfully skirt the edge of the precipice for the time being. Many soldiers would agree that they were kept sane by some moment or other of rough humour, laughing almost hysterically at events or comments which would not seem funny in another environment. Some such tension-breaking moments are still remembered with a grin.

The Maisonneuves still laugh at the story of the hungry dispatch rider (DR) who saw a fat pigeon and dreamed of pigeon pie for dinner. He drew his gun, took careful aim and shot the pigeon down. It was only then that the horrified DR noticed that the pigeon had a green container on its leg, and that there was a message inside the container. The DR hastily and penitently carried this additional message to battalion HQ where both pigeon and message were speedily 'evacuated to brigade'.

A group of Royals had been digging-in with picks and shovels just behind the FDLs. Suddenly a spade struck something solid which shone like highly polished gold in the sunshine. Surely this must be buried treasure. They doubled their speed of digging. There emerged the brass driving band of a huge unexploded 14-inch naval shell! Panic and exit at the double!

Maj Jacques Ostiguy was now used to taking prisoners and carrying out the first brief interrogation. 'What regiment are you? Where are your tanks?' He saw his batman coming towards him, herding another prisoner before him. Approaching him the batman said:

'Sir, I've brought you a Chinaman.'
'You've what?'
'Yes, a real Chinaman, sir.'

Somewhere, at some time, the migrant Chinaman had been conscripted into a Nazi labour battalion and, now wearing a baggy nondescript uniform, had been working on the Atlantic Wall overlooking the beaches. He had become embroiled in a conflict of which he knew absolutely nothing.

As the Camerons were coming to the climax of their Fontenay battle, Ostiguy and the remainder of the Maisies were forming up close by, ready to push the enemy further back towards Falaise. Lt Charlie Forbes was a platoon commander whose men might be described as 'semi-walking infantry'. They had close tank support from the Canadian Grenadier Guards (22 CAR). Charlie was commanding 18 Platoon, there was a sergeant in charge of 17 and 16 was non-existent. There was a shortage of French-speaking reinforcements for Le Regiment Maisonneuve and Les Fusiliers. As the platoon officer Charlie had the privilege of riding on a tank. He was thankful for the relief from foot-slogging for a mile or two but cautious about the Sherman's ability to attract the attention of the biggest enemy guns. Their objective was a village called Quilly and this involved an advance over terrain still similar to that in the Verrieres area.[11]

Unlike the ominous starts of Atlantic and Spring, the Maisies were suddenly optimistic and enthusiastic. For the first time they were given explicit written orders, 'like the scenario of a stage show. It was all there – what was going to happen, all worked out. We really began to believe that this was going to work.' True to the scenario, at H Hour, 8 August they saw bombers coming over at 1,000 feet. They could see the bomb doors open. They could see the bombs dropping. 'We were scared they would hit us. I dismounted ready to dive. But they had a long trajectory, dropping about half a mile ahead of us.'

Then the artillery barrage opened up in full force. 'The noise was fantastic, sucking the air out of our ears. There was excitement everywhere. We were anxious to go.' The colonel later reported that 'the artillery set the wheatfields afire so that the attack was made dramatically through a flaming desert'. Spotlights came on and the whole scene was illuminated. They had taped lines to follow and even little lights to guide. They started to move in the second wave at 0400 and passed through the dug-in first wave. At that point the taxi ride was over and Charlie became involved in action:

At first light the Germans were coming out of the hayfields. I saw three about to attack our tank. I tried to reach the phone [an outside phone through to the tank commander] but I had forgotten to pull it out of the box [on the side of the tank]. Panic – I threw a grenade. Hit them: one killed, one wounded, one prisoner. I walked to him holding my pistol. My first face to face encounter with the enemy. As I did, a grenade was thrown by another. It fell at my feet: a potato-masher – there was time to throw it back! The scare and terror were coming out of us, leaving us. We kept moving.

At 1000 Charlie's company could see their objective defined by the church tower at Quilly. Then anti-tank guns in Bretteville, a little farther away, opened up, 88 mm guns, picking out their tanks. 'Clouds of smoke. Tanks brewing. Horrible to look at.' They could see the main defences on the ridge now. Quilly was in a dip between the platoon and the church spire. No progress could be made as one by one Shermans blazed and crews bailed out. The company commander said not to worry as a new bomb attack was coming. At 1200 the heavy bombers came over again and, as it seemed, bombed Bretteville out of existence. Charlie's platoon, lying flat and watching, found it paralysing even at the distance:

Huge clouds of dust and smoke. Half an hour later dust so bloody thick you still couldn't see if there were any houses left. Equally the panzers couldn't see us. Again we advanced. Towards the hill above Quilly, trees on the ridge. Thick belt of trees.

In the next few minutes Charlie Forbes endured the extremes of terror and farce, as could sometimes happen in battle. His platoon plodded up the hill towards the mystery of the dark trees silhouetted against a bright sky – just a black mass of indistinguishable branches and leaves. As they drew near his limbs shuddered to a halt, his brain went blank, and the blood seemed to freeze in his veins:

There was a panzer in among the trees, gun sticking out a few yards away from me, pointing right at me out of its camouflage. I was so damned scared if it fired the shell would go right through me and there was nothing I could do: must be people inside and machine guns and why doesn't it fire? Panic again and stupidly I threw a grenade at it. The whole tank BLEW UP and caught fire.

I was shocked. A 36 grenade blow up a tank? I must be dead in Hell dreaming it. Then slowly I realised that this was a cardboard model of a tank, exactly shaped and camouflaged to perfection as a decoy. Still shivering we descended into Quilly. Threw grenades into first house. House caught fire. Two Germans emerged yards away. I was so surprised I forgot all the German phrases we had learned for this moment. *Hoch die Hande!* So I fired my gun in the air. More effective.

The exultant company of Maisies, having suffered much in the recent past, now surged through the village and Charlie's platoon quickly captured the fine chateau. 'Going to sleep in luxury tonight,' they laughed. 'Sleep in the Chateau de Quilly'. Unfortunately as the Germans retreated Brig Megill and his staff advanced and claimed seignorial rights over the beds of the Chateau. Charlie Forbes concludes the episode by saying, 'Yes, I did sleep at the Chateau de Quilly that night. But in the pigsty of the Chateau.'

Jacques Ostiguy had a shock and a surprise at about this time. The corps commander, Guy Simonds, while respected as a strategist, had for some people a reputation of being rather dour, harsh and unbending. At the beginning of phase 2 of Totalize, USAAF heavy bombers had released a load of bombs near Caen on rear echelons and artillery batteries. Men had died. On the army grapevine the news very quickly became known. It needed only one DR eavesdropping and all ranks knew the story. Jacques Ostiguy realized that his brother was in one of the batteries which was badly hit with serious casualties. He began to worry and to wonder how, in the middle of a battle, he could get news of his brother. Then a messenger came to him from battalion HQ with a personal message from Simonds: 'Tell Ostiguy his brother is safe. Make sure he gets this message!' Ostiguy has never again considered that Simonds was unfeeling.

Another kind of emotion awaited some of the surviving Camerons who were clearing up around the Taraud mine shafts, between Rocquancourt and Fonetnay, always anticipating that an enemy sniper might be holding out in a suicide mission. They heard movement in a mine entrance, pointed their guns, cocked them and shouted a challenge. Voices responded in French. A Highlander shouted 'Bras en l'air!' Some thirty French civilians emerged, almost afraid to believe that the uniforms they saw above them were not German. The group was led by M. Tesson, the chief engineer of the mine, who during the evacuation on 14 July, with a number of similarly-minded civilians, had gone down into the deepest gallery where the enemy soldiers could not reach them. Life was almost impossible, constantly staying at that depth, with intense cold and lack of nourishment. From time to time Tesson made his way cautiously to the surface. At last on 9 August it seemed that the battle had calmed. And the uniform he saw: 'ce sont des Canadiens', he remembered exclaiming.

The Canadians, for their part, saw a bedraggled group of refugees, frozen, pale, and extremely feeble in movements after having been immured for so long. Compassionately, the soldiers quickly found food and, while the refugees ate greedily, summoned battalion ambulances to transport the sick and frail survivors to the Abbaye aux Hommes in Caen.[12]

The refugees from the mine survived but those small mining villages counted up a list of forty-six of their number who had been killed before or during the battles to liberate their homes. Twenty-five of them had succumbed to air bombardments which could not discriminate between friend and foe. Another twelve also suffered from air attacks, being machine-gunned by fighter bombers. Four were killed by artillery shells, one by a land mine, and one in a pit accident. Two went missing and were never heard of again. One, a union leader, died after being deported to Auschwitz concentration camp. A number of those who died were miners pressed into service working on German defences. A bus arrived every day in the period before D-Day to take the conscripted miners to work on the beach defences.

The deep intensity of resentment and hatred engendered by foreign occupation of people's homes and communities is evidenced by the lack of recrimination expressed by the local inhabitants towards the liberating soldiers who so violently destroyed their homes. Indeed it is still highlighted by the warmth of welcome extended by all generations of civilians in the villages to veterans returning to the tragic scenes of their youth.

A young French poet, Pierre Samson, looking at the hundreds of shattered trees around these villages in 1945, saw them as a symbol of human suffering and wrote:

> These denuded trees, without branch, without foliage,
> Have all lost their soul in losing their verdure,
> And all without willing it; before them we recoil:
> Dead but erect at their posts, they all have a proud bearing.[13]

CHAPTER TEN

Tilly – Deadly to the Last

The Britons begin by driving all over the field. . . . Then, after making their way between the squadrons of their own cavalry, they jump down from the chariots and engage on foot.

(*Julius Caesar, 55 BC*)

It was like winning the Lottery and then losing the ticket or forgetting to check the winning number. For two weeks, platoons and companies and battalions had crossed those wheatfields, aiming for the ultimate prize: the capture of Tilly-la-Campagne.

Then at about midnight on 7/8 August, a single Sherman tank of 148 RAC grumbled over the railway track, trundled along the top arm of the T junction and halted, its engine mumbling, outside the church. No Stiller, Wolff or Thorn waited to greet it. For a moment the commander was bewildered: 'What the Hell? There's not supposed to be any village here. Let's look at that map. Railway . . .? Church . . .? Houses . . .? This must be . . . it can only be Tilly. Which is wrong, me or the map? Anyway we're not supposed to be here. Driver, advance, Step on the gas.'

L/Cpl Bill Deeming in a lead tank of 148 RAC had commented on the utter tumult to be heard on the tank's wireless headphones when directional signals were being sent out.[1] Overhead, the Bofors tracer was a clear but very imprecise indicator of direction. In the darkness with sunken roads and collisions and tanks brewing up, it was easy to move away from the columns for a moment and get lost. The 148 RAC route at one point went within 250 yards of the tiny railway station at Tilly. There the regiment did a slight swing to the right. The stray tank went straight on. It had been thought that there would be no route through the fortified villages. But the 148 Sherman found a way through and its commander might have become a great hero, if he had fired his guns, if other tanks had followed him in his error, if the defenders had been so confused by the hundreds of tanks going past the village that they had laid down their arms and surrendered to the intruder.

All those 'ifs' were not to be. Yet another infantry onslaught would be needed before the history book closed on Tilly. And this time the Scottish Highlanders would be taking over from the Canadian Highlanders, but against a new foe. The 1st SS Panzer LAH had now disappeared to the south and the 89th Horseshoe Division was in residence. Col Rossman's numerically strong 1055 Regiment held the ground around Tilly, La Hogue and Garcelles-Secqueville. Its II and III Battalions were forward. But this was their first taste of actual battle. It was a reasonable assumption that, as the Highland Division historian put it, 'the Germans in the front line, knowing that British armour and infantry were in full action behind them, would clear out [of Tilly] as soon as they could. But the enemy stayed to fight, and very tough they proved.'[2]

When the Totalize plans were finalized it was believed that the stronghold villages would have to be by-passed by the tanks, leaving the walking infantry to clear the routes through villages for later traffic. On the left flank it was 152 Brigade which would walk at the same time as the armour and head for Tilly (objective of the Seaforths) and Lorguichon (earmarked for the Camerons). In their perilous sandwich route between two columns of armour, 2 Seaforths would advance on Tilly from a different direction to those taken by the Calgaries, North Novas and others. The Scots would leave Hubert-Folie, crossing the railway diagonally as it were, and entering the village through the thick belt of orchards to the north-west.

The Seaforths had as their CO Lt-Col G.L.W. 'Geordie' Andrews. His then intelligence officer, Hugh Cuming, remembers the CO from a close-up view, sharing slit trenches. A very young colonel, still in his mid-twenties, Andrews was always remarkably immaculate and a very precise planner, leaving nothing to chance. He was an inspirational leader, tough and determined. An example of this was when he was quite badly wounded a little later and confined in a field hospital. After thirteen days he discharged himself prematurely because on the fourteenth day of absence he would have lost his battalion.[3]

Later Andrews recalled his first sight of Tilly in the company of 152's brigadier:

Jim Cassels and I went forward to the Canadian front line at the little village of Hubert-Folie to reconnoitre for the attack. Just outside the village stood a white house in some trees, not quite a chateau but more than an ordinary farmhouse – I was glad to see it was still there unchanged when I re-visited the scene in 1974. A straggly hedge ran from it across our front and from behind this we peered through our binoculars at the objective. On rising ground some 1,500 yards away stood the houses of Tilly, separated from us by open fields. Across the front ran a single-track railway on a low embankment, beyond which an orchard fringed some farm buildings. In recent weeks Tilly had twice been entered by Canadian troops . . . and their unburied dead could still be seen lying along the railway.[4]

It was impossible to pick out the German positions but it seemed likely they would be holding the embankment and the orchard beyond. Rightly or wrongly . . . I decided to establish my leading company on the embankment and pass another company round each flank to converge on the orchard and village. I hoped that the noise of armour on our flanks would hide our movement and therefore chose a 'silent' attack without prior artillery preparation.

In the intelligence section, Pte (later Major) James Nairne was making illicit notes about the pre-battle scene. (Soldiers in battle were prohibited from keeping diaries or notes although numbers of them did so.) On 6 August the battalion had moved from Anisy to Bras. The weather was very hot and on the afternoon of 7 August final preparations were made for the set piece attack. Battalion HQ had visits from the brigadier, various gunner officers, and squadron and troop leaders from the tanks, 'all looking very professional with their map boards, chinagraph pencils and field glasses'. They were attended to by the 2 i.c., Maj D.A. Blair.

At 1800 hours, Nairne accompanied the intelligence sergeant, D. Adams and Pte F. Kidd on another reconnaissance through the FDLs to some higher ground where they could look over to Tilly:

> Our main task at zero hour was to lay strands of white tape from rear Bn HQ which would be located at Bras, to a cross track close to the railway line some six hundred yards distant, as a guide for our jeep vehicles carrying the wounded back to our regimental aid post. On our return from this recce we passed through our forward companies who had been resting most of the day in their slit trenches and who were now talking in groups, smoking or preparing their equipment for the night attack. One platoon commander, Lt Brain, was reading out a pre-battle message from the Commander-in-Chief.[5]
>
> Everything was very quiet; there was a beautiful sunset and it looked like a fine warm night with another hot day to follow. After a hot meal in the late evening most of us settled down for a few hours final rest. At about 2300 we started to hear the noise of tanks and the kangaroos moving up on our flank. We ourselves were to receive no immediate tank support. At precisely the same time a steady stream of aircraft, flying high, could be distinctly heard, which got louder and louder and very soon the sound of exploding bombs became deafening as they dropped their bombs ahead of us. This lasted for about forty-five minutes.

Listening to the bombing in the outskirts of Hubert-Folie, together with his intelligence officer, Hugh Cuming, Lt-Col Andrews checked his watch one last time before giving the signal for yet another attempt to breach the rubble ramparts of Tilly-la-Campagne. Then:

At 23.50 hrs on 7th August 'D' Company, directed on the embankment, crossed the Start Line, followed by 'A' who were to pass round their left and then by 'B' who were to go right. In the pitch dark I saw them over the Start Line and then followed 'B' with my Tactical HQ, leaving 'C' in reserve. For a while there was no sound as we advanced, except the clatter of armour on our flanks.

But, as soon as 'D' approached the railway, Spandau fire broke out and soon afterwards the German artillery defensive fire came down, heavy and accurate – a nasty experience in the open. The No. 18 manpack radio with me was soon put out of action by a splinter and we had to send the operator back for a replacement. Meanwhile the only contact with companies was by runner, and in the dark it was difficult to discover what was going on.

The route forced on the Seaforths like a tight collar by the flanking armoured columns gave them farther to walk than their Canadian predecessors, but for the first few hundred yards of their advance the defenders must have been more concerned about the possibility of a massive incursion of tanks. Col Rossman's men were having their first experience of battle. They had no way of knowing that Tilly was not a target of the tanks. They had no way of knowing from which direction the assault on the village would come. In common with almost every infantryman before or since they had no way of translating into local tactics the noise, the tempest of bombing and artillery fire, the shuddering of the abused earth in a vast unnatural earthquake, and the blinding, searing and dulling plethora of coloured light and flame in the heavens above. Within the space of a mile the elephantine tanks were trumpeting their defiance as they crashed and clattered past on either side of the village. From which angle would dozens of those tanks break off and crush the village? It was a miracle that any of the defenders stayed to fight. But stay they did. It was a wonder that they ever spotted the silently advancing, tiny figures of the Seaforths. But they did. And the furious fusillade that followed pinned the Seaforths close to the railway.

Pte Nairne and his group were unusual and conspicuous in that their orders were to retreat, or at least to move in the opposite direction to the advance:

At about midnight, the Intelligence Sgt, the Intelligence Corporal and myself moved off with our rolls of white tape. We had timed it well and we reached the tail end of 'C' Company (Maj A.M. Gilmour) who were the reserve company just as they were leaving their trenches to move forward. Our artillery had by this time opened their barrage and, looking back, it was a spectacular sight to see the flashes from what appeared to be hundreds of guns spread along the Canadian and 51st (Highland) Division sectors. We carried the heavy rolls of white tape and followed slowly behind 'C' Company. It was not long before firing started from the German defenders in Tilly. Bullets were whistling about in all directions and they were also putting up Very lights.

We moved past the reserve company and started to unroll the white tape. It seemed strange to unroll the tape *backwards* towards rear Bn HQ and the few men in the rifle companies who saw us thought so too! We had no pegs, so to prevent the tape blowing away we placed stones on it at intervals. The first casualties being carried in a jeep came along our taped lane and passed us, and we came across some stragglers lost in the dark from the rifle companies. Lt T. Harvey, the carriers officer, had sited himself about midway between Tilly and Bras and rallied most of the stragglers together. Some were walking wounded and others had genuinely got lost.

For officers, map in hand and briefed in O groups, it was a bewildering wilderness of trackless fields, or of tracks which went in the wrong direction, in a vision-blurring disembodied universe where darkness and light appeared to be waging their own separate war. For the ordinary foot-slogger relying mainly on leadership and clear communications there was a constant sense of blundering through clogging high wheat or undergrowth towards objectives which were only darker blurs on the unreal landscape.

Lt-Col Andrews was, for a brief while, encouraged when, at around 0130 'D' reported 'on objective'. A few minutes later 'B' also reported success. It was only later that it became clear that 'B' had veered to the right of the correct line and were not opposite the main part of the village. At the same time 'A' company having crossed the railway could not penetrate into the orchard where heavy fire was coming from positions invisible within the trees. The CO had to pause and think again:

'A' were held up short of the orchard and reported heavy casualties. It looked as if we were getting stuck. I ordered 'C' to come forward and complete 'A' company's task. But soon they too were finding the opposition in the orchard too strong. My rear-link radio to Brigade had also packed up by now, but I was eventually able to get in touch with Jim Cassels via the Artillery net.

On hearing my news he sent forward 'D' company of 5 Seaforth under Grant Murray to reinforce us. As the orchard on our left seemed so sticky I directed them to make for the village from the right flank. They disappeared into the night and for a long time I could not tell how they were getting on.

James Nairne witnessed at close hand the difficulties at rear HQ because of the breakdown of communications:

It appeared that there was a breakdown in wireless communication at Tac.Bn.HQ which was caused by machine-gun and mortar fire that had put out of action the control wireless set. As a result of this setback communication between Tac.Bn.HQ and the forward companies and Rear Bn.HQ was very limited. The fighting was confused and the defenders of Tilly-la-Campagne were putting up very strong resistance.

As dawn broke on 8 August a thick mist lay across the fields, the railway embankment and the orchards. The situation was unclear and difficult to assess as the defenders continued to avail themselves of the Germans' apparently unending supply of mortar bombs and machine-gun bullets. Explosions glowed red in the ghostly fog and at times machine-gun bullets appeared to visibly tear the fog into interlinking skeins of blank air. The only certain thing was that 89th Division's green troops were earning their spurs at Tilly and were still dug-in amid the ruins.

'Geordie' Andrews reported to Brig Cassels who now, at 0310 hours, brought Lt-Col J. Walford of 5 Seaforths into the action. The narrow attacking front available to the Seaforths was still constrained by the two-way traffic now hustling along the armour's ploughed lanes from the Night March. This again meant that, as with former Canadian actions, the attackers had not yet confronted Tilly's defenders with the overwhelming numbers of rifles generally regarded as necessary for this kind of assault. Cassels determined to make this a two battalion action with heavy artillery backing. Walford considered that a mass attack in the dark would be a recipe for disaster but agreed that after he had been able to recce the ground his battalion should be briefed and launched as soon as possible.

Meanwhile, the extreme left flank march of 1NY and 1 Black Watch had been on their objective since 0300, taking the key village of St Aignan-de-Cramesnil at dawn, demonstrating that Simonds' audacious master plan had worked. The double column of 144 and 148 RAC had encountered more delays but 144 was also on its objective at Cramesnil with their Argyll comrades. 148 had turned off short of 144 to carry 7 Black Watch into Garcelles-Secqueville and now stood relatively unemployed. (1NY and 144 RAC were poised to repel counter-attacks). Cassels contacted Brig H.B. Scott, who had commanded the armour with such success, and asked for tank support.

During the night tanks would have been of minimal support for firing at precise targets, but now Scott was able to detach a squadron of 148, one of whose tanks had already inadvertently toured Tilly.

The reserve squadron of 148 had only a mile to drive in their 30 mph Shermans and, as an artillery concentration heralded the forward move of the two Seaforth battalions, the Shermans smashed in through what might be termed the back entrance of Tilly. Resistance melted away, some defenders retreating through woods and along hedgerows, others dying in their slits and a few remaining in the confused tumuli of rubbish that had been Tilly. Records suggest that the tanks of the 148 squadron drove back and forward through the village, although where nineteen Shermans found room and routes to drive around tiny Tilly is not explained. Probably one troop entered the village while the rest encircled it. (Unfortunately that excellent regiment, 148 RAC, together with 2nd Northamptonshire Yeomanry, was broken up a few days later on the grounds of 'juniority' to reinforce more senior regiments, and reminiscences of the regiment are in short supply.)[6]

At last, at long last Tilly had fallen. Only twenty days since the waves of Goodwood desperation had washed back from the steep shore of Tilly. Less than three weeks, but an eternity, figuratively speaking, for those who were engaged on both sides. An eternity, literally speaking, for many. In the ranks of the Seaforths there was more sad reflection than giddy exultation. At 0215 Capt Grant Murray, popular and efficient officer of 5 Seaforths, led his 'D' company to support the 2 Seaforth, arriving at the level crossing near the village railway halt. Heavy fire was coming through the mists from farther down the railway so Murray took his men in a right curve beyond the village, eventually attacking a wood where defenders were well dug-in.

Next morning Murray's body was found surrounded by both Scottish and German dead. His company had gone into action with only forty men. He and ten others were killed and another ten seriously wounded. 'Geordie' Andrews learned on return to battalion

HQ of Murray' death and wrote, 'it upset me to think that he should die while under my orders: he was a particular friend from Desert days' and, like many, had survived the rigours of desert war only to fall in the verdant woods and orchards of Normandy. Among those who died in the 2 Seaforth ranks were Capts Robinson and Tannahill. Again, Andrews grieved to think that he had just moved Tannahill from the intelligence officer's job and sent him to his death leading a company. Hugh Cuming had taken over as intelligence officer and survived. The dice of war were surely loaded at times.[7]

James Nairne remembers counting two German officers and forty-nine other ranks as prisoners at the capitulation of the Tilly garrison. The story which found its way into official history was that as the tanks of 148 prowled around Tilly a young German lieutenant emerged from the ruins and asked for time to consider surrender. He said he was the only officer left. Lt-Col Walford was called and gave the young officer a stern warning and a brief time limit. Those waiting checked their watches as, at 1050 hours on 8 August, the lieutenant appeared again out of the ruins of Tilly with about thirty of his men. It is likely that the German officer was Lt Katthge.

The defenders of Tilly had operated in a disciplined and selfless manner in contrast to those described by Panzermeyer as being seen running away. 1055 Regiment battle casualties were heavy. Their 5 Company was totally destroyed. Capt Marbold von Kalm lost an arm and was taken prisoner. Their 6 Company lost ninety-four men between Tilly and La Hogue on 8 August. To make matters worse for their wounded, the medical doctor Leidenfrost of 1055 Regiment was himself killed during the fighting. Although the division ceased to exist as a fighting formation at Falaise, Lt-Gen Heinrichs was able to reform it later when he himself was killed in a street full of American soldiers near Liege. By the end of 1944 Col Rossman was writing to von Kalm saying that nobody was left in the division from the time of Tilly and that the 1055 Regiment was 'burned to a cinder'.[8]

The Seaforths, together with the Canadian battalions at May and Fontenay, bore the brunt of the 'walking' role during Totalize but other battalions of the 51st Highland Division carried out lesser but not pleasant tasks of a similar nature. Those often forgotten men of the medium machine-gun and mortar battalions, in this case 1/7 Middlesex, fired off a total of 250 bombs from each mortar and 44 belts of ammunition from each machine-gun during the first phase of Totalize. 152 Brigade had formed a firm base for the armoured columns, but when the armour had been established on the objectives five miles on, the battalions of the brigade walked into other intermediate villages, taking numbers of prisoners. The 1 Gordons and 5/7 Gordons each had good success.

The other battalion of the brigade, 5 Black Watch, was unfortunate enough to be underneath some of the American heavy bombers which caused havoc by bombing Allied troops near Caen. Two jeeps, those of the CO (Lt-Col Bill Bradford) and the adjutant were blown over and Sgt Dewar, the medical sergeant, was wounded, as were three others. The HQ party managed to resume after dusting itself down and the battalion headed for the trouble spot of La Hogue. Nobody was disappointed when a patrol from the Gordons reported that the enemy had vacated La Hogue. 'A' company marched into the village and found a few Germans still hiding in the ruins. The battalion found the streets to be so cratered and mined that it was some hours before their own transport could enter.[9] This tends to justify Simonds' decision not to try to push the armoured columns through the villages in the dark. In any case, even today, the bends on some main streets in Soliers, La Hogue and Bourguebus will only take one fifty-four seater coach going one way at a time, as many veterans will recall.

The 5 Camerons had just been taken over by Lt-Col D.B. Lang, MC, and whereas the other 'walking infantry' battalions were charged with clearing intermediate villages, 5 Camerons received the anomalous role of marching to an objective on the line of the 'deep thrust' – the key main road village of Lorguichon. This was the junction of Canadian and British troops. The route, fairly clear in the dark as it flanked the main road, would be a hard two mile trek between the two main masses of armour. It also meant a fifty metre climb between Bras and Lorguichon. The way was through the extensive cornfields along the road and was luridly lit by the flames from tanks which had gone up on mines.

For two hours the battalion slogged and coughed and cursed. The cornfields proved good hiding places for snipers who had to be found and driven out one by one. Thirty-five prisoners were taken en route in this way and by 0430 the battalion had split up and the individual companies were on their respective objectives. Digging-in at the crossroads they were not to know until later that they were formed around a bridge which had been time-bombed. Fortunately the bomb seemed to have been badly timed and the engineers came to the rescue.[10]

The Allied front now stood firm and clear some five miles beyond the previous FDLs which, in terms of Normandy fighting to-date, represented a huge advance. Inevitably later criticism has suggested that the advance to Falaise should have been completed in less time and that an earlier junction with the American Third Army moving north would have trapped many more enemy troops in the eventual pocket. Gen Patton who was commanding those Americans would certainly have agreed with that criticism.

It will always appear to 'those who were there' that such criticisms fail to take into account the reality of warfare in 1944. Often the criticism seems to ignore the problems of fighting against a superb army with weapons of overwhelming power on terrain of their own choosing. It must also be realized that Simonds' masterpiece plan of the Night March was not only a mission of tanks into unknown territory, it was also a launch into planning and battle hazards which constituted an incredible risk at the time. So much could have gone wrong that it was a miracle so little went wrong.

Some historians also doubt if an earlier junction between Patton and Simonds could have been maintained. One commentator has pointed out that a thin line of junction at that time (say 10–12 August) would have had to contend with counter-attacks from 1st, 2nd, 9th, 10th, 12th, and 17th SS Divisions as well as a division of paratroopers. And on 16 August a German engineer battalion on its own proved to be a redoubtable fighting unit. So, an earlier link-up might, said J.S. Lucas, have resulted in 'a Balaclava in Normandy'.[11]

As to the last attack on Tilly carried out by the Seaforths, James Nairne, who was there had some doubts. He says:

> At this distance of time I feel the casualties of 2 Seaforth and 5 Seaforth could have been largely avoided at Tilly-la-Campagne if these 2 battalions had been allowed to wait until the Tanks over-ran the village on their way back after de-bussing the 154 brigade. 2 Seaforth could have been made to move towards Tilly in an advance to contact plan, but NOT to get mauled if the opposition remained strong which it was. After the operation was over I remember the CO's batman saying to me 'the place could have been taken with a troop of tanks', a point shared by others. I think that the Divisional Cdr was hoping that resistance in Tilly would crumble quickly when the Germans heard our tanks by-passing them.[12]

It is always difficult to reconcile the loss of good comrades with the need for haste on the battlefield. It is probable that the Highland Division commander was conforming to Simonds' insistent demand for the earliest possible opening of two-way traffic routes for the thousands of vehicles involved in Totalize. The villages of Tilly and Rocquancourt were perched on either side of the main road so that a German force remaining in those villages could cause havoc with the mainstream of supply and reinforcement. It was therefore considered imperative to attack at night before tank support could be made available to the Seaforths.

Tilly had been liberated and destroyed. The author spent the night of 8 August in Hubert-Folie, ruined like the other neighbouring villages. He described that village from which the Seaforths had advanced:

The buildings are, almost without exception, ruined. There are roofless cottages and floorless cottages which have sunk into deep pits. There are buildings with three walls, two walls, one wall. Doors hang loose, doorways have been enlarged into ragged gaps, windows jut askew, oddly positioned new apertures give the walls the appearance of having been designed by crazy architects, dwarfs or giants . . . an almost unbearable stink of burning rubber sterilizes the normal stench of putrefying flesh.[13]

In May of 1960 the author was organizing earthquake relief in the Chilean city of Valdivia, which had been hit by the most severe earthquake ever recorded on the Richter scale, and the port of Corral, which had been swamped by a Tsunami so huge that it recoiled through the ocean depths to kill people on the shore of Japan, 7,000 miles away. While the cathedral in Valdivia had been reduced to a pile of stones there was no devastation so total and complete as seen in these Normandy villages after Liberation. The wrath of nature was more selective or haphazard, even though inhumanly violent. Human anger sought out every square yard of enemy territory and systematically, with moronic persistence, obliterated it.

Tilly was the epicentre. Riding his Norton motor-bike down the main road next day, Sgt W.R. Bennett, who had doubted his own survival on the ridges, 'stopped to look at Tilly-la-Campagne . . . a short man could see across the whole village as no structure was left standing to block his view. As we turned into the farm compounds at Lorguichon an eerie quiet had replaced the continuous roar of battle – as though we were waiting in limbo for the final judgement.'[14] For nearly three years twenty brewed-up iron monsters around Tilly continued to pollute the fertile fields.

CHAPTER ELEVEN

The Other Terrible Tilly Twin

Hotly contested fights took place in various parts of the field and continued for a long while without decisive results. . . . the infantrymen dispersed themselves among the squadrons and fought with great steadiness.

(Julius Caesar, 51 BC)

By one of those grim coincidences of war two of the Normandy villages most costly in Allied infantry casualties and most devastated by repeated battles were both called TILLY.

There was Tilly-la-Campagne on the Bourguebus Ridge and Tilly-sur-Seulles, deep down in a pretty bridgehead valley at a vital crossroads. The name Tilly is therefore in itself a reminder of the sufferings shared by Allied infantry in similarly unrewarding battles, that is to say locally unrewarding but each contributing to the eventual elimination of the enemy. Other infantry voices might well point out that to match Fontenay-le-Marmion, on that reverse slope of Verrieres, the British had their Fontenay-le-Pesnel, the latter being only a brief march from Tilly-sur-Seulles, just as Fontenay-le-Marmion was a brief march from Tilly-la-Campagne. And while the eponymous village of Verrieres stood on its ridge and gave its name to a series of actions, the village from which the final Tilly-sur-Seulles attack was launched by 50th (Northumbrian) Division was also called . . . Verrieres!

This shared infantry travail also serves as a reminder that while the Canadians were fighting their way along the bank of the Orne from Caen to May, other British infantry battalions were shedding blood to clear the opposite bank of the Orne, with the dominating hills which culminated in Mont Pincon, another name of sad and dramatic significance.

The German formation which would counter-attack phase 1 of Totalize, Hitlerjugend, was despatched to Tilly-sur-Seulles on D-Day + 2, 8 June, as 50th Division was pushing beyond Bayeux. This was Hitlerjugend's first battle move but 50th Division had fought in the Western Desert and Sicily. Although retrained for D-Day it still contained many veterans of those previous campaigns and was one of the three most experienced British divisions in Normandy.

Conditions in the Bocage were vastly different to those of the wide open desert. In the network of tiny fields, some of them hardly big enough to provide a tennis court, troops became intermingled and nobody was safe from an enemy emerging at any time from the hedgerows. It was said that cows milked by men of the Panzer Lehr Division one day could be milked by men of the 50th the next. Dispatch rider Pte Mawson had dismounted when his motor-bike chain broke. As he was bending over the machine he felt a tap on the shoulder. It was a German wanting to surrender. The German helped Mawson repair his bike before riding off on the pillion into captivity.[1]

On 8 June men of 1 Dorsets reached Tilly-sur-Seulles but in too small a group to hold on. After the initial probe of Hitlerjugend, the Panzer Lehr moved into the counter-attack. On 14 June, 6th and 9th Durham Light Infantry (DLI) assembled at Verrieres to advance some 4,000 yards to the main lateral road through Tilly. In the Bocage they had found that Germans would hold their fire until a patrol was no more than ten yards away and then unleash devastating fire. On 14 June the ground was more open but at 150 yards the defenders again opened up with fire which suggested there was no lack of ammunition.

69 Brigade picked up the attack again on 16 June and by 18 June their 6 DLI and 2 Essex had fought into the outskirts of Tilly which was cleared next day. It had been bombarded by mortars and artillery, and bombed and strafed from the air, and blasted by the massive shells from the big guns of the battleship HMS *Warspite* out beyond the landing beaches. It was, like the other Tilly, almost a total ruin. The division had suffered 673 killed, 3,072 wounded, and 1,236 missing of whom only 505 were ever accounted for.[2] But over 3,000 prisoners had been taken.

A divisional history aptly sums up the episode stating that these struggles around Tilly had been:

a phase without spectacle or glitter. In week of difficult fighting, which had yielded no great gains, measured in distance, the 50th division had slowly ground the enemy into impotence. From becoming incapable of effective counter-attack he passed to the stage where he could no longer hold his line. And back he went, not in rout but carefully and steadily with the usual array of booby traps and mines in his wake. We followed pressing him.

Among many personal recollections of the Tilly-sur-Seulles battles one of the most poignant is that of Pte Tateson of 7 Green Howards:

The two leading companies came under heavy mortar and machine-gun fire and their commanders, Majors Bowley and Boyle, were both killed. I heard on my radio the signaller accompanying Major Bowley desperately pleading for the Medical Officer to come to the Major's aid as he was dying. The sudden loss of these two officers had a terribly depressing effect on us all, and particularly on those who had served with them in the battalion all through the Western Desert and Sicily campaigns.[3]

The exhausted infantry who had finally liberated May, Tilly-la-Campagne, Fontenay and Verrieres had at least the satisfaction of dovetailing into the brilliant Totalize break-in which, with relatively little delay, led on to the great mantrap of the Falaise Pocket. The exhausted attackers at Tilly-sur-Seulles had to sustain another month or more of minor, niggling, blood-letting exchanges before they saw any light at the end of their tunnel.

The author was called forward as a reinforcement to his tank squadron after one of those niggling 'local attacks' near Tilly-sur-Seulles on 26 June. The tanks of the Northamptonshire Yeomanry were ordered to advance with a company of Green Howards for about 1,000 yards through a baffling maze of tiny fields, huge hedges and dense orchards. One troop leader later remembered waiting for his group of infantry to move forward with the tanks in support. When nobody moved, the tank lieutenant got down to find out what was wrong. He reported that the infantrymen were like zombies or robots. Having been in almost constant action since D-Day they were so exhausted that they were almost unable to think or respond to orders. However, when the tanks moved forward on their own the infantrymen somehow managed to drag their limbs out of their slit trenches and join in what, at that time, was regarded as a successful advance: 1,000 yards.[4]

Whether it was the British Essex at Tilly-sur-Seulles, or the Canadian Essex Scots at Tilly-la-Campagne, or those other battalions storming up Mont Pincon,[5] there was a commonality of purpose and understanding of one fact. 'Attrition' – that comfortable word for generals – meant that you were going to eliminate the enemy eventually. But, of your own fighting rifles, the final war total of casualties would be more than the full front line strength of your battalion on any one day. In your dicing with death that would give you odds which no gambler would want to take.

CHAPTER TWELVE

Reasons and Recriminations

If anyone is alarmed by the fact that the Germans have defeated the Gauls and put them to flight, he should inquire into the circumstances of that defeat. . . . his victory resulted from his stunning strategy.

(Julius Caesar, 58 BC)

When you've been shot and wounded and then patched up in order to be shot again . . .

when you've lived, slept and eaten in pits which, under pouring rain, become sumps of living human sewage and dead putrifying wastes . . .

when you've gone days without proper food or sleep and weeks without undressing to get rid of the lice . . .

when you've pored over indistinct maps, and considered one hundred possibilities and reached a decision to send some of your comrades, and probably yourself, to death . . .

when you've gone up against the finest army the world has seen, armed with overpowering weapons, and defending impregnable strongholds, and yet pushed that enemy back and finally broken his ranks . . .

and then are told you should have done better . . .

and years afterwards you read what seems to be irrelevant, uninformed, carping criticism: it can hurt as much a shard of tearing shrapnel, or a burning bullet, or the blast of a mortar bomb.

It is not surprising that some Canadian veterans nurse a grievance because criticism points to an unnecessary cost in casualties and a few days delay in reaching Falaise. It is doubly sad because a Canadian started the fashion of writing off Operations Atlantic, Spring and Totalize as, to a significant extent, unsuccessful. It was none other than C.P. Stacey, the official historian, who dug the knife into the wounds and twisted it. Others lined up behind Brutus with sharper knives.

J.A. English described Operation Spring as, 'by any measurement it was an unmitigated tactical debacle . . . It would seem that the lives of so many soldiers were unnecessarily cast away.'[1] Of the 'it could have been otherwise' school of thought, Blumenson opined that 'Patton . . . would take absolute hold of the operation and surround and destroy all the Germans in Normandy with resolution and finality.' He alleges against the Commonwealth generals personal incompatibility, too strict adherence to the original invasion plan, and lack of forcefulness from Bradley and Montgomery.[2] Although to some extent valid, that criticism might have better resonance if it did not emanate from a paean of praise for Patton, that most incompatible of generals.

The critics have correctly noted that not all the objectives of Atlantic, Spring and Totalize were achieved, or, when achieved, some delay was involved. They therefore, perhaps less correctly, judge that those operations failed, or that the balance of the outcomes tended towards failure. A current Canadian historian, Professor Terry Copp, has stated that a new paradigm of success and failure is needed in judging historic battles. But before setting out on the proposition of a new paradigm it is necessary briefly to review the realities of the operations described in these pages.

Commencing from the dictum of 'know your enemy!' there are certain facts about the German Army in Normandy in 1944 which are virtually unassailable. First of all, German battle equipment was generally superior to that of the Allies. This is particularly true in regard to tanks and the 88 mm anti-tank gun, although in some situations the Sherman Firefly with its 17-pounder gun vied for the champion's role. Not only tank crews but infantrymen in their slits were appalled by the power of the 88. George Cooper of the Regina Rifles remembers, 'German weapons were fearful weapons when we first encountered them. Their 88 we could only respect for its velocity, its smokeless propellant, and its versatility. The sound was terrifying – the muzzle blast and the exploding shell at a distance like two almost simultaneous thunderclaps. We could only duck.'[3]

The supremacy of German armour was enhanced, or exacerbated according to where one stood, by the structure of the panzer units. A total fusing and blending of all arms into a cohesive unit, because it was born, grew, fought and died as an independent Arm of Decision, unfettered by outmoded rules and the curbs of the traditional Cavalry, Infantry and Artillery arms, it (the panzer formation) instituted a unique brand of armoured warfare.

The evil reputation for atrocities of some SS units has sometimes made it difficult to give military credit where due to front line SS panzer divisions. A modern British general, who has commanded troops of several nations, has no such inhibitions in assessing the 1st SS Panzer:

[The LAH] was an incredible organisation. In only ten years it had developed a spirit and fighting reputation second to none. In this short period it had achieved what most armies and regiments strive for but take decades and even centuries to attain; moreover, it had gone even further and formed something never before achieved in any army: a division of all arms – infantry, armour, artillery, engineers, etc., but with the same badge, spirit and sense of 'family' as a regiment. To this was added the advanced military thinking current in the Wehrmacht generally at this time, thinking which had developed the tactics of the blitzkrieg, produced the necessary equipment to practise it, and maintained a cooperation on the battlefield between the different ground elements, and even between air and ground elements, unknown to other nations.[4]

Most allied soldiers at the sharp end had no illusions about the quality of the enemy confronting them. To take two Canadian examples: M.G. Berry of the Royals found that, 'German infantry fighting in a defensive role were very good, difficult to locate, lots of ammunition and machine-guns. They could also call for very heavy and accurate mortar fire on any group of men. The German tanks were frightening.'[5] Don Ripley of the North Novas agrees, for 'the Germans had the versatile 88 mm gun which, in my opinion was the "weapon of the war". . . . Then there were the "Moaning Minnies". We had nothing to compare with the Tiger tank. . . . The German troops were, in my view, methodical and generally predictable.'[6]

One of the Germans' main problems was the number of non-nationals within their ranks, many of whom were not sympathetic to the Nazi cause. Several references have already been made to this phenomenon. On 25 July the prisoners taken by the Calgaries included Poles, Ukrainians and Russians. On 1 August three deserters presented themselves to the Rileys from 9th SS Panzer Grenadier Division Hohenstauffen. Two were Poles who stated that there were foreigners in every platoon, and all wanted to desert but the SS NCOs kept a vigilant watch. The SS NCOs also very cleverly advised the foreigners that if they surrendered in their SS uniforms they would be shot by the Allied troops who took them prisoner.

Not all comments on all German troops were complimentary. Capt Watt at Fontenay wondered why the enemy had missed an easy opportunity to capture the Camerons' mortar positions. The vigorous Maj Dextraze was not too impressed saying, 'Jerry is no good at night. He needs only noise to frighten him away. On one occasion a burst of Bren fire aimed into a field caused him to pull out of the area.'[7] (That obviously did not apply around Tilly!) Brig Foster thought that, 'The German attacks were launched without any semblance of tactical sense

. . . where a carefully conceived flank attack might have been deadly, the enemy flung himself straight against the strongest points.'[8] Lt R.H. Pelly, in his clumsy flail Crab near Rocquancourt, was fired at three times at short range by an anti-tank gun, once when the Crab was static and twice when moving slowly, and the enemy gun missed all three times. The author had a similar experience when an unusual battery breakdown on his Sherman allowed the enemy three free shots while the turret was being traversed manually – and again all three missed. Such things happened in battle. But it would be an extremely foolish Allied soldier who would go into battle actually expecting a German gun to miss.

Questions have been asked as to why, when the war was apparently lost, German morale remained so high. It must be remembered that the power of Hitler's personality and the perverted brilliance of Goebbels' propaganda (unequalled until the arrival of the 'spin doctors') still convinced many German soldiers that something would happen – such as another miracle weapon – to stave off final defeat. One observer of the Second World War German Army has pointed to:

> peer-group pressure and dogged conformity within the group, careerism, a general all-encompassing xenophobia unrelated to any specific racial or national group, deference to authority, draconian discipline and the motivating role of junior officers and NCOs . . . [however] the armed forces of the Reich contained . . . individuals ranging from teenagers to octogenarians. Each generation carried with it into the theatre of war . . . markedly different attitudes to National Socialism and differing life experiences. The Wehrmacht was not a homogeneous entity.[9]

As already stated, unreliable foreign conscripts were closely watched and harshly disciplined by totally incorruptible NCOs. There were also the legions, nearly 50,000 of them, of Nationalsozialistischer Fuhrungsoffizier in army uniform, repeating the propaganda messages at unit level.[10]

German tactics were often surprising and extremely effective. An instance was the way in which their artillery fired into the Canadian barrage behind which the Calgaries were advancing on Tilly, and sending shells just beyond the barrage itself. This gave the impression to the infantry that their own shells were dropping short and they asked for the barrage to be halted. The colonel himself was convinced that the rogue shells were German but the calls from the leading troops were so insistent that the barrage was indeed halted. It was only then that it became apparent as to what the enemy was doing, and this had resulted in a halt, even though only temporary, to the friendly barrage.

Such ingenuity was apparent at the lowest and highest levels. The 4th Canadian Infantry Brigade reported enemy at Tilly moving about in soft shoes rather than boots, and placing small stones on the railway ties so as to hear the approach of patrols as the latter kicked the stones. During this period the Germans also sprang the surprise of the 'mobile mines', the small heavily armoured vehicles packed with explosives from which the drivers ejected before directing the vehicles at defenders' FDLs.

On 5 August the Maisies reported 'all kinds of jamming in the air' and it was apparent to them that the enemy was systematically interfering with the weak signals from the 18 wireless sets. There was also the incident where, on evacuating a headquarters house, the Germans had left behind a wireless receiver which appeared to be wired to send out direction signals when the receiver was switched on: a 'booby trap' which summoned precisely ranged mortar fire. On several occasions the enemy 'opened the door', let the attackers in and then counter-attacked from behind. At Etavaux and at May, among others sites, patrols found an empty village but when an occupation force advanced it was greeted with the usual 'wall of fire'. 'One problem was continually present', reported one CO, '– that of the enemy reappearing in areas that had been cleared. On one occasion our tanks riddled the factory area but when they withdrew more enemy appeared', in the latter case out of the iron ore mines.[11]

At times the Germans' adherence to proven battle doctrine worked to their own disadvantage. A prime example of this was the demise of the tank ace Wittmann. The automatic response of Wittmann, Panzermeyer and the like, on an enemy break-in was to attack immediately. In the majority of cases this was successful. As the Night March forces consolidated on the launch sites for the second phase of Totalize, Panzermeyer sent Wittmann's small Tiger troop hurtling over the disputed ground to counter-attack a force which had over thirty of the new Sherman Firefly variants within 17-pounder shooting range. While myths have grown up around Wittmann's heroic last stand, the facts, as those of us who were there can testify, is that his valuable elite Tigers were wiped out with very little harm to the Northamptonshire Yeomanry or the Sherbrookes. On the other hand, if Wittmann's Tigers had been held under cover in counter-attack positions, phase 2 of Totalize could have taken very much longer to break through to Falaise and with much higher casualties. A continued study of this episode leads one to wonder if Wittmann that day ever expected to achieve anything with his hopeless advance, except perhaps his own demise.

Historians from both sides of the Second World War fence have commented on the problems encountered in the field by German formations because of the interference of Hitler in minor details. Apart from his own conviction that he was an infallible military strategist, Hitler often made decisions on outdated information because of the distances and difficult communications involved. Gen Warlimont of Hitler's own Supreme HQ wrote of some of the problems with the Hitler style of command, speaking of late July 1944:

Even in this pressing period Hitler and Jodl could not be seen before 11 am. Any decision had then to go through the process of endless discussion . . . decision unlikely to be reached before early afternoon. Supreme Headquarters insisted on laying down itself every detail in every theatre of war.[12]

Warlimont also commented that in spite of the fact that the Americans had broken through as far as the Avranches defile, Hitler's objective was 'to keep the enemy confined to his bridgehead . . . to wear him down and finally destroy him'. Another indication of the remoteness of Hitler, even within his own HQ, was that when Warlimont was sent urgently to Normandy on 31 July, he was briefed personally by Hitler for the only time in his five years of service in a room next door to the Fuhrer.

As opposed to the Germans' highly and precisely trained elite troops the Allies' attacking troops were not always as well trained as they might be – often for very good reasons. Lt-Col MacLaughlan had apposite views on this, pointing out that training space in England was very restricted. Food was scarce and thus infantry in training were not allowed to trespass into wheatfields and trample on valuable grain. So they were not able to practise finding trampled tracks in the grain or locating fields of fire in wheatfields, or learning the advantages and disadvantages of burning grain fields.[13] These conditions could not be tested until actual battle in Normandy when Essex Scots reported difficulties in treading softly on ripe grain at night.[14]

Some officers felt that there was insufficient training of armour and infantry together, with some units jealously guarding the independence of their arm of battle. Maj Don Learment points out that before Normandy the North Novas shared the same camp with the Sherbrookes, including the same messes. Consequently good rapport was achieved. The two units had no problems with cooperation in the field. This was a rare instance which might have been made universal in Britain before D-Day.[15] There also appears to have been too small a number of persons per battalion with previous battle experience. Col John Martin remarks that in October 1943 the Lincoln and Welland Regiment sent five Officers and five NCOs to Canadian 1st Infantry Division in Italy to obtain battalion experience pre-D-Day in Normandy. Only one of the cadre returned to the 'Lincs'.[16] Responsibility for these failures can only be charged to the highest level of command.

The 5th Black Watch, out of the line for a day or two and receiving large numbers of reinforcements, found it virtually impossible to do weapon training in the confined and over-crowded beachhead. In desperation they borrowed two bulldozers and constructed a set of thirty yard butts at the end of the field, much to the discomfiture of 7 Argylls who were in the next field and were collecting some of the 'overs' from the Black Watch practice. Legend has it that the Argylls retaliated by firing their own practice into the rear of the Black Watch butts.[17] Funny? – but not the stuff of serious war. The author and others who had to fire the Firefly 17-pounder, found that it was almost impossible to find space to check the gun sights at the requisite 1,500 yards range, much less actually practise with a new war-winning piece of equipment on which each 'expert' gunner had been able to have only one shot before embarking for Normandy. Not the regimental CO's fault! This training disparity was highlighted when Allied soldiers were able to see the German Army training areas ruthlessly expropriated from farmers and foresters.

Battle exhaustion was also a problem for the Allies, as the legendary First World War tactic of 'the little Lieutenant with his revolver' driving on the men was not feasible in the Second World War. Two experts who studied this phenomenon found that:

Battle exhaustion . . . was largely an infantryman's problem. More than 90 per cent of known cases were among infantrymen. The large majority . . . exhibited acute fear reactions and acute and chronic anxiety manifested through uncontrollable tremors, a pronounced startle reaction to war-related sounds and a profound loss of self-confidence. Conversion states such as amnesia, stupor or loss of control over some physical function . . . described as 'shell shocked' in the First World War, were rarely seen in the Second World War.[18]

Like Gunner FOO Blackburn, mentioned elsewhere, platoon commander M.G. Berry remembers that 'one thing I found difficult was to ensure that men in forward positions did not fall asleep. I spent many nights without sleep when we were in dangerous positions. Fortunately, the Germans did not always seem too keen on night operations.'[19] Another platoon commander, Charlie Forbes, made the interesting comment that 'city gents' were often not suitable for infantry point work and that country boys from the bush, loggers, fishermen and hunters did better and could put up with the extreme physical strain.[20] It is perhaps relevant that SS recruits tended to come largely from rural areas.

One anonymous veteran commented on two COs present in Normandy, whom he termed 'dug-outs'. Traditionally a dug-out colonel is a retired officer who returns to the ranks in an emergency and usually serves with zeal. But the anonymous veteran said that in this case the 'dug-outs' were so called by their men because they were never seen outside a deep dug-out well behind the lines. Both 'dug-outs' mentioned were soon 'dug-out' of their command and sent packing by Simonds.

However, in spite of criticism of a few officers, the casualty lists support the conclusion that most officers were up front and taking risks with their men. For instance, the Reginas' list of 557 men killed shows the obvious numerical preponderance of riflemen (342) but relative sharing of risk by 65 corporals who gave their lives, as well as 17 sergeants, 8 company sergeant-majors or quartermaster sergeants, 16 lieutenants, 5 captains and 4 majors. The battle at Fontenay revealed how dangerous battle could be for battalion commanders. By December 1944 69 per cent of Canadian officers in North-West Europe of major rank and lower had become casualties compared with 51 per cent of other ranks. That could be called sharing the risks.[21]

It was in the area of equipment that the attackers on the ridges were most highly disadvantaged. Much has been said about the vulnerability of the ubiquitous Sherman tank. Research revealed that in order to knock out a Sherman a German tank needed only an average of 1.63 shots on target, and 62 per cent of German hits knocked out the enemy tank. In a survey of 65 hits only 3 out of 53 hits by German 75 mm shot failed to penetrate the Sherman armour and all 12 of the 88 mm shots penetrated.[22] This contrasts with stories of Sherman shots bouncing off Tiger and Panther armour like tennis balls. So the Panzers and Tigers could, to a certain extent strut the ridges and their panzer grenadiers could strut behind them, unless a Firefly came on the scene or the infantry's own anti-tank guns could be brought up quickly enough.

While some soldiers saw advantages in the crudeness of the Sten gun others recalled it with horror. Its 'back street workshop' production process rendered it unreliable. Maj Dickin of the South Saskatchewan's recorded:

> On one occasion my corporal pulled the trigger of his sten at the same time as the Nazi fired his rifle. Both triggers clicked, the sten was out of ammo and the German rifle jammed. So the corporal hit the Nazi over the head with his sten and then shot him with his own rifle after clearing the jammed bullet.[23]

Some troops complained that the German maps were much better than 'ours'.[24] Perhaps of more general concern was the poor broadcasting quality of the infantry wireless sets and the fallible batteries which were supplied. 'B' Company of the Calgaries at Tilly at 0232 on 1 August, 'B' and 'C' Companies of Les Fusiliers Mont-Royal on both 19 and 20 July, and the Maisies towards May at 2230 on 5 August, were only a few of those who had reason to curse the set or batteries or both. When it is remembered that as long ago as 1917 the British Army was experimenting with a wireless tank, it is amazing that as late as July 1944 the point infantry were restricted to manpacks of dubious quality and perilously susceptible to shrapnel or stray bullets.

Certain queries arise about the level of intelligence preparation at high level. While the D-Day beaches seem to have been adequately surveyed, the iron ore mines around May-sur-Orne were totally missed and were mapped as factory buildings. A more positive factor was the impressive quality of Allied radio intercepts. The Enigma intercepts were available to Simonds and his own headquarters also had a good service of its own. Fred Pollak was a lieutenant signals analyst for Simonds. He recalls:

> My unit was involved in monitoring and copying German traffic for some 3 years. Hence we became fairly knowledgable in our job. . . . Eventually we could tell one [enemy] service from another. Many of these units developed characteristics which we recorded. The other source which proved in France of great importance was DF, direction finding. We could narrow down the location of the source of a signal reasonably well. We could tell the arrival of a new formation before POWs or other evidence became available. Towards the end of the Falaise battle we identified two new divisions in our area from up north.[25]

The most favourable aspects for the Allies in the balance of forces were the effectiveness of their artillery and the command of the air. Lt-Gen Horrocks noted that 'the core of the Royal Artillery . . . was the fantastic accuracy of the survey units. . . . Neither the Germans, nor the Russians, nor even the French who were always supposed to be the masters of artillery systems, could approach the accuracy or weight of concentrated fire-power which I had at my disposal within minutes.'[26]

Stacey and others have criticised divisional, brigade and battalion commanders during the July and August infantry battles. Indeed a number of commanders were sent home, although this has happened in all armies much of the time. One observer, who himself moved into that level of command, disagrees with the general criticism. Brig Denis Whitaker, DSO and bar, one of the most decorated Canadian soldiers, thought of the brigade in which he served as a battalion commander, 'it was a very well commanded Brigade in those days. And other people at other levels of command were pretty damned good.'[27]

Simonds himself was critical of some of the units under his command but added, 'I find analysis of an operation like the attack of the Black Watch at May-sur-Orne a most distasteful task for it means criticism of some who, whatever mistakes they made, made them in good faith and paid the supreme sacrifice in the course of duty.[28]

Terry Copp has probably pointed to the nub of the problems when he suggested that:

The Allies had simply not created a force large enough to confront the German army. . . . In the spring of 1944 the British-Canadian component of the Allied Forces available for the invasion included formidable strategic and tactical air forces, a naval commitment of unparalleled power and a small army which was especially deficient in infantry.

It was well understood at the time that the purpose of many of the attacks in Normandy was to hold the German troops on the Caen sector in order to allow for an American break-out farther west. As the Reginas' war diarist put it in a moment of weary cynicism, 'it was this unspectacular but vital role that Canadian forces carried on while the glamorous armored Spearheads spread their arrows over the front page of newspapers the world over.' To quote Copp again, 'under these conditions the battle of Normandy remained a battle of attrition and there are no reasonable grounds for believing it could have been otherwise.'[29]

Another Canadian historian, Marc Milner, has summed up the situation in terse words:

Given the German doctrine of counter-attack, the Canadian response (much as it had been in 1917–18) was to seize ground, lay on defensive supporting fire, move the anti-tank guns up and kill Germans. It worked, but it wasn't fancy and analysts have carped about it ever since.[30]

Reflecting also on 1917–18, on the ridges in 1944, the Canadians were called upon to shed blood at the same rate employed pro rata as in the more lauded First World War battles of Vimy Ridge and Passchendaele. Some have suggested that the Russians or the Americans (or even the Germans) would have made a better job of the assault on the ridges. To suggest this is to ignore the realities, the major one of which was the German Army fighting on known and prepared ground, against Allies who were governed by the restrictions of democracies, so that every Canadian who fought at Verrieres had to volunteer twice, once to join the army and once to be sent overseas.

One of the lessons of these battles was the superiority of the all arms panzer system. The British Army appears not to have learned that lesson in time for the Falklands War when infantry were again sent across open country directly at machine-gun posts as in 1916. It was better planned for the Gulf War, although the standing armoured regiments had been so denuded that they had to be reinforced even before the battles commenced. By the time of the Kosovo encounter it seemed that infantry was no longer needed. Air power would suffice. Television cameras showed the Serbian positions apparently being destroyed by air power alone. The same cameras later showed the Serbian armoured columns happily emerging unscathed from their hides after the planes had gone home.

As for a new paradigm of success in battle, this should commence from the hypothesis that the normal result of attacks is either defeat or a too costly gain of territory. A gain of land without spillage of blood is a freak occurrence. The battle should be judged not on the stated proposals of the planners but in relation to an expectation of failure. At the same time it is relevant to study the accuracy of the planners' projections.

This kind of approach would allow due credit to be given for all those who served loyally, were wounded and killed, irrespective of whether their efforts produced an outcome precisely as the planners forecast.

In criticising battles in Normandy it is only too easy to take the generals' forecasts or targets as the yardstick for success. Yet hindsight reveals again and again either that there were circumstances over which the generals had no control or that their staff training required them to infuse into their plans illogical expectations. These might have been permissible in a war game on Salisbury Plain but often had little bearing (except perhaps as very minor footnotes) in the uncontrollable chaos that was launched at each real H-hour on each real D-Day. Simonds was restricted by his allotted narrow front. However, Montgomery *could* have sent two British armoured divisions on the left of Totalize to close the Falaise gap via St Pierre-sur-Dives.

Marc Milner again summed it up when, reacting to the tide of criticism, he observed, 'Those slow, bumbling, artillery-addicted soldiers in Normandy found a way to beat the best, and they should be judged by their accomplishment.'[31] Or perhaps a survivor of Verrieres Ridge, Reg Dixon of the Glens, said it just as well – 'What did they expect us to do? Fly?'[32]

Fifty years later two panzer survivors of Tilly, Ustuf Stiller and tank driver Thorn, stood with a North Novas Tilly veteran, Colin Nelson, at the Cintheaux grave of Colin's comrade, Thomas Douglas whose dog tag Stiller had preserved amid the flames of ultimate Hell. They observed a minute's silence together. Stiller still ponders:

And if I look at the photo of any young soldier today, I am seeing the numbers of young Canadians fallen and wounded in front of the railway-crossing at the west end of Tilly. I can only say 'Why . . .? Wherefore . . .? For what reason . . .?' But *that* may have been *then*, and we may have grown wiser . . .'[33]

Notes & References

Many references are from unit war diaries or regimental histories and are noted below only if the quotation is especially unusual or contentious. Other basic and not always specified sources include the 'official history' – Stacey, C.P., *The Victory Campaign*, The Queen's Printer, 1960; Roy, Reginald, 1944 – *The Canadians in Normandy*, Macmillan of Canada, 1984; Copp, Terry, *The Brigade*, Fortress Publications Inc., 1992, and Copp, Terry, *A Canadian's Guide to the Battlefields of Normandy*, Wilfrid Laurier University, LCMSDS, 1994.

Chapter Headings are from Caesar (trans. Handford, S.A.) *The Conquest of Gaul, (58–51 BC)*, Penguin Books, 1951.

1. In the Foot-slogger's Boots

1. Sgt Percy Howse, Lincoln and Wellands, letter, 10 October 1999.
2. Anonymous rifleman letter, October 1999. Three veterans were happy to be quoted but did not wish their names to be mentioned.
3. Quoted in Williamson, *Loyalty is my Honour*.
4. Verney, *The Desert Rats*.
5. North Novas' regimental history.
6. Blackburn, *The Guns of Normandy*.
7. McAndrew, *Normandy 1944: The Canadian Summer*.
8. Recorded by Neil McCallum and quoted in Ellis, *The Sharp End*.
9. Cpl later Sgt Kipp, letter, 12 October 1999.
10. Evert Nordstrom (Reginas), statement, June 1993.
11. Major W.R. Bennett, *Vignettes* of the Royal Regiment of Canada.
12. Blackburn, *op. cit.*
13. Colonel John G. Martin, interview, 25 October 1999.
14. Whitehouse, *Fear is the Foe*.
15. Major W.R. Bennett, *op. cit.* and interview, 23 October 1999.

16. Anonymous, phoned conversation, 3 November 1999.

17. Reg Spittles, taped for Bovington Tank Museum.

18. Guy Merle, personal correspondence, 4 October 1999.

19. McAndrew, *op. cit.* and interview, 22 October 1999.

20. Whitehouse, *op. cit.*

21. Jack Belden quoted in Ellis, *op. cit.*

22. Black Watch report, 28 July 1944.

23. Taylor, *Tommy Cooker*, unpublished.

24. McAndrew, *op. cit.*

25. Blackburn, *op. cit.* and conversation, 21 October 1999.

26. Taylor, *op. cit.*

27. John Williamson, interview, 25 October 1999.

28. Lincoln, *Thank God and the Infantry*.

29. Kipp, letter, 12 October 1999.

30. Taylor, *op. cit.*

31. Hillsman 1948 quoted by Rawlings, Bill in *Canadian Military History*, 6.1.92.

32. Blackburn, conversation, 21 October 1999.

33. Ripley, letter, 15 November 1999.

34. McAndrew, *op. cit.* and interview, 22 October 1999.

35. Copp, *The Brigade*.

36. Lt-Col Charles Forbes, tapes, by favour of Jacques Ostiguy.

37. In frank interviews with Professor Terry Copp.

38. This summary relies on various sources but Copp, *The Brigade*, Chapter 4, is essential reading.

39. Shaughnessy, interview, 26 October 1999. Bennett, interview, 23 October 1999. Ostiguy, interview, 20 October 1999. Anonymous, letter, 26 November 1999.

2. Departure Point 'Despair'

1. These two quotations enlarged on later in chapter.

2. Mitcham, *Rommel's Last Battle*.

3. Hastings, *Overlord*.

4. Stacey, *The Victory Campaign*.

5. D'Este, *Decision in Normandy*.

6. Maczek, *Avec mes blindees*.

7. Jones, *Sixty-four Days of a Normandy Summer*.

8. Tout, *A Fine Night for Tanks*.

9. Berry, letter, 1 November 1999.

10. Now Maj Learment, interview, 26 October 1999.

11. Tout, *op. cit.*

12. Cooper, letter, 22 October 1999.

13. Blackburn, *The Guns of Normandy*.

14. Maj Dickins' report, 23 July 1944.

15. Capt Chapin's report, 4 August 1944.

16. Lt-Col MacLaughlan's report, 28 July 1944.

17. Forster, J., 'Motivation and Indoctrination in the Wehrmacht' in Addison, *A Time to Kill*.

18. Meyer, *Grenadiers*.

19. Tout, *op. cit.*

20. Intelligence Summary, II Canadian Corps, 2 August 1944.

21. Westphal, *The German Army in the West*.

22. Roy, *1944 – The Canadians in Normandy*.
23. Reynolds, *Steel Inferno*.
24. Ellis, *The Sharp End*.
25. MacAndrew, *Normandy 1944*.
26. Lt-Col Ostiguy, interview, 20 October 1999.
27. De Guingand, *Operation Victory*.

3. Operation Atlantic – in Deep Water

1. Mein, *Up the Johns*.
2. W.L. Keating, letter, 16 October 1999.
3. Merle, statements and phone conferences, September 1999.
4. Statement by favour of Geo Cooper, 1999.
5. Cooper, letter, 28 October 1999.
6. Nordstrom, statement, June 1993.
7. Regimental history, 1962.
8. Charlie Martin, DCM, MM, CM, *Battle Diary*.
9. Verney, *Desert Rats*.
10. Lt-Gen M.S. Dempsey, orders 17 July 1944 for operations 18 July 1944.
11. Sid Jones, telephone conversation, 12 March 2000.
12. Gordon Brown, letter, 31 October 1999.
13. Radley-Walters, phone conference, 24 October 1999.
14. Cooper, as 5 above.
15. Nordstrom, as 6 above.
16. Brown, as 12 above.
17. Blackburn, *Guns of Normandy*.
18. Professor J.L. Cloudsley-Thompson, letter, 23 October 1999.
19. Maj Edmondson's report, 23 July 1944.
20. Lt Matthews's report, 23 July 1944.
21. Maj Dickin's report, 23 July 1944.
22. Ray White, letter, 3 March 2000.
23. 'Goodwood' loss of 400 tanks had been generally quoted but there is now a tendency to 'downsize' this considerably.
24. Kitching, letter, 11 October 1999.
25. Radley-Walters, as 13 above.
26. Ostiguy, interview, 20 October, 1999.
27. *Ibid.*
28. As 4 above.
29. Cloudsley-Thompson, *op. cit.*
30. Col A.J. Hodges, MC, CD, letter, 4 February 2000.

4. Tilly – the Epicentre

1. Manfred and Hazel Toon-Thorn, correspondence, January 2000.
2. Maj J.K. Nairne.
3. Mayor and 'adjoints' of Tilly, May and St Martin.
4. G. Merle, statements, October 1999.
5. Stiller, conversation, 22 January 2000.
6. Brown, letter, 5 December 1999.
7. Maj D. Learment, DSO, interview 24 October 1999.
8. Merle. *op. cit.*
9. Brown, *op. cit.*

10. Manfred Thorn as 1 above.
11. Maj R.R. Dixon, CD, the Glens' war diarist, papers, November 1999.
12. North Nova's war diary, 25 July 1944.
13. Dixon, *op. cit.*
14. Merle, *op. cit.*
15. North Nova's war diary.
16. Ripley, Letter, 5 November 1999.
17. *Ibid.*
18. Graham, *The Price of Command.*

5. Operation Spring – Unsprung!

1. Based on Lt-Col MacLaughlan's Report, 28 July 1944.
2. See also Copp, *A Canadian's Guide to the Battlefields.*
3. Granatstein, *Bloody Victory.*
4. *Ibid.*
5. F. Pollak, letter, 7 November 1999.
6. College Paul Verlaine, *Histoire d'un Pays Minier.*
7. From Capt/Maj Bennett's own report.
8. Cooper letter, 28 October 1999.
9. Maj-Gen Rockingham account, 27 October 1948, reprinted in *Canadian Military History*, Spring 1993.
10. Shaugnessy interview, 23 October 1999.
11. Rockingham, *op. cit.*
12. Granatstein, *op. cit.*
13. Sternbecke in Reynolds, *Steel Inferno.*

14. Blackburn, *Guns of Normandy.*
15. Berry, letter, 17 October 1999.
16. War diary and Sgt later Maj W.R. Bennett, *Vignettes.*
17. Berry, *op. cit.*
18. Bill Robertson, Gordons 51 HD, conversation, 16 January 2000.
19. W.R. Bennett, *op. cit.*
20. *Ibid.*
21. Royal's regimental history.
22. Lt-Col Charlie Forbes' tapes per J. Ostiguy.
23. Martin, *Battle Diary.*
24. Essame, *Normandy Bridgehead.*
25. Granatstein, *op. cit.*
26. Graham, *The Price of Command.*
27. Reynolds, *op. cit.*
28. Pollak, *op. cit.*

6. Tilly – Encore Plus!

1. German view based mainly on G. Stiller and M. and H. Toon-Thorn correspondence, December 1999 / January 2000.
2. Col A.J. Hodges, MC, TD, 18 August 1950 / letter 4 February 2000.
3. Blackburn, *The Guns of Normandy.*
4. Calgaries war diary more descriptive than many.
5. Stiller, letter, 25 January 2000.
6. Lehmann, *Die Leibstandarte.*
7. Bennett, *Vignettes.*
8. Tout, *A Fine Night for Tanks.*
9. Dunlop, letter, 29 September 1999.
10. Whitehouse, *Fear is the Key.*
11. Hayes, *The Lincs.*

12. Martin, interview, 22 October 1999.
13. Howse, letter, 6 October, 1999.
14. Kipp, letter, 12 October 1999.
15. Thorn, correspondence, January 2000.
16. Brown, interview, 20 October 2000.
17. Kipp, *op. cit.*
18. Histories of 10 Canadian Infantry Brigade and Argylls.
19. Entire poem in Lehmann as 6 above.

7. *Operation Totalize – Eating Dust*

1. Tout, *A Fine Night for Tanks.*
2. Jarymowycz, R.J., *Canadian Armour in Normandy*, in *Canadian Military History*, 7, 2, 1998, pp. 19–40.
3. Jolly, in *Royal Armoured Corps Journal*, vol. 2, 1948, p. 94.
4. Burn, Lothian and Border Yeomanry reports, 9 August 1944.
5. Tout, *Tank!*
6. Graham, *The Price of Command.*
7. Jarymowycz, *op. cit.*
8. McAndrew *et al*, *Normandy 1944 – The Canadian Summer.*
9. Restricted circulation digest of Simonds' lecture, 1947.
10. This and more details of Kangaroos, Tout as note 1.
11. 51st Highland Division history.
12. Eason, Lothian and Border Yeomanry reports, 9 August 1944.
13. Jolly, *op. cit.*
14. Tout, *Tank!*
15. Lothian and Border Yeomanry reports, 9 August 1944.
16. Tout, as 14.
17. Kitching, letter 28 October 1999.
18. Beale, *Tank Tracks.*
19. Blackburn, *The Guns of Normandy.*
20. Col A.J. Hodges, statement/letter 4 February 2000.
21. Col Neitzel (89th Infantry Division), 1944 report on 'Totalize'.
22. Radley-Walters, correspondence 1997–9.
23. Freeman, *The Mighty Eighth War Diary.*
24. More on Wittmann in Tout, note 1 above.
25. Von Kluge, 7th Army telephone log, 8/9 August 1944.

8. *May – Tilly's Murderous Sister*

1. Anonymous corporal, interview, 22 October 1999.
2. *The Daily Telegraph*, 26 July 1944.
3. Both Crerar and Montgomery were guilty of uttering or failing to deny such statements.
4. 6 CIB war diary and *Historie d'un Pays Minier.*
5. Copp, *The Brigade.*
6. Black Watch war diary.
7. *Maisonneuve* war diary.
8. Ostiguy, phone conversation, 5 February 2000.
9. Lt-Col Gevert Haslob, only surviving senior officer of 89th Infantry Division

10. Most of details based on report by Maj Brochu and Capt La Mothe, 12 August 1944.
11. *Ibid.*
12. *Ibid.*
13. Roy, *1944: The Canadians in Normandy*.
14. Dom G. Auborg, translated by the author.
15. College Paul Verlaine, *Histoire d'un Pays Minier*.
16. Auborg as 14 above.

9. *Fontenay – Fatal for Officers*

1. S. Saskatchewans' war diary.
2. Blackburn, *Where the Hell are the Guns?*
3. Lt-Gen Sir Derek Lang, phone conversation, November 1999.
4. 6 CIB war diary, Queen's Own Camerons war diary (Appendix 6), and also Roy, *1944: The Canadians in Normandy*, and Tout, *A Fine Night for Tanks*.
5. Burnside, 11 August 1944, in Cameron Appendix 6.
6. Capt W.S. Watt, 11 August 1944, *ibid.*
7. Roy, *op. cit.*
8. Marks, statement, 17 June 1946.
9. Roy, *op. cit.*
10. S. Saskatchewans' war diary.
11. Lt-Col Charles Forbes, taped memoirs, per J.W. Ostiguy.
12. College Paul Verlaine, *Histoire d'un Pays Minier*.

13. *Ibid* (published with authorization of Mme Philippe).

10. *Tilly – Deadly to the Last*

1. Tout, *A Fine Night for Tanks*.
2. Salmond, *History of 51st HD, 1939–45*.
3. Todd, *The Elephant at War*.
4. Brig G.L.W. Andrews, CBE, DSO, unpublished memoirs.
5. Maj J.K. Nairne, statement, 13 September 1999.
6. Tout, *op. cit.*, and Borthwick, *Battalion*.
7. Todd, *op. cit.*, and Col Hugh Cuming, interview, 10 January 2000.
8. Lt-Col Gevert Haslob, letter, 17 December 1999.
9. Battalion history, *Spirit of Angus*, per Dr Tom Renouf.
10. *Records of the Cameron Highlanders*.
11. J.S. Lucas, *Daily Telegraph*, 24 August 1981.
12. Nairne, letter, 14 October 1999.
13. Tout, *Tank!*
14. Bennett, *Vignettes*.

11. *The Other Terrible Tilly Twin*

1. Barnes, *The Sign of the Double 'T'*.
2. Clay, *The Path of the 50th*.
3. Barnes, *op. cit.*
4. Recollection of Lt Tony Faulkner.
5. See also Jary, *18 Platoon*.

12. Reasons and Recriminations

1. English, *The Canadian Army and the Normandy Campaign*.
2. Blumenson, *The Battle of the Generals*.
3. Geo. Cooper, correspondence, October 1999–February 2000.
4. Reynolds, *Steel Inferno*.
5. Berry, letter, 17 October 1999.
6. Ripley, letter, 5 November 1999.
7. Dextraze, statement, 30 July 1944.
8. Quoted in McAndrew, *Normandy 1944*.
9. Schulte, T.J. 'The German Soldier in Occupied Russia' in Addison and Calder, *Time to Kill*.
10. Forster, J., 'Motivation and Indoctrination in the Wehrmacht' in Addison and Calder, *ibid.*
11. Lt-Col MacLaughlan (Calgaries), statement, 28 July 1944.
12. Warlimont, *Inside Hitler's Headquarters*.
13. MacLaughlan, *op. cit.*
14. 4 CIB war diary, 3 August 1944.
15. Learment, interview, 22 October 1999.
16. Martin, interview, 22 October 1999.
17. Battalion history, *Spirit of Angus*.
18. Copp and McAndrew, *Battle Exhaustion*.
19. Berry, *op. cit.*
20. Lt-Col Forbes, taped memoirs, by kindness of J. Ostiguy.
21. Geoff Hayes in *Canadian Military History (CMH)*, 8.1. p. 4.
22. Details from REME, 6 June to 10 July 1944, in *(CMH)*, 7.1. p. 73.
23. Dickin, statement, 23 July 1944.
24. D.W. McIntyre in *CMH*, 7.1. pp. 68 and 70.
25. Pollak, correspondence, November/December 1999.
26. Horrocks, *Corps Commander*.
27. Whitaker, interview, 23 October 1999.
28. Simonds, statement to the Minister of National Defence, 31 January 1946.
29. Copp in *CMH*, 7.4. p. 4.
30. Milner in *CMH*, 7.2. p. 17.
31. Milner in *CMH*, 7.4. p. 10.
32. Dixon, letter, 29 November 1999.
33. Stiller, letter, 15 February 2000.

Bibliography:
Sources & Further Reading

Only a selection of regimental histories is included here.

Addison, P. and Calder, A., *A Time to Kill*, Pimlico, 1997

Barnes, B.S., *The Sign of the Double T*, Sentinel, 1999

Beale, P., *Tank Tracks*, Sutton, 1995

Bennett, W.R., *Vignettes*, Royal Regt. Association

Bird, W., *No Retreating Footsteps (North Novas)*, Kentville, n.d.

Blackburn, G., *The Guns of Normandy*, McClelland & Stewart, 1995

——, *Where the Hell are the Guns?*, McClelland & Stewart,1997

Blumenson, M., *The Battle of the Generals*, Wm Morrow, 1993

Borthwick, A., *Battalion (orig. Sans Peur) – 5 Seaforths*, Baton Wicks, 1994

Boss, C., *The Stormont, Dundas & Glengarry Highlanders*, Runge, 1952

Brown, K., & Greenhous, B., *Semper Paratus (RHLI)*, Regt., 1977

Buchanan, G.B., *March of the Prairie Men (South Sasks)*, Regt., 1957

Castonguay, J, and Ross, A., *Le Regiment de la Chaudiere*, Levis, 1983

Cent ans d'histoire d'un regiment canadien francais – Les Fusiliers Mont Royal, Editions du Jour, 1969

Clay, E.W., *The Path of the 50th*, Gale and Polden, 1950

College P. Verlaine, *Histoire d'un Pays Minier*, Evrecy, 1999

Copp, T., *The Brigade*, Fortress, 1992

——, *Canadians Guide to the Battlefields of Normandy*, LCMSDS, Wilfrid Laurier University, 1994

Copp, T., and McAndrew, B., *Battle Exhaustion – Soldiers and Psychiatrists in the Canadian Army. 1939–45*, McGill-Queens, 1990

Copp, T., and Nielsen, R., *No Price too High*, McGraw-Hill Ryerson, 1996

De Guingand, F., *Operation Victory*, Hodder & Stoughton, 1950

D'Este, C., *Decision in Normandy*, Wm Collins, 1983

Ellis, J., *The Sharp End, The Fighting Man in World War II*, Windrowe and Green, 1990 (rev.)

English, J.A., *The Canadian Army and the Normandy Campaign – A Study of Failure in High Command*, Praeger, 1991

Essame, H., *Normandy Bridgehead*, Ballantyne, 1970

Fletcher, D., *The Universal Tank: British Armour in the Second World War*, HMSO, 1993

Fraser, R.L., *Black Yesterdays*, Argyll Regt. Foundation, 1996

Freeman, R., *The Mighty Eighth War Diary*, Arms & Armour, 1990

Furbringer, H., *9 SS-Panzer-Division*, Munin-Velrag, 1987

Goodspeed, D.J., *Battle Royal*, Royal Regt., 1962

Gouin, *Bon Coeur et Bon Bras (Maisonneuves)*, Bibliotheque de Quebec, 1980

Graham, D., *The Price of Command*, Stoddart, 1993

Granatstein, J.C., and Morton, D., *Bloody Victory*, Lester & Orpen Dennys, 1984

Hasting, M., *Overlord*, Michael Joseph, 1984

Hayes, G., *The Lincs*, Alma, 1986

Horrocks, B., *Corps Commander*, Griffin House, 1978

Hutchinson, P.P., *Canada's Black Watch*, Regt., 1962

Jackson, G.S., *Normandy to the Rhine*, St Clements, 1948

Jackson, H.M., *The Argyll & Sutherland Highlanders of Canada*, Regt., 1953

Jary, S., *18 Platoon*, Odiham, 1987

Jones, K, *Sixty-four Days of a Normandy Summer*, Robert Hale, 1990

Keegan, J., *Six Armies in Normandy*, Penguin, 1982

Lehmann, R., and Tiemann, R., *Die Leibstandarte IV/I*, Munin Verlag, 1986

Lincoln, J., *Thank God and the Infantry*, Alan Sutton, 1994

Luxton, E., *1st Bn Regina Rifle Regiment, 1939–1946*, Regt., 1946

Macksey, K.J., *Panzer Division*, Ballantyne, 1968

——, *Military Errors of World War Two*, Cassell, 1998

Maczek, S., *Avec mes Blindees*, Presses de la Cite, 1967

Martin, C.C., *Battle Diary*, Dundrun Press, 1994

Mason, D., *Breakout: Drive to the Seine*, Ballantyne, 1968

McAndrew, B., Graves, D.E., and Whitby, M., *Normandy 1944: The Canadian Summer*, Art Global, 1994

Mein, S.A.G., *Up the Johns*, Turner-Warwick, 1992

Meyer, H., *History of the 12 SS Panzerdivision Hitlerjugend*, J.J. Fedorowicz, 1994

Meyer, K., *Grenadiers*, J.J. Fedorowicz, 1994

Mitcham, S.W.J., *Rommel's Last Battle*, Stein and Day, 1983

Reynolds, M, *Steel Inferno: 1SS Panzer Corps in Normandy*, Spellmount, 1997

Rogers, R.L., *History of the Lincoln and Welland Regiment*, Regt., 1954/89

Rohmer, R., *Patton's Gap*, PaperJacks, 1981

Roy, R, *1944, the Canadians in Normandy*, Macmillan, 1984

Salmond, J.B., *History of the 51st Highland Division, 1939–1945*, Blackwood, 1953

Shulman, M. *Defeat in the West*, Secker & Warburg, 1947

Speidel, H., *Invasion 1944*, Regnery, 1950

Stacey, C.P., *Canada's Battle in Normandy*, King's Printer at Ottawa, 1946

——, *The Victory Campaign (Official History of Canadian Army in Second World War, Vol. III)*, Queen's Printer at Ottawa, 1960

Todd, A, *The Elephant at War (2nd Seaforths)*, Pentland, 1998

Tout, K., *Tank!*, Robert Hale, 1985/95

——, *A Fine Night for Tanks*, Sutton, 1998

Verney, G.L., *Desert Rats*, Hutchinson, 1954

Warlimont, W., *Inside Hitler's HQ*, Praeger, 1964

Westphal, S., *The German Army in the West*, Cassell, 1951

Whitehouse, S, and Bennett, G., *Fear is the Foe*, Robert Hale, 1995

Williamson, G., *Loyalty is my Honour*, Brown Books, 1995

Wilmot, C., *The Struggle for Europe*, Collins, 1952

General Index

Index of Units Mentioned